EXTRAORDINARY TRAVELS
of an
ORDINARY HOUSEWIFE

Diane Jones

Copyright © 2022 by Diane Jones

All rights reserved. No part of this book may be used or reproduced by any means, graphic, electronic, or mechanical, including photocopying, recording, taping or by any information storage retrieval system without the written permission of the publisher except in the case of brief quotations embodied in critical articles and reviews.

The views expressed in this work are solely those of the author and do not necessarily reflect the views of the publisher, and the publisher hereby disclaims any responsibility for them.

Cover: Head hunting arrows from the Asmat region, Irian Jaya

For my grandchildren
Indy, Jake, Thomas and Katie

and for the Kenworthy kids
Adam, Natalie, Dylan and Anna

Acknowledgments

I greatly appreciate the encouragement and assistance of my long time friend, Wendy Bonus, and the support I have had from Alan Kenworthy and my son, Tom Jones. Many thanks to Heather Morin for the book cover, and Kathryn Willms for facilitating the book through to final publishing.

INTRODUCTION

As a wartime baby growing up in Scotland in the 'forties and 'fifties, travel meant a month each summer in a simple crofter's cottage, on a remote white sand beach of the West Coast Highlands. We caught the train to Arisaig and loaded bikes and two hampers filled with clothes, camping and fishing gear for the last stretch of our journey which was on the back of the local coal lorry. I didn't realize, in those early years, that I was surrounded by some of the most beautiful scenery in the world.

Food rationing, hand me downs, make do and mend, secondhand bikes were of no consequence to my childhood happiness. I could save my pocket money and buy a fat envelope of used stamps from all over the world. Hours would be spent soaking them in a saucer of water to peel off the torn piece of envelope, carefully pressing the stamps between blotting paper and finally placing, by country, into my treasured stamp album. What strange country names there were: Bechuanaland, now Botswana; Nyasaland, now Malawi. A dog-eared World Atlas was my favourite companion and I would browse its pages for hours to find each stamp's origin and imagine what it would be like to visit these exotic sounding countries. This must have been where my travel bug came from as my parents never saw any need to travel abroad, even in later years, when their income and family circumstances would have allowed. Graduation gifts of around the world airline tickets and financing of Gap Years were not even on the horizon by the mid-fifties and certainly would not have been an option on my father's civil service income. Perhaps if I had had such an offer I would have continued at my grammar school but, instead, I quit at sixteen with passable marks in English, French, Geography and Arithmetic. Fortunately these subjects have since proved useful when writing about world travel on a shoestring budget.

In those days a girl need look no further than a few years as a shorthand/typist until she got married, had a family and became a full time housewife. I followed the shorthand typist route for a couple of years until I was old enough to follow my dream of travelling the world as an airline stewardess for British Overseas Airways. To my dismay, my hopes were dashed at my Heathrow interview when my "passable" French came up short. Instead I became involved in the fashion business for many years which took me to London in the swinging sixties. Here I met and married my first husband, Peter, and where my two sons were born. His job required many extended business trips abroad to all corners of the world whilst I, quite happily, fell into the role of child rearing and household management and resolved that my exploration of the world would come later when my children had left the nest. In 1976 we emigrated to Canada and we all became outdoor and fitness enthusiasts, buying cross-country skis, bikes, camping gear and a canoe to explore the wilds of Ontario and I downgraded my fashion wardrobe to track suits, bug proof clothes and hiking boots. But my enthusiasm for world travel did not abate and I replaced my old atlas with National Geographic and followed the travels of my favourite authors, Bill Bryson and Redmond O'Hanlon.

In 1985 I spotted, in the newspaper, a very cheap promotion by British Airways for a two-week trip from Canada to Russia to celebrate the opening of their new route to Moscow, with a flexible few days stopover in the UK. This meant I could make it an excuse to include a visit to my widowed mother. I had been waiting for this day as my two sons had pretty much flown the coop and I had completed evening courses in WordPerfect and H&R Block tax return preparation and by now had my own small part-time income. I was off on my first solo adventure.

The following year, there was no stopping me. When I arrived in London in 1986 for my family visit, I walked into Thomas Cook's office on Regent Street, announced to the agent my limited budget and time frame and asked what was the most exciting trip she could offer. She rose to the challenge, almost as excited as I, and found a last minute discount on a week's camping safari in Kenya with a flight to Nairobi two days later. Just enough time to get a water bottle, malaria pills and borrow a sleeping bag.

My expeditions to Western New Guinea in 1989 and Borneo in 1994 were both exploratory trips when travel companies were looking to expand to other lesser known parts of the world to market under what we would now term Adventure Travel. My costs were more than recouped by my published articles and lectures in the years that followed. I kept a daily log of my travels with an eye to the funniest and most ridiculous moments, as it would have been impossible to get through some of the tougher days without good humour, flexibility, determination and, not least of all, stamina. These logs I turned into journals, slideshows and photo albums in the many years that followed and which have been the basis for this book. I wanted to share these adventures with future generations as these stories, going back almost forty years, seemed too good to be forgotten.

When my first husband, Peter, retired in the late nineties we resolved to join the Gap Year kids on their lengthy trans-continental truck journeys. We were happy travelling on a limited budget because it meant we could travel further and for longer. I still have a record of the cost of our five years of travel in the Southern Hemisphere over the long winter months by overland truck and backpacker bus. Twenty years ago the cost was $75 to $100 each per day for absolutely everything, including our international flights. Almost cheaper than staying home, and no need for an expensive wardrobe or haircuts. Over the years I have got packing down to a fine art. Mountain Equipment Co-op produced a soft bag that exactly measured the maximum dimensions for a carry-on, plus it had two flat padded shoulder straps concealed in a rear pocket that could turn it into a backpack when required. In Kalimantan I made separate compartments to hold my thermarest, tropical sleeping bag, mosquito net, change of clothes and bog roll. Since every square inch of space counted, I remember rolling up the exact number of sheets of toilet paper I would require. One large hockey bag was all we needed for our overland truck camping trips which held our tent, mats and warm sleeping bags, plus space for shoes, quick dry clothes and personal gear. I owe a debt of gratitude to my black moisture-wicking underwear. The long-sleeved top with a sarong came in handy for impromptu parties and when paired with the long-johns, they have come to the rescue in chilly climes whilst also serving as a sun-protective wetsuit when snorkeling. Not to be forgotten are my comfortable ear plugs that don't require a search party next morning.

Faced with physical limitations and divorce in my seventies, I moved to Ottawa to be nearer to grandchildren. Here I met my soulmate, Alan, who shares my life and enthusiasm to explore faraway places, albeit at a slower pace. We have happily spent the past eight years together, sailing the southern oceans in our winter months with Holland America, whose smaller ships and unusual itineraries appeal to us. However, global warming and good conscience may limit our future travel plans. That makes me appreciate my good fortune in being able to travel to so many corners of the world in my lifetime. My motto "Don't put off till tomorrow what you can do today" has proved its worth many times, as several destinations I visited later erupted with political unrest, or suffered extreme weather incidents. There is no doubt that travel broadens the mind as it helps us to understand, appreciate and respect the many other societies and cultures that share this planet with us.

And so I say: On your way! Off you go!

CONTENTS

IRIAN JAYA EXPEDITION	1989
KALIMANTAN EXPEDITION	1994
MOROCCO Backpacking and Explore Jebel Sahro Trek	1996
NEW ZEALAND Backpacking	1997/98 & 2003
AROUND SOUTH AMERICA By Tucan and Dragoman Overland Trucks	1998/99 & 2002
AFRICA KENYA TO THE CAPE By Exodus Overland Truck	1999
TURKEY Istanbul and The Turquoise Coast Backpacking and Explore Hiking Tour	2000
AUSTRALIA Camping Tour & Backpacking	1993/2000/01 & 2003
LAO Backpacking	2001
VIETNAM Hired car and driver	2001
CAMBODIA Hired car and driver	2001
NEPAL Peregrine Trek	2003
A-Z of MY MOST MEMORABLE MOMENTS (MMMMs)	
WORLD TRAVELS SUMMARY	1956-2020

"Dani tribesman all dressed up for Jiwika's Sunday Market"

Extraordinary Travels of an Ordinary Housewife

IRIAN JAYA

EXPEDITION

October 1989

Diane Jones

PART 1

THE BALIEM VALLEY - BACK TO THE STONE AGE

As our plane touched down in Wamena, the proud native Dani hardly spared us a glance as they casually wandered along the landing strip on their way to the town's market. The women, wearing only low slung grass skirts, were bent over with the burden of their long net bags suspended from their foreheads and bulging with market produce. The men, unencumbered, chose to walk apart and were naked except for their penis gourds and colourful feathered headgear.

Wamena is a small government town in the centre of the Baliem Valley, a forty by ten mile fertile plain at an altitude of 5,000 feet. It is hidden within the Central Mountain Range of Irian Jaya, the western half of the equatorial island of New Guinea. The valley, surrounded by this wall of mountains, is home to approximately 40,000 natives of the Dani, Lani and Yali tribes and, as the only access to these remote areas is by air, these people have remained virtually unchanged since Stone Age times. Their thatched roofed huts in small village compounds, surrounded by banana groves and carefully cultivated raised hiperi fields (these sweet potatoes are the staple of their diet) dot the landscape as far as the eye can see indicating an agrarian and peaceful lifestyle.

The latter was not always so as it is only since the late sixties that the missionaries and Indonesian government have been able to stamp out the ritualistic tribal warfare that was once such a dominant part of the valley's culture. However, in the southern Asmat lowlands, much of the area remains unexplored and head hunting and cannibalism may still be practised. When I heard that an environmentally aware Canadian led group of adventurers planned to attempt to be the first expedition to climb south over the 12,000 ft mountain ridges that isolate the Baliem Valley and follow native trading paths south into these swamp jungle lowlands in search of these remote tribes, I was determined to participate.

I flew out of Toronto mid October to Biak International airport in west Indonesia to meet up with our expedition's assistant guide, Kevin, from Vancouver. Fellow Canadians Nipper and Wally, both experienced in climbing and extreme travel, were on this flight along with Nancy from Washington who would be my roommate. She had been a White House travel secretary, now looking for a mid life crisis adventure. Alan and Jeannie from California were a delightful older couple but I did wonder if they had read the same small print as I about the extreme travel conditions we were going to endure. Jim, from Nevada, already had some previous experience of travel with this group but he didn't spoil their fantasy at this point. Ernest, waving the Union Jack for

England, had just dropped in from Singapore and, to prove how experienced he was, showed us all the leech bite scars he had endured on a trip in the Malaysian jungle. So that made eight of the group's maximum ten participants. The other two were already trekking near to the mission station at Korupun where the expedition was to start along with our Head Guide, Jim and partner Jean who would be a second assistant guide.

After changing a few US dollars for a wheelbarrow load of 100 rupiah notes at the bank in Biak, we took the short flight to Jayapura, the capital of Irian Jaya. We were required to stop overnight in this disappointingly shabby tin roofed town in order to have our visas for the interior processed before boarding a small plane early next morning for the fifty minute flight south over the steep jungle covered mountains that encircle the Baliem Valley.

Of course, I had read everything I could lay my hands on about these Stone Age people, especially the books written by members of the Harvard Peabody Expedition of 1961 who had been the first to document, over several months, these warring tribes of the Baliem Valley. For the past three months I had adopted a strenuous fitness programme in order to pass the required medical at which time I was also given needles, pills and many dire warnings. My excitement perhaps blurred my misgivings about such a venture but, in retrospect, if I could have seen exactly what was ahead of me I would never have thought I could possibly survive such a journey. Of the 13 participants (which included our three Canadian guides) only four of us were to complete the entire trip. Fortunately I was one of the four.

Our itinerary would allow us to spend only a couple of days with the Dani in the Baliem Valley before we flew east to the mission station of Korupun for the start of our trek, and we were anxious not to waste a moment of that time. We walked the few hundred yards to our losman (inn) on the edge of town, followed by an entourage of curious Dani children anxious to help us carry our packs.

Few tourists reach this area and the losman is mainly for visiting anthropologists and Indonesian government officials. Judging by the standard of the accommodation, tourists are not encouraged. I was glad to have the safety of my own mosquito net, not only to protect me from flying insects, but also from the huge cockroaches, rats, and lizards that were already established residents. Also something with large teeth that came out and gnawed the soap bar at night!

Without delay we headed for the marketplace. It was an astonishing sight. Even though it was now mid afternoon it was still packed with Dani tribesmen who seemed to be there purely to socialize as their produce by this late in the day was limp and long past its best. Also everyone seemed to be selling much the same vegetables (hiperi, greens, peppers, tomatoes) and nobody seemed to be buying. I suspect they just took it all home that night and ate it themselves having thoroughly enjoyed a day's gossiping in town.

The bare breasted women wore a wrap skirt of faded cloth or a lush grass skirt, both of which were slung low and almost drooped off their buttocks. They used their foreheads to support their nokens (long net bags) which covered their backs and were part of their everyday dress code whether empty or filled with produce for the market. Some had babies slung somewhere down in the folds and often a baby pig as well! The women being the producers were also the traders and they squatted and displayed their wares wherever they could find a vacant spot amongst the vermillion splashes of chewed betel nuts. Hands were always busy weaving net bags from fine strips of bark or spinning twine on their big toe and dying the string with an assortment of roots and berries, all the time cuddling and nursing little children and apparently the piglet if required.

Evidence of the old custom of Ike Palin was to be seen on the hands of most of the older women. This was the ceremonial amputation, below the second joint, of one or several fingers of young girls as a mourning sacrifice. In many cases these women had lost all four fingers and often another couple on the other hand. But they still managed to handle their weaving and spinning and smoke their rolled cigarettes with considerable dexterity using their thumb and remaining stumps, and were extremely proud to show off their hands if one showed the least sign of interest.

The Dani males by tradition do little work. Gathering wood and preparing new hiperi fields for the women to manage is about the extent of their chores since going to war had been banned by the government. They take great pride in their appearance and the majority were there to be admired, from their heads in an assortment of hairnets, feathered and seed head dresses and braided greased dreadlock wigs. Their penis gourds came in all shapes and sizes. These were supported by a fine string around their waist or their chest to hold the penis rampant style, whilst the bottom of this dried carrot shaped, hollow gourd was anchored by a string around the scrotum. Apart from various armbands and neck chokers made from anything and everything such as braided orchid fibre, fur, shells, boot laces and broken zippers, their only other accessory was a small net shoulder bag to carry their tobacco and perhaps their boar's tusks which they would obligingly thread through their pierced septum when proudly posing to be photographed.

Their penis gourds, being much too brittle to afford protection, were more an expression of individual character, with their curves and curls. The Lani from the north of the valley were easily identified by their enormous gourds which were both large in length and diameter and required a cloth waist sash for support.

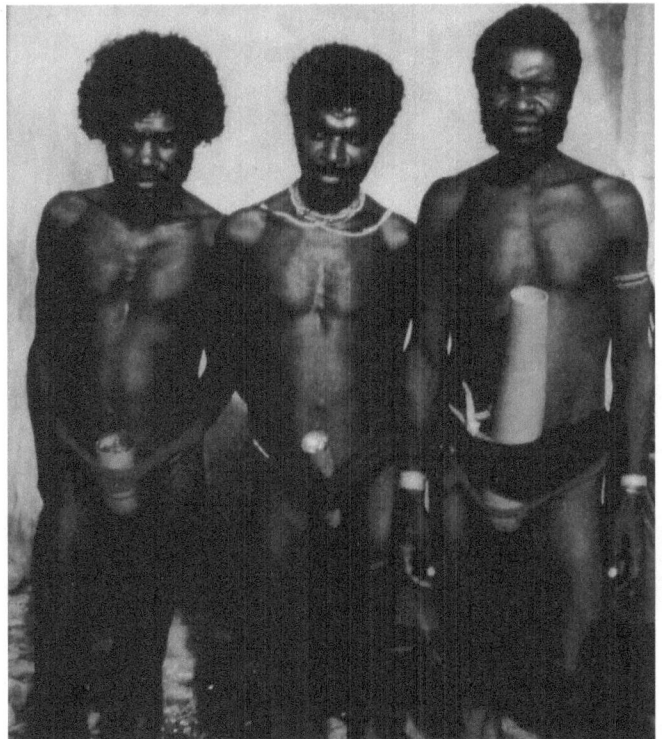

Three Lani tribesmen at Wamena market

Dani warriors with spears outside their village men's hut

Kim Yal porter with his stone axe at Deibula

They used the upper end of the gourd to store their tobacco, etc. instead of the string shoulder bag of the Dani men.

Flights were planned for the following morning to Korupun using small planes belonging to the Missionary Services (M.A.F.), but the flights were cancelled due to poor weather for landing. Instead we headed northwest to the village of Jiwika and the start of a strenuous two hour climb up the steep mountain wall to visit the natural brine springs and the only source of salt in the valley. Dani women soak strips of unravelled fibrous banana stalks until they are saturated and then carry these heavy bundles many miles back to their villages where the salt is retrieved by drying and burning. Salt, we were to find, was a valuable trading item and we had stocked up on this, plus tobacco, at the market's Indonesian stalls.

We returned to the valley down the same steep path and then hiked across the hiperi fields, past several village compounds and finally squeezed through the narrow raised entrance (which keeps the pigs out) of the village of Sompaima. Here we had heard there was an old preserved dehydrated corpse crouched in the traditional cremation chair's fetal position. Kain (chief) Konona and his wife were proud to have him brought out into the sunlight from his revered place in the village men's house. I must say the deceased was in extremely good condition for his age. Blackened and shined up with pig fat, it was an extremely solid skeleton, but the gruesomeness of it left us all somewhat silent.

Kain Konona's wife was the first woman we had seen wearing the traditional married woman's skirt, the yokel, which was lovingly made by her intended when he wasn't off to war. This consisted of many many strings of braided orchid fibre in its natural shades of browns, reds and ochres, which were gathered at each side and slung low from the hips in many loops across the front and even lower across the back below the buttocks. It was her only clothing except for the ubiquitous net bag suspended from her forehead and all the way down her back to below her bottom.

From here we headed to the village of Wuperaima, made up of several adjoining compounds with nine or ten families in each. This village was closely studied by Peter Matthiessen, a member of the Harvard Peabody Expedition in 1961, and his book "Under the Mountain Wall" documented their experiences with these warring tribes and I had memorized many of the personal names of the local people. This gave me a special rapport with U-mue the village chief, and several of the children, now adults 28 years on, who appear in the book's many photographs. We had a copy of the book with us. He must have thought I had close connections with some of the expedition's members and I received many welcoming embraces. This made up for the lack of any language communication and I was honoured to be invited into the men's hut. Women are normally never permitted to enter. It was a tight squeeze through the small doorway into the smoky gloom, and I could just discern the central fireplace between four posts which supported the roof. My hair caught something tucked into the woven boughs which formed the floor of the sleeping loft above and I found myself struggling to free myself from the jawbone of a pig. No, not a human skull!

The men and adolescent boys sleep and eat quite separately from the wives and younger children and all intimate contact is reserved for private moments in the fields and forest. The women have their own round, heavily thatched sleeping huts down one side of the oval compound. On the other side was a long, low thatched cooking hut where each woman had her own allotted cooking fire which may number up to nine or ten. None of the huts had windows nor chimneys and the smoke just leached out through the thatched roofs. Pigs are highly valued and determine the number of wives a man can afford, and their shelters abutted the compound wall with a small access door. During the day the pigs would roam freely outside under the watchful eye of a young boy. The walls of the compound were also covered with a thatch of dried grass which protected the wood from rotting due to the constant winds. We were to experience some of these sudden torrential but warm downpours as we hiked back to town and negotiated a fragile looking suspension bridge of sagging planks across a raging river.

I had been adopted by a small boy, about 10 years old, who took my hand and, with some encouragement, sang as we marched along. When we parted at the edge of his tribal territory he touchingly took off his bracelet of braided orchid fibre and, with little ceremony and great difficulty, managed to push it over my much larger hand onto my wrist. It would prove to be my lucky charm.

WAMENA TO KORUPUN MISSION STATION

It now looked unlikely that we would be able to reach our expedition's starting point at Korupun by small plane, not only because of the unreliable weather, but because the runway at Wamena was rumoured to close for repairs over the weekend. Not only were we anxious not to have to delay our expedition's scheduled start, but some members of a previous group, who had spent the last ten days hiking from the eastern Baliem Valley up to Korupun, needed to be flown back to Wamena. Two of this group were to continue on with us. It was decided that we should incur the expense of renting two of MAFs helicopters. We returned that night to our hotel to pare our equipment and supplies down to the bare minimum, as weight would now be all important as it was to cost $900 for every round trip. We would need at least three flights for passengers and hopefully, at most, one to bring all the supplies.

Nancy, Nipper and Ernest took off at 5.45 a.m. and the chopper returned with three of the men from the previous expedition that had reached Korupun. One was a doctor from a town near my home, so I asked him if he would call my husband when he got back to Canada and confirm I was fit and looking forward to my trek. He said that was just as well as he had found the topography very demanding and of the two men in their group that planned to carry on with us on the second stage down to the lowlands, one had decided to drop out and so our group would be reduced to nine. Jeannie and Alan and Nevada Jim took the second flight and Wally and I the third flight. Kevin came in an essential fourth with the rest of the supplies.

It was one of those little glass bubble choppers and you almost seemed to hang from the front seat looking down through this fish bowl. We had the most magnificent panoramic view during the half hour flight. We flew southeast out of the valley by the Baliem River's dramatic gorge, then due east up and down over the steep ridges, keeping fairly close to the dense jungle canopy. Little villages were perched on these upper slopes and we passed the village of Soba that had been wiped out by an earthquake two months earlier when the sides of the mountain collapsed. These huge landslides were clearly visible all around and would have been devastating in a less isolated area.

We dropped down into the valley of Korupun just after nine. It is a small mission station approximately 100 miles east of Wamena and 150 miles west of the border which neatly slices the island of New Guinea down the middle. The runway was not only very short but on a steep gradient and it is little wonder that winds and weather must be just right for a small plane to land. The helicopter was a much more reliable, if expensive, solution.

Four very substantial wooden clapboard houses with corrugated metal roofs formed the central core of Korupun. There was the Mission House, which an Australian missionary nurse and a linguist from the States shared, the small clinic building, the school-cum-church and the Mission Guest House which we were to occupy for the night. Across the grassy runway was the original village of the Kim Yal people of this area and on the slopes above the mission station, the Bible Village. Here would be teachers and their families from outlying villages would come to stay for as long as it took to teach them to read their native language. When eventually they could understand the simple bible picture books the linguist prepared, they would go back to their own village and "spread the word". This mission station was one of many sponsored by The Regions Beyond the Mission Union, a Protestant Christian movement formed in 1873.

The Kim Yal were also naked except for penis gourds and the women wore voluminous grass skirts under plump bellies. However they were much smaller than the Dani, their average height being just over five feet. They crowded in curiosity around the guest house, but if you ventured out with your camera they would scatter and women especially were very shy. We were a little unnerved to see, from the windows, a human skull skulking under a bush and even a little more unnerved to see it moved to various bushes around the house that day, but there was no explanation available. Perhaps they were protecting themselves from any evil spirits we may have brought with us. Our concern was that it had been only five years since four of the missionaries in this area had been killed by the Kim Yal.

We had now caught up with the ninth member of the group, another Jim from Philadelphia, to be known as Jimbo, who had completed the trek up from the Wamena Valley along with our chief guide, Big Jim, a whopping 6'5" giant of a man. His partner, Jean, was to be an assistant guide along with Kevin. In addition we were required to have an Indonesian guide, Bob, who could translate into English from Henke, our Irian Jayan guide, plus our Indonesian cook Agung and his helper Scorpio.

We all found our overnight spot on the floor of the unfurnished guest house, in my case a lucky find of a foam mattress in one of the rooms. After a preliminary introduction about our "expedition plans" from Big Jim, we all adjourned to the Mission House for a slap-up lunch of roast pork and local vegetables including beigi. This is the flower top of a type of wild cane but could almost pass as asparagus. We had barely finished when Big Jim announced that we would all follow him on a training and test hike down the gorge and back to get an understanding of the terrain. I was laughed at when I asked if we would be waiting until the rain - which was falling by the bucketful - stopped. So with my umbrella up and my rain jacket fastened, and sulking that I was getting my new boots wet (little did I realize then that my boots were not going to be dry again for the next two weeks), I set off at an enthusiastic pace. It was such a steep drop down a very slippery, muddy path that I handed not only my umbrella to a little native follower so that I could hang on with both hands as I slithered downwards, but my rain jacket too, as it was as wet on the inside with perspiration as the outside was with the rain.

I made it to the bottom and back up again still with a smile on my face to find that we were being graded for the seven day trek. Big Jim announced that I had passed but, not surprisingly, Alan with his extra weight and his wife Jeannie did not fare so well and both realized that they were well out of their depth in this kind of terrain. Nipper, Nevada Jim and Wally also passed but Nancy was told that she would have to think carefully if she could really handle mountains which were going to be ten times more difficult than this training hike. Ernest had attacked the trail with great determination but took a bad fall and split his forehead and his knee when he dropped twenty feet down through the undergrowth. He was patched up that evening by the nurse and assured everyone that he would be setting out with us in the morning. Jimbo was permitted to take a well earned rest that day, but he was able to tell Nancy and me how difficult the trail had become in reaching Korupun, and that it was going to be as bad or worse for the next few days, as our expedition attempted to scale the 12,000 ft ridges between Korupun and the lowlands. We could see the mountain through the mist that we would be climbing the next morning and it looked extremely forbidding. The alternative, for those that didn't feel up to the next seven days of climbing, was to fly on later that week and meet up at the trek's finishing point at Dakai on the Brazza River where we would all continue the expedition by dugout canoe. As we went to bed that night, it was still undecided as to which of the nine of us would pick up the challenge.

PART 2

OVER THE MOUNTAIN WALL
KEEPING ONE'S HEAD IN HEAD HUNTING TERRITORY

TREK FROM KORUPUN TO DAGI

Nancy awoke and announced she was not going! Alan and Jeannie had already backed out but Ernest, despite his injuries from the day before, seemed determined to continue. I was surprised, as he did not seem to have the agility that surely would be required for this trip. At 7:00 a.m. Henke called for porters from the Kim Yal villagers. The guest house had been surrounded by them since dawn as obviously word had spread about our planned journey and, as our first few days of travel would be within their own Kim Yal territory, they were all enthusiastic to participate.

Big Jim suggested that I ought to hire myself a personal porter to carry my small pack for the first day. When I saw my little umbrella carrier from the day before amongst the crowd outside the house, I signalled to him and offered him my pack. He smiled broadly and promptly ran away and I was just thinking I had better look for another when he returned with a supply of sweet potatoes in his net bag and obviously his mother's blessing. He can't have been much more than fourteen and his name was Sawcop. There was a bit of an embarrassing moment as I showed him how to fasten on my pack as the waist belt got in the way of his penis gourd. However I let him sort that one out.

There was great excitement as we all assembled on the runway: Jimbo, Nevada Jim, Nipper, Wally, Ernest and I; plus our three Canadian guides, Big Jim, Kevin and Jean; Indonesian guide Bob; Agung and Scorpio our cooks; plus thirty-seven Kim Yal and Dani porters. It was by now seven thirty and Big Jim was anxious to be off. Henke, the Irian Jaya interpreter, had been appointed to stay behind with Nancy, Jeannie and Alan. Bob, our Indonesian guide, would manage the porters, and so we all bid our farewells.

We walked to the end of the runway and immediately dropped down 1,000 ft of very steep muddy paths to the Wamena River in the gorge below. This was a tributary of the Erok River we had descended to the day before. I managed to scramble on all fours over our first of many flimsy bridges when Big Jim called a halt, and after a quiet talk with Ernest despatched him back to Korupun. This initial descent had been too difficult for him and Jim felt, if he was struggling now, there was no hope he would be able to continue. I know Ernest was terribly disappointed and I wondered if I would be next to get the chop, so I set out on our climb at an enthusiastic pace to show I could keep up with the best of them.

Our ascent to the summit of the shoulder at 8,000 ft took us till lunchtime and the last couple of hours' climb was straight up a very slippery path that was much like climbing a ladder as so much of it was across the tangled roots of trees. Little Sawcop hauled me up a good deal of the way and often the stretch was so great I had to get one knee up on the ledge and have him pull me up from a kneeling position. The altitude also didn't help matters and I found myself praying that we would reach the top while I could still catch my breath. By now it was pouring which made the mud thicker and the moss that covered everything else even more treacherous.

Little Sawcop had by now introduced me to his "nan". Was this an uncle, godfather, mentor? I had established it was not his father. Sepnyat was a little wizened man probably only half the age he looked. He had been signed up as a group porter and he hung back and took it upon himself to adopt this crazy woman who, apart from our young assistant guide Jean, was the only female member of the expedition. Obviously he thought I should have stayed behind in Korupun cooking sweet potatoes. I was certainly glad of both his and Sawcop's outstretched hands and also relieved to see that Wally was behind me and not making any faster progress. It was just the most awful climb one could imagine through dense equatorial rainforest, and the main problem was that the path went almost straight up the mountainside with no traverses. What a relief when my nose came over the final ledge and I saw our lunchtime campfire on the shoulder of the summit.

We didn't take long over lunch, partly because we were damp and cold sitting around at that altitude, and also because Jim knew we had some distance still to go before dark, judging by the anxiety of the porters to continue. They didn't want to be caught out in the jungle after dark. I, too, was anxious to get this nightmare over with and so we started our descent down an equally treacherous trail; this time I was being caught from below by the faithful Sawcop and Sepnyat as I slithered from rock to root to rock. It took almost three hours to drop the 4000 ft to the valley floor and then we found that, after we had struggled for an hour through dense swordgrass along swampy paths, we had another 1000 ft climb to reach the village of Dagi where we would spend the night.

Nipper, Nevada Jim and Jimbo were obviously pleased to see Wally and I limp in at five-thirty just before dusk, as they had found it challenging and wondered how the two weaker ones would cope. I had enough daylight minutes left to stumble down to the nearby stream to wash my socks, boots, insoles and gaiters before changing into my long sleeved shirt and pants and getting my mosquito net attached to my hat before night fell at six on the dot. Amongst the village's round pandanus roofed huts there was an empty wooden school building which would have been brought in by MAF's helicopters in anticipation of one day supplying the village with their own bible teacher. We found these single room buildings in most of the villages we passed through and, although they were in various stages of dilapidation, we were glad to have a hard dry floor and a roof over our heads. Tents erected in the wet mud of the compound in these villages were not an attractive alternative.

Sawcop and Sepnyat busied themselves getting a drying line erected for me between the rafters and seeing me unpacked and settled before they went off to join the other porters in the village huts. Sepnyat seemed to have done some incoherent nattering with Big Jim whilst pointing at me and Sawcop. It became clear that he considered Sawcop was not going to be up to the task ahead. Jim agreed that perhaps it would be for the best if Sepnyat took over as my personal porter and young Sawcop return to Korupun. So I bade farewell to little Sawcop, paid him his daily wage of 2000 rupiah ($1.20) and he seemed delighted that he had done a man's day's work. When I discovered what was ahead it proved to be a wise decision.

Jean was now very busy with what would be a daily pre-supper medical clinic for us all. Bob was suffering from a wound on his shin which had become septic and required hot compresses to try to release the poison which was beginning to travel up his leg and he already had a fever as a result. He had been advised to go to the clinic in Korupun for a shot of penicillin but had not related to Jim that they had refused him treatment. We hoped it was because the missionary nurse was not aware of the severity of his infection rather than that she was anxious not to give help that would encourage future outsiders, especially Indonesians. Jim had already experienced unwillingness in these parts to give assistance no matter how serious the situation. There is a certain (and perhaps understandable) negative attitude on the part of the missionaries towards anyone whom they feel may be a threat to their control in that area. But it seems a rather uncharitable and unChristian attitude and I was not overly impressed with their work as we continued our journey. Too much saving of souls for the next world, instead of improving the quality of life in this one! Everyone had cuts and scratches to be attended to, but mine were minor and mainly caused by the high swordgrass that had swiped my ear and were enough to stop me sleeping on that side. Some purple iodine cured that and also lent a little colour to my visage which, fortunately, I never saw in a mirror for a whole two weeks.

I had fallen over a couple of hobbled chickens when I arrived at the Dagi Hilton, and Agung deftly despatched, plucked, cooked and served them up for supper. They were still putting up a fight it seemed when we tried to chew them, but they were a welcome repast. The others were too tired to bother erecting tents but I was determined to sleep under netting. I knew malaria was not a problem at this altitude but I wanted to keep out the many other creepy crawlies. Our guide Jim had asked me to give my little personal mosquito net to Nancy, as she was going to be without a tent when they got to Dakai and would need some protection and, provided I could always be inside a tent during our trek, I agreed. We had small two man domed free standing tents with a floor, and with walls and roof entirely of mosquito netting, plus a waterproof fly that could be used when erected outdoors. They were ideal for this climate. And so, with my water bottle filled with hot water to comfort my aching thigh muscles, I crawled under my sleeping sheet relieved to have survived what we had expected to be the most difficult part of our trip.

DAGI TO KOBBOKDUA

It was my first morning of trying to drag on soaking wet socks and boots. Attempts to get anything to dry in this humid climate were fruitless. I must say I was feeling far from refreshed and my leg muscles so contracted I could have pinned my socks to my earrings. However I reckoned that nothing could be as bad as the previous day and, once I got moving, I would be okay. I seemed to be much slower than the rest in getting packed up and was still trying to do up my gaiters when we set off.

The porters led; they were the only ones who knew our route, since no topographical maps exist of this area. Big Jim was trying to make one with his compass and altimeter as we went along. Kevin went ahead as the lead guide, followed by Nevada Jim, Jimbo and Nipper, then Jean in the middle, followed at an ever increasing distance by myself and Wally. Big Jim would always bring up the rear, which was a comfort and wise guiding. Bob and Agung would move up and down the line keeping an eye on the performance of the porters.

Sepnyat had been waiting for me at the door that morning with an air of importance. His group pack had been redistributed but he would continue to be considered a senior porter and paid accordingly. He popped my thermarest into his large noken along with his supply of hiperi (soil and all). This he slung from his forehead and balanced on the top of my personal backpack. Again there was the confusion about whether the waist strap should go below or above his penis gourd string. He also found the snap buckle mighty confusing as well and was forever undoing it and rushing back to me with the buckle bits in his hand for reassembly. He was like a little monkey with arms almost as long as his bandy legs, which were continually on the move running along the path and then running back when he remembered about me. His feet had a large spread between the first and the big toe which allowed him to use them like claws to wrap around roots and logs and give him balance. Nattering incessantly in his incomprehensible dialect, he would look up at me, his face full of expression, and I felt I knew every word of encouragement he was surely giving me. His only word of English was Mamma, which was the name I was to share along with the Virgin Mary, and I just hoped I was going to be able to pull off a few miracles to match.

My recollection of this day's trek is a little hazy, for it was to be one of the toughest days of my whole life. Again we had an absolutely horrendous ascent, this time to 8,600 ft, and most of the way in rain cloud. My lungs were bursting and I would manage about ten steep steps before I would have to rest to catch my breath. The vegetation was dense with wet moss everywhere and tangled roots to manoeuvre or clamber through, and my only consolation was that Wally wasn't faring much better. Sepnyat literally dragged me up most of the way, cooing encouragingly and faithful as a little dog. When I pulled out my trail mix for a quick fix of energy he would almost sit on his hind legs and beg his share. At this rate it wasn't going to last me two days, far less two weeks. All my reserves of energy had been used up the day before and I was running on empty.

I had hardly the strength to spread some jam on my cracker crumbs at lunch when we finally reached the top. Obviously one of the porters had been using our box of perishable goods as an occasional armchair and our total supply of lunchtime water biscuits had suffered accordingly. However, we managed to glue them into a ball with the daily ration of one tin of sardines, a tin of corned beef, a jar of jam and one of peanut butter - which amongst nine was never enough. Bread had been included in our rations, but it had gone mouldy by day one. It was realized early on that our Indonesian food suppliers for the expedition had miscalculated badly. As our breakfast every morning consisted of nothing more than a bowl of porridge, with occasionally a little dried fruit added, there was no way we could replenish the kind of calories we were expending. We all lost many pounds in the next two weeks.

Sepnyat seemed anxious that I start out again before the others finished lunch and I agreed that the sooner this day was over the better. So I tottered off with him to be confronted with a descent down an almost sheer cliff face. Some of the vegetation was clinging to the rock and some came away in your hand as you inched downward, searching for every toe and finger hold. The last thing I ever wanted to be was a rock climber and here I was one but without a rope. The natives, over the years, had cleverly placed logs across the front of some of the smoother faces and these you inched along, knowing that you just dare not slip. All I can remember was that I was continually wailing "Oh no!" as every section seemed to offer yet another horrific descent. This cliff face dropped for 2,400 ft without a break and it took a good two and half hours to reach our first piece of non vertical ground and the more normal 90 degree slither and slide down the last 3000 ft. Yesterday was a bad dream. Today was a nightmare.

It was, of course, pouring with rain during this whole descent but there was no question of trying to constrict oneself with rainwear and really a bit pointless. Sepnyat was obviously finding, with the slow pace, that he was getting cold. The large tropical leaves that he tucked under his tumpline to lie over his back were not as effective as my umbrella, which he suddenly discovered tucked down the side of my pack. So he absolutely skipped along with glee when I unfolded it for him and, when we reached the lower firmer slopes, he ran away with it and I was on my own to follow the path. It was about an hour before he reappeared by the river in the valley, whooping with delight that we had met again. I felt he had been a little derelict in his duties and wondered if it was only because he had closed my umbrella and now couldn't reopen it that he had returned at all. But then I discovered he had lit himself a little fire under an overhang by the river to warm himself and realized that my slow pace was too chilling for someone who was only clad in a penis gourd.

We had long since been overtaken by the rest of the expedition and even Wally, with his mountaineering experience, had passed me by muttering that he had never made such a difficult descent in all his climbing career. Jim, however, had stayed at the back with me and so we brought up the rear with little Sepnyat encouraging me to quicken my pace as we started to climb the next ridge towards Kobbokdua. It took another two and a half hours over arduous, rolling terrain at a jogging pace, as it was gone five thirty and we were all anxious to not be be caught out in the dark that descends so suddenly

I think they all cheered when I showed up at the village. I'm not sure. I have never been quite so exhausted in my whole life and I had been running on sheer guts and will power for most of the day. Every step had been an agony of stretched and painful muscles. So often I had just wanted to sit down and say I couldn't go on, but I knew I had to. It didn't surprise me to hear that a German expedition, which had previously attempted the same crossing of the Mountain Wall, had retreated back to Korupun after the first day.

I forced myself to eat supper and drink lots of tea and hot chocolate as I knew I had to replenish my body. I was so glad to find that Kevin had put up a tent for me in an adjacent rickety building and I barely remember collapsing into it.

KOBBOKDUA TO DEIBULA

I was so terribly stiff the next morning. Sepnyat had to help me lace my boots and my gaiter zippers were so clogged with dried mud that I had to wash them

Diane Jones

in the only available puddle which a pig had kindly just provided. At least the sun was shining and I was still alive.

This was another Kim Yal village with several round huts, thatched with pandanus palm leaves, arranged at random in a fenced compound. As in Dagi all the houses were raised about eighteen inches on stilts so obviously the mud is a permanent problem. Much of it is a slime green, the contribution of the many pigs which are highly prized by the natives and are the basis of their wealth and power. Each village would also have a tame cassowary strutting about in addition to some rather mangy looking chickens. The villagers were fascinated by us and watched our every movement. I had to dress with a crowd of them peering at me through the open doorway and when I tried to find a little private spot in the long grass beyond the compound, avoiding a big boar who claimed it was his territory, they would follow along to see what I was doing. It was a few days before I discovered that to push one's arm towards someone with the palm open meant quite the opposite to them and was a sign to follow.

Big Jim encouraged Wally and me by suggesting that we all might take it a little easier today and stop for the night at a village a half day's journey away. Wally had taken a bad fall on "the cliff" and bruised his back, so although his legs were in better condition than mine, his back was causing him some pain. Mentally I felt positive, for I knew that nothing could be as bad as yesterday ever again, and the fact that I had come through it and survived buoyed me up. There were no more 8,000 ft ridges ahead of us, but with the limestone terrain it meant that every river and stream we came to had eroded a very steep gorge, and this meant many steep descents and an equally steep climb on the other side. Every bend of the knee was agony but my faithful Sepnyat helped me down and pulled me up all the way. Good news was that the sun was shining and the views were magnificent.

We did indeed reach the village of Sisepna before noon and not too far behind the others, but hopes of staying there for night three were voted down as everyone else, including the porters, were anxious to continue. However our cook had managed to buy the hind leg of a freshly cooked pig, straight out of the communal pit oven. So shortly after, when we came to a mountain stream, we all had a good wash and laundry session before tucking into a roast pork lunch. It was delicious. The natives love pork, especially the fat, and they all sat around us drooling. I was very tempted to slip a little piece to Sepnyat who was watching my every bite, but we had been advised not to show our porters any favouritism in front of the others or they would be ridiculed and so I let it be. The remains of the pork leg and all the fat was given to the head porter for distribution that night and I was pleased to learn from Sepnyat, through our sign language, that he did get his share.

That afternoon started with a pleasant path through tall grasses and stands of pandanus palms, and you could see the long line of our porters by the sacks they carried on their heads. Being at the rear I felt that I would be unlikely to come across any unfriendly animals in my path as they would already have been scared away by those ahead. But later Leo, the head Dani porter, who was directly behind me, let out a great whooping as a large snake slithered into the undergrowth beside the spot I had just walked. Surprisingly, that was to be my only close encounter with any wild animals on this trip. The jungle and the upper canopy are so dense that it is very difficult to spot wildlife, and although you can hear exotic bird calls at all times, it is seldom that you can actually spot the bird. That was a disappointment for me as I expected to have the opportunity to see some birds of paradise which frequent these mountains or even see the many prolific parrots and cockatoos.

We faced another ridge but this had entirely different jungle vegetation. Instead of a muddy path we had to negotiate a trail made up almost entirely of felled tree trunks. This allowed the porters to travel above the forest floor which had such a build up of rotting vegetation and bushes as to be sometimes indiscernible. This is where Sepnyat's claw like feet were at their best and he could literally run along the narrowest of these logs which were often many feet above the ground - that is if there was any firm ground down there. With hiking boots it was a different story and, although I mastered the wider tree trunks with his steadying hand, sometimes our path was reduced to a narrow log or branch that any tightrope walker wearing size eleven boots would have found difficult. The slippery conditions that were always present created a tense and challenging journey for us all and we would name some sections "No Falls" when it would have been very dangerous to lose one's footing.

At this lower altitude I also discovered we had entered leech territory when I felt a persistent itching up the leg of my shorts. The first moment I was able to balance myself and free my hands I had a look-see, and am quite ashamed to say I just stood there and screamed. This was quite the most revolting pest one could ever meet. It was about two inches long and hooked onto my skin with two little barbs on either side of its mouth. When I tried to remove it, it just went into a perpendicular corkscrew squirm and hung on. Leo, who was still behind me, took the matter of the offending leech into his own hands and, after great difficulty in detaching it, gave it a thoroughly good send off by crushing it between two stones. Flinging it a couple of yards into the bush was not sufficient punishment obviously. I was left with a nasty bruise and treated the haemorrhaging holes immediately with the antibiotic cream I had learned to carry with me in my pocket. A little later I had the same sensation but this horror had crept up and beyond the bikini line. Sepnyat answered this scream and I shed all modesty and insisted he deal with this creature, and he too gave it its comeuppance between two rocks.

Diane Jones

These loathsome creatures actually climb the vegetation and lie in wait for a warm blooded victim. There can be so many hanging from one stalk that they look like the fringe of a lampshade. They drop onto you and travel undetected towards the warmest area of the body, needless to say the crotch. The leeches were to be an ever increasing pest when we reached the jungle lowlands. On one occasion Kevin, being on lead, counted thirty that he had to pull off his upper legs in half an hour. I defeated these creatures by foregoing my cool shorts for long pants tied tightly with a drawstring at my waist, pulled my gaiters tight round my lower legs and by wearing what I found to be my indispensable cotton gardening gloves, I was able to brush them from my clothes before they could reach my skin. I also think that my wide brimmed straw topee, that I wore all the time, deflected many of them.

By mid afternoon I was very weary again and Sepnyat would coo sympathetic sounds when I had to stop for a short break. He had fallen head over heels in love with me, I think, for he would hold my hand in his and pound his heart and blow little kissing noises up at me, and then clutch my hand to his cheek and nuzzle it. Of course, my fellow trekkers ribbed me unmercifully about "my affair". I guess it could be rather erotic, being continually behind a little bare brown butt, and occasionally having to duck the 18" rampant penis gourd when he swung round to grasp my hand. I was quite amused to wonder what other middle aged women would think if they found themselves in such a situation.

The log walking had slowed all of us today so I wasn't quite so far behind the guys when we reached Deibula in the late afternoon. The village was balanced on a cliff edge at 4,500ft and afforded a magnificent view of our descent to the lowlands below. However our initial view of our night's accommodation was not so hot. The only hut available was not much bigger than a hen house and certainly no cleaner. The village compound of a dozen huts sat on the ubiquitous sea of slimy mud and it was raining cats and dogs. There was no point in descending to the creek a hundred feet below to wash as you were going to be just as muddy by the time you stumbled back. Instead we got wise to hiring the little village kids to take our socks and boots and wash them for us. A fine job they did too for a pinch of salt or a 100 rupiah note, which was more an attraction for its pictures than its trading value.

Our circumstances were certainly grim that night, but our sense of humour would come to the fore as we all squeezed together in this 12'x10' hut on stilts and laughed ourselves to sleep. No hope of putting up any tents in this confined space so we just pulled the mosquito netting of one of the tents across our heads, as being at this lower altitude meant we were in malaria territory, and kept ourselves inside the safety of our sleeping bags. Concern had been growing over the worsening condition of Bob's leg wound and he developed a high temperature and was delirious that night. We had made him more comfortable by putting him on an upper platform under the roof with Kevin beside him.

DEIBULA TO UPPER DEIBULA

The noise of a helicopter awoke us next morning and we all squeezed to look out our hen house door. It flew off down the valley but returned shortly after and landed, or rather perched, on the cliff edge of the village compound. Out hopped Ernest who, with the other three, had unfortunately taken the advice of the linguist at Korupun that our group would, by now, have reached a point on the expedition that would be easy enough for the four of them to rejoin the group. So they arranged to charter the helicopter to fly them, two days earlier than planned, to search for us in the interior, instead of waiting for the MAF plane to take them direct to Dakai in the lowlands to regroup. It was an awkward situation as Jim knew they would still be unable to tackle the final descent which we could see was going to be very tricky. But they didn't need much persuasion when they saw the conditions and topography we were dealing with and it gave us an opportunity to swap Henke, who was with them in the chopper, for Bob, who needed to be evacuated in order to reach medical help in Dakai.

The pilot had been able to tell Jim that there was a much better village, drier and with a new empty school building, further along the ridge. This was where they had expected to find us, so we set out with the knowledge that we had only a tough couple of hours' hike and we could then take the rest of the day off. We all badly needed a break. I still had agonizingly painful leg muscles and a sprained elbow which discouraged me from using my hiking stick for support. Wally's bruised back was needing a rest and Jimbo's foot rot was worsening.

When we arrived at Upper Deibula in the late morning in the sunshine, I thought we had died and gone to heaven. The empty school building was new and very large. Plenty of room to erect all the tents and lay out all our gear to dry and air. It was perched on the summit of a ridge that extended out towards the lowlands and, from 4,700 ft, offered wonderful views. The bare ground was well drained and dry so we could wear our sandals in the warm sunshine. Several adjacent village compounds dropped off down the mountain so there was an unending stream of visitors coming to inspect us.

This outlying post of the Kim Yal tribe afforded us the chance to spend some time observing them and they us. There was only one woman in a ragged dress. All the rest of the women were in grass skirts and the men, some of whom looked quite Neanderthal, wore nothing but their rampant penis gourds. We always broke the ice with a few inflated balloons which had the children, followed by the adults, running all over the place laughing and screaming with delight. Jim also had a crocodile puppet and would give a show from one of the window openings. As we were within trading distance of the lowlands they knew about crocodiles and so the puppet's antics caused much amusement and I think that, rather than invading them, we gave a little brightness to their lives that day. We also made sure to collect all the burst balloons as we were travelling on the "leave no impact" principle. I should note that we were beginning to notice many ginger haired children in these villages and wondered if it was caused by a parasite or a diet deficiency. It wasn't particularly noticeable in the adults and, on the whole, they looked very healthy although most had the distended belly that can be caused by malnutrition. The hiperi (sweet potatoes) were still their staple diet. I noticed a small circular cage of sticks with a thatched roof just beyond the fence when I was venturing forth for a jungle toilet stop and noticed an old man crouched inside. His noken was suspended from a branch just beyond and I wondered if he could have been isolated for some health reason or as a punishment and depended on donations of food being dropped in his bag. I should have got in line as it turned out to be the village privy.

We were going to have to change porters here as our Korupun ones would not go any further, although I think by this time Sepnyat would have gone to the ends of the earth with me. The Deibula Kim Yal were used to trading in the lowlands with the Momina tribe at Dakai and we needed them as guides, whereas the Korupun Kim Yal were much too afraid of malaria to ever venture further than the edge of the mountains. Agung and Henke took the opportunity of buying up as many fresh vegetables as possible as this would be our last village before Dakai in three days time at best. Henke called for our new porters to assemble the next morning. There had never been an expedition through this area before so portering was a new thing for them, but we depended on the previous porters to pass on the information as to what was expected of them and we still had the nine Dani porters with us to set an example.

We were all in very good spirits next morning and had become very close to one another under what had been some very trying situations. We all had strong personalities and would react in different ways when stressed, but we felt we could totally depend on each other and indeed often had to for both moral and physical help. Being the only woman amongst all these men I had to put up with a great deal of ribbing and, suffice to say, a considerable lack of privacy. I don't include Jean because she was not only young and super fit but also, as Jim's partner, very much under his protection. I almost considered it a compliment that I was treated as one of the boys. Usually I was able to top their cheeky remarks but I knew I had also gained their considerable respect and that they were proud that I had survived the past few days with good humour. Or were they just relieved that I hadn't broken down, either mentally or physically as they had probably suspected I would, and thereby hold up the expedition. Even Big Jim, who could be rather remote and preoccupied, seemed to enjoy and even seek out my company. They would tease me mercilessly for the next couple of nights by drawing straws to decide who would have to share a tent with me and, of course, it was always the short straw.

PART 3

CROCODILE FEARS
HEADWATERS OF THE BRAZZA RIVER
UPPER DEIBULA TO THE LOWLANDS

Sepynat had crept into our building at dawn and was squatting outside my tent when I awoke. He was here to say a final goodbye before he started out on his return journey to Korupun. He seemed somewhat dismayed to find that Jimbo, who had chosen the short straw, was sharing my tent and jabbered away at him. Jimbo said he was offering to buy me for a pig but I ought to refuse and stick with the expedition. I felt really sorry to say goodbye as Sepnyat had been the most devoted porter I could ever have wished for and we had been through some tough times together. I had given him lots of little goodies and paid him well and his final gesture was to introduce me to his successor whom he had personally selected for me. His name was Belman, and I don't know where he appeared from as he was wearing shorts and a tee shirt and we hadn't seen any of the men with western clothes. Perhaps he saved them for trips to the lowlands to help protect from the mosquitoes. So with Sepnyat still nuzzling my hand whilst murmuring sweet nothings and helping me into my boots and gaiters for the last time, Belman put on the backpack, produced a stout stick and by 6:30 a.m. we were underway.

My legs felt so much better after our rest day and, with the knowledge that it would be mostly downhill from now on, we were all in good spirits. However, before long, the rains came and it was back to the usual slither and slide. Five of our new porters quit after a couple of hours and the guides had to carry their packs until we could redistribute the loads at lunchtime. Belman was definitely the strong silent type and it made a change from Sepnyat's constant nattering, but he was every bit as attentive and was obviously very familiar with the trail. We were at 1,200 ft by lunch break and the rain stopped for the rest of the day.

We had to cross a couple of fast running tributaries before we finally came to the headwaters of the Brazza River by about 3:30 p.m. It was only about fifty feet wide but waist deep and fast running. The Kim Yal are nervous of water except for a few experienced traders like Belman who were always first to cross. Jim rigged a rope across at the narrowest point for the porters to hang on to but, of course, the strong current was enough to whisk the odd penis gourd off its perch which caused much hilarity amongst the porters when he emerged on the other side with it dangling from its tether. It took an hour to get everyone safely across and, as we were on an open pebble beach well above the river, we decided to make camp for the night.

Immediately all the porters seemed to know what to do and, better than any military exercise, they felled trees using their traditional stone axes, built a frame for our tarps and a large shelter for themselves covered with the huge leaves from the felled trees. These jungle skills then produced a large domed hut by bending saplings and lacing them altogether with jungle vines before cladding them with palm fronds. It was all accomplished within the hour and it took us almost as long to level the beach stones and erect our free standing tents. Jimbo's foot rot was getting worse and some of the others were suffering from infected sores but I was in very good shape and felt that, now we were on flat ground, I could hold my own. I had a terrific night's sleep and can confirm that rocks can be more comfortable than the flat ground if you get the contours just right. We were now into hot and humid temperatures with little fluctuation at night so we could lie on top of our sleeping bags for additional padding. Our altitude had dropped to 400 ft and we were still 150 miles from the Arafura Sea!

The route from now on was, as often as possible, down the banks of the river and moving into the jungle only when there was no shoreline or pebbled dry riverbed to walk on. Our jungle path had to be cut by the porters with parangs (machetes) and Belman would be one of the leaders who always seemed to know the way. They would leave notches in tree trunks and break saplings to mark the route for their return as the vegetation is so lush that it will grow back with alarming speed. The ground under foot was very wet and we would often find we had to wade waist deep through depressions left in the dry riverbeds. You had no idea what you were treading on below the muddy water and what might be lurking there or in the lush undergrowth. There are no predator mammals in New Guinea but reptiles are another matter and crocodiles our main fear.

When we had to cross a vast stretch of dry riverbed we were exposed to the fierce sun and I was glad to have my umbrella for shade. We criss-crossed the Brazza River several times before coming to a particularly wide and turbulent section. The porters were very nervous and our guides spent a good hour searching for a safe crossing point. It was much too wide to stretch a rope and we had to settle for a three stage crossing with one of the sections being chest deep with a very strong current. We put on our own packs for added weight and Kevin, Wally, Nipper, Jimbo, myself and Nevada Jim linked arms and locked hands and inched our way slowly across, slanting our line gradually downstream. One or two lost their footing but were supported from either side and were able to recover and, of course, the water was not cold, just wet.

Belman had disappeared back upstream looking for his own route but returned, conceding that this was the best we were going to find as the river was running high, and he and several of our Dani porters started ferrying all our equipment across. But about half the Deibula porters were so scared they started to leave and refused to come back when called. Big Jim, on seeing that we were about to lose them, promptly caught up with one, swung him up on his shoulders and carried him across. With his height and strength he was able to make this crossing on his own and, when the porters saw that one of them was now stranded on the other side of the river, they hesitated. Jim just went back, grabbed another one, and gradually he and Kevin, by roping the remainder between them, brought them safely across plus the remaining supplies. It had taken two and a half hours. If our Deibula porters had left us at this stage our expedition would have been in trouble so we gave them much praise and promised a pay bonus. They seemed pleased at having conquered their fear of the river.

Belman had a severely swollen right arm by now and I remembered him having taken a bad fall the first morning. It didn't seem to be broken but we gave him some anti-inflammatories and I fixed up a sling with my small towel and the elastic from my money belt, which he wore with pride.

We had only covered a few miles that day but now had only a couple of hours left before we had to find a campsite and our hopes of reaching Dakai tomorrow did not look promising. Our choice of a huge sandy bank by a bend in the river was not ideal, but we made the best of it. Jimbo's feet were very raw and swollen even across the instep. Nipper, Nevada Jim and even Jean were also showing signs of foot rot. Belman helped me put up the tent for Jimbo to rest a little higher up on a secondary pebbled beach, but there wasn't much room and the rest of our tents were spread out over the sandbank. The porters soon had their own huts built from scratch, this time by pulling the growing canes of tall beach grass over one another until they formed cosy domed shelters high up on the bank.

Agung got a good cooking fire going under our tarp and, as it hadn't rained all day, we didn't mind the sudden thunderstorm as we were well sheltered. Jimbo and Jean required room service for dinner that night and the rest of us were just scraping the last mouthful from our plates when Belman came, tugged my arm, and pointed in the direction of the river which was invisible in the pitch dark. Kevin volunteered to investigate and came scurrying back shouting that we had to move the camp immediately as the river was rising fast, and we had a flash flood on its way. We grabbed all the tents and equipment from the beach whilst the porters dismantled the kitchen. Almost immediately the water swept right across our campsite and carried our campfire off down the river with the logs still flaming brightly. The tent with Jimbo inside was now on the front line, about a foot from the river's final highest point. Belman chose to become our nightwatchman with my raincoat and umbrella. The other tents had to layer themselves on what small piece of bare ground behind us they could find.

The following day was to be our first day without torrential rain but the many river crossings made sure we were never dry. The river would often split into many channels, some of which created bayous within the jungle and again we kept a close lookout for crocodiles as we waded through these. After five hours of hiking we were in impenetrable jungle making only as fast progress as the porters could slash a trail. Often the porters would set up a whooping call that would be answered further along the line and especially if something alarmed them, so it was nothing new to hear this Wha Wha Whaaing in the distance. But what we didn't know was that this wasn't our porters but some of the Momina from Dakai that had been sent out as a search party. They suddenly came crashing through the jungle looking slightly menacing with their bows and arrows, but soon everyone was covered in smiles and we knew we were on the home stretch.

It was another hour's fast walk but not difficult now that we could follow the Momina trails. I felt very strong and in good shape, but it was a difficult struggle for the ones with bad feet and the leeches were particularly obnoxious. The last couple of miles were mainly across the scorching river beds and our winding file of thirty odd porters was well spread out and tiring. However, our pace quickened when we saw the roofs of the village, and it was just after four when we staggered, in ones and twos, into the village to a wonderful reception from Alan, Jeanie, Ernest, Nancy and a now fully recovered Bob, our Indonesian guide.

Beyond the village was a beautiful clear swimming hole in a fast flowing tributary stream, and we wallowed in it for the next hour and gorged ourselves on fresh papaya.

Diane Jones

PART 4

DOWN RIVER BY DUGOUT
IN SEARCH OF THE TREEHOUSE PEOPLE

DAKAI TO PATIPI

The village of Dakai sat in fairly open cleared land with the mission's grass runway dividing it into two sections. About ten rectangular houses on metre high stilts, with walls of palm bark and roofs of pandanus leaves, occupied the main area and another four clustered at the far end of the runway. This mission had a resident Indonesian bible teacher and possessed not only a schoolhouse but also a church. The villagers probably totalled about fifty and at all times seemed to be crowded around the schoolhouse where we had set up camp and where the remainder of our group had been living for the past four days.

It was concerning to see that the Momina were covered in ringworm and another skin disease called cascada. Most males were wearing ragged shorts, many of them old Y Fronts, most of which were in such tatters that their genitals were hanging out. One had to wonder if there was any point in the missionaries trying to clothe them. The rags were so filthy that they probably contributed to the unhealthy skin conditions and seemed totally out of place in this hot, humid climate. The males' traditional dress was a small leaf which they tied over the end of their penis but there were only one or two older men "dressed" like this. The women wore attractive traditional skirts of many many strands of braided jungle twine which swung like a heavy kilt when they walked.

Bob had recovered with the few days of rest which had allowed the antibiotics to cope with the infection. There was no medical facility here and a filthy little hut that said "Clinic" on the door looked as if it hadn't been used for decades. The bible teacher didn't seem to mind us using his schoolhouse and, as it was Sunday morning, we sent all the Dani porters to his church service. No point in us going as we wouldn't have understood a word and we didn't want to squeeze in with all that ringworm. We were allowed a wonderful lazy day and spent the scorching afternoon mostly in the swimming hole. We watched a beautiful sunset from the river bank and dined on fresh crayfish and papaya.

Tomorrow our porters would leave. We had come into Dakai with 28 of them remaining, nine of whom were the original Dani from the Baliem Valley. It would take them seven or eight days to return to Wamena at twice our speed, and the Kim Yal from Deibula would probably be home in three. Belman's arm was much less swollen and on the mend but he was happy to continue to sport the sling. He wanted to keep my umbrella, but I knew I would need it as a sun shade in the dugout. He was well paid and happy to settle for my shorts and a tee shirt. If he was going to wear clothes, better some decent ones than the ragged ones he had set out in, and as he was so tiny the shorts were baggy and long enough to give him some protection from the mosquitoes at night, as he could draw his legs right up inside them. Our packs had been so continually soaked both by rain and submersion that everything was mildewed and I knew I would not be taking much of my gear back home.

Jim announced that tomorrow we had two choices: either we start our journey down the Brazza in the dugout canoes, or join him and Bob on a two to three day excursion southeast towards the Obini tribes, who had had little contact with white people. The teacher told us that there had been a tribal war in Obini territory a day or two earlier and tried to discourage this plan, and it certainly discouraged me. Anyway I felt I was not quite ready for such an expedition and the thought of bobbing off down the river in a canoe was very appealing. Nevada Jim said that he would go if his foot rot had improved by the morning.

At dawn our porters all came to say goodbye and it was an emotional moment as we had treated them well and they in turn had given us faithful service. We would never know how our Kim Yal fared on their return to Daboulah but I felt confident that Belman's arm would heal. Six of the nine Dani porters got back to Wamena in exactly one week. We met them whilst we were in transit at Wamena from Senggo to Jayapura. They were in good shape and they expected the other three the following day. It was good to know they had all returned safely.

Nevada Jim decided his feet were not in good enough condition, but Jimbo decided his were much better and he would go on the hike to find the Obini. He, Big Jim and Bob saw the rest of us packed into six dugout canoes with eighteen Dakai natives to paddle. The whole village walked to the river bank at the other end of the runway to see us off and it took about an hour to get us all loaded. Wally, Kevin and I in one; Jeannie, Alan, Nancy and Ernest together; Jean, Nevada Jim and Nipper in a third; and Henke, Agung and Scorpio, his Dani assistant, monitored the other three which were loaded with all the packs and supplies.

I was glad to be facing the rear as it wasn't the quiet bob-along I had expected. The river was very fast and we had many rapids caused mainly by stranded logs that had to be negotiated, but in my rearview position I didn't have the horror of seeing what was coming up. Only by the noise could I tell that it was going to be a hairy scary ride. Our three paddlers seemed to be rookies and did not inspire us with confidence. They stood to paddle; one precariously perched on the very narrow bow, the other on the equally narrow stern and one with trembling legs in the middle. Frequently one of them fell in and we had to head for the bank with him in tow as it was impossible to climb back in without tipping the whole canoe. We had to sit on the floor in a varying amount of water depending on how often we bailed. The dugouts were just that; tree trunks with the centre core hollowed out with a stone adze. They were about twenty to twenty-five feet long, with a very long and sharply pointed bow and stern. You daren't move or you upset the balance and, after a day in this position, your bottom was numb and your knees bruised from bracing them against the gunwales. I got wise to the sore backside and used my inflatable neck pillow to sit on and was the only one smiling by the end of the day.

Our plan was to stop at Sepanna where the Cain tribe live in communal treehouses. Big Jim had discovered the village when he was exploring the Asmat lowlands the previous year. But there was no sign of any habitation and we decided to continue without stopping for lunch in the expectation it would be around the next bend. However by four o'clock we thought it best to set up camp as we had come to the confluence of the Brazza and the Saris Rivers which indicated it was too far to reach Patipi village where we had intended to spend the night.

We set up camp where there had been an old fishing shelter, but there was little room for all our tents and it meant we had to clear some of the dense vegetation which, we discovered, was covered in fire ants. As soon as you brushed against them you were immediately stung as if seared by a flame, but fortunately the sensation didn't last long if you quickly flicked them off. It was the first time Alan, Jeannie, Nancy and Ernest had had to camp in rough jungle country and, as Jeannie's pack was sodden, having fallen in the river when Agung and Henke's dugout had capsized, they quickly found out that it could be pretty rough and uncomfortable.

We were beginning to be seriously short of food having pretty much consumed all that was available for sale in Dakai. However our paddlers had frequently stopped during the day by sandy banks with turtle prints and had excavated more than a hundred eggs. So it was rice and boiled turtle eggs for dinner. The eggs had a very rich yolk but interestingly the egg white remained liquid. Not very appetizing, but having had no lunch that day we all tucked in.

PATIPI

After another three hours down the Brazza River, which was now much deeper and had fewer rapids, we arrived the following morning at the government village of Patipi, having still not seen any sign of Sepanna. Patipi consisted of two rows of twenty wooden cabins, only about one third of them finished and occupied. The Moluccan bible teacher's house sat at the end facing down the "main street" and our idea was to persuade him to take our party onwards down the river in the mission's huge dugout which could be fitted with a highly prized outboard motor. It would mean the difference between a ten hour trip down to our destination at Senggo Mission Station or a three to four day paddle changing canoes and paddlers several times along the way.

Patipi was an interesting place, as the natives, who had been persuaded to come in from the jungle, were living in what we might consider squalor in these unfamiliar western style homes. They had even pulled up the flooring so that they could continue to build their fires inside on the earth below. Apparently the government and the missionaries are trying to centralize the natives in this way in order to have better control over them. But as they expect them to bring only one wife with them and to adapt to a more western lifestyle, they are not having much success in filling these sterile communities, (I'm glad to say). Again the natives, who were mainly of the Cain tribe, were covered in skin disease and filthy rags. We set up our tents by the teacher's house, hardly able to perform the task with the whole village crowding curiously around begging for cigarettes. We were also careful not to leave things lying around because of Bob's warning about "light fingers" and indeed some of our steel axe heads, that we had for trading, disappeared. It seemed they were picking up some of western culture's bad habits.

None of us wanted to have to stay in Patipi longer than was absolutely necessary. We were very anxious that the bible teacher be persuaded to loan us his canoe, but he was terrified of using the motor without superior authority as his instructions were that it must be used for mission business only. However a sufficient financial inducement was all it took and it was agreed he would set out with us the next morning.

What was going to happen about Jim, Jimbo and Bob was a problem solved when they showed up that afternoon in a dugout which they had hired not much farther back up the river. Their trek to find the Obini had to be aborted when their porters from Dakai refused to go further than the first village. Indeed there was still a war in the territories ahead and they wanted no part in it as it would then involve their own lives and families in Dakai being at risk. So they had basically walked to Patipi in little more time than it took us to canoe because of the many tight loops the meandering river takes.

Dinner again was turtle eggs and rice, but we had some breadfruit for the first time. These melon sized rough skinned fruits are baked in the fire and then split open to allow you to pull out the large round seeds, peel them like a lychee and eat the core which tastes somewhat like a chestnut. In fact the breadfruit tree, with its huge leaves, was next to our campsite and we were amused to see the scruffy chickens climb a ramp, which had been placed against the trunk, and roost for the night high up in the branches. The little chicks were hoisted up on the ends of poles and more often than not fell back down again.

The bank of the river was very steep and muddy and was pretty useless for bathing as you were just as dirty by the time you scrambled back up to the village. However, for the first time, I could sit with my binoculars by the river and spot some magnificent parrots, as well as the ubiquitous Sulphur Crested Cockatoos. The dugouts were much too unstable to allow me to focus my binoculars and I preferred to keep them inside their waterproof bag along with my camera while we were on the river. Hornbills, which you would hear before you could see them, frequently flew over the river but sadly no Birds of Paradise were to be seen in such dense jungle. Glorious butterflies would often alight on our skin, attracted by the salt, and give you a wonderful close-up. The Blue Morph, the world's largest butterfly, was commonly seen during our trek.

Big Jim, disappointed by his aborted side trip to find the Obini and hearing that we had not found Sepanna, decided that he would launch another exploratory trek to see if we could find this treehouse village of the Cain. One of the natives in Patipi, the son of a Sepanna chief, communicated to us through Henke that they had abandoned their riverside village and moved further back into the jungle and that if we wished, he would lead a visiting party. So our choice this morning was to take the motorized dugout down to Senggo or join Jim on what was expected to be a day trip to try to find Sepanna and then to continue to Senggo when the teacher came back. It would mean two trips for the canoe, but we couldn't all fit in the large dugout anyway. I decided to join Big Jim, but the only others game enough were Nevada Jim and Kevin. Henke and Scorpio were assigned to come with us. So we waved farewell to the dugout, heavily loaded with the rest of the group and all our packs, keeping only a small daypack each and two tents.

SEARCH FOR THE SEPANNA TREEHOUSE

We immediately set out in two dugouts with six paddlers back upstream. It was very hot and I was glad I had kept my umbrella with me for shade. We continued up river for almost seven hours with only a brief break for lunch when we ate all the food we had, a packet of crackers and a jar of jam. We went well past where we had camped two nights before and finally, about three o'clock, we pulled into a hidden backwater where several canoes were moored. Despite Henke as our translator there was very poor communication with our paddlers-cum-porters and obviously this was going to be more than a day's outing.

We followed the natives through the jungle in a rainstorm, which had already soaked us in our last half hour in the canoes and, as there were plenty of leeches, I was glad I had the protection of my long pants. The natives continually brushed their legs with alternate feet to sweep them away and seemed to know instinctively when they were being attacked. After the first half hour our path became entirely one of fallen logs and, without a break, we inched along this precarious route for almost two hours. After the first hour we had come to a clearing with two huge tree houses built on twenty foot stilts. But they were abandoned and we continued along the trail till we came to a second clearing. We would never have found the way without our native guides as there was no defined path, and I would never have managed some of the smaller logs if I hadn't had Scorpio take my hand to steady my balance. It would have challenged any tightrope walker and required a great deal of concentration.

It was almost dusk when we arrived. There were two treehouses each supported by approximately eighty stilts, some of them live trees, twenty feet above ground level. But there wasn't really any ground, rather a tangle of fallen trees and vegetation and inhospitable "don't fall" swamp. The houses were enormous, measuring thirty-five by twenty-five feet, with a verandah at either end reached by two broad ladders sloping up from underneath the centre of the structure outwards to each of the verandahs. The only daylight was through the four doors, two on either side of each verandah, and the roof of sago palm leaves was supported by side walls of woven palm bark which were about four and a half feet at the sides rising to an apex of ten feet at either end. Inside there were six fireplaces down the centre plus two at either end on one side and one centred on the other side. Only about six of the fireplaces were in use indicating that probably many of the inhabitants were away in the forest hunting or collecting sago, the staple of their diet. There were thirty to forty men, women and young children huddled around the fires, and several dogs and baby pigs roamed freely, plus millions of cockroaches covered the ceiling and walls. The interior walls were also covered with bows and arrows, fish scoops and unidentifiable tools. We settled against the wall (and the cockroaches) in one corner feeling a little uncomfortable as we were pretty well ignored by the occupants. Our porters mingled with the families and hopefully passed on the word that we were not a threat and, as it was almost dark outside, it was obvious we were stranded for the night.

Sepanna Treehouse

Jim blew up some balloons and this broke the ice a little and one elderly man settled down beside us. Kevin introduced me to Chief Big Balls, which was very naughty of him, as the man was almost crippled with elephantiasis with its symptomatic swelling of the lower body. The old man seemed intrigued that I was a woman and beckoned me to follow him out onto the balcony where he pointed out the second treehouse about fifty yards across the clearing and indicated I follow him there. If I thought I could have managed the obstacle course of logs I might have succumbed to my curiosity, and so I declined and waved goodbye. Jim casually mentioned afterwards that this was a wise decision as our native guide had said we would not be well received in the other house. We don't know why but wondered if only men and older male children occupied it.

It was now dark and we were hungry, so we sent Scorpio to try to scrounge some food. He came back with some sago crust on which we spread the last of our jam. A damp ball of sago starch is kept continually in the ashes of the fire and, as the outer layer is cooked, it is peeled off and the ball returned to the fire. It tasted like damp wallboard and was very unappetizing, but not so unappetizing as their next offering. This arrived wrapped in a parcel of green leaves and when we opened it we found a row of large fat white sago grubs staring up at us. They are a great delicacy in the lowlands and we realized they would be offended if we refused their generous gift. I decided that, as I had survived the frightful journey to get here, the least I could do was sample the hosts' favourite dish. The grubs were about the size of my thumb and went splat in your mouth and then there seemed to be a kind of crunch when you got to the head with its big black eyes. Probably just my imagination. Our heroic gesture certainly turned all eyes on us. We learned later that they are usually eaten roasted! I haven't kept the recipe.

Although it was only about six thirty, the occupants seemed to be settling down for the night, so we found enough room to put up our tents and did likewise. I chose the spot nearest the door because it was very hot and, with no chimneys and six fires continually burning, it was suffocating. It would have been difficult to sleep anyway as there seemed to be continual coming and going out to the verandah, probably for a breath of air. It was unnerving to know they were stopping to stare down at us through our mosquito net tents. Also there was a great deal of noise of crying babies, grunting piglets, barking dogs, hacking coughs and the incessant sound of tree frogs living in their very own treehouse. Of course the tree frogs act as the perfect warning signal since they would immediately stop singing if there was any disturbance on the ground below. Now and again, during this long night, one of the fires would be stoked and a group would gather round for a spot of sago and a gossip, then all would quieten down again until some other fireplace would decide to hold a party. It was unnerving to know that they were probably discussing their visitors but not know if we were considered friend or foe. Later I was told by anthropologists that our white skin may have indicated that we could be returning ancestors and therefore treated with respect rather than hostility.

At dawn we folded our tents and tried to stuff down a little sago sans jam and shared a couple of little packets of instant porridge that Big Jim had in his daypack. With what daylight was now coming through the doorways, I was able to pick my way around a little more safely as there were many holes in the floor which we suspect were used as latrines. I think my kidneys seized up when I swallowed the sago grub for I hadn't dared descend the ladder for a comfort stop before bedtime, nor did I fancy squatting over a hole in the floor either. If I recall I actually hung on till I got back to safe ground by the river, probably dehydrated

I took the chance to join the group of women at each fire and offered a little salt and some colourful embroidery threads which seemed to delight them. I admired their babies, naked except for a cowrie shell tied around their necks, and I looked the women straight in the eye and gave them a big smile and evoked a similar response. There were only one or two men present in the house this morning and either most of them spent the time in the other treehouse, or had already left to hunt in the forest. The Cain men were naked and wore a single cowrie shell in their hair over one temple and the woman wore a length of soft inner bark looped back to front on a waistband of braided jungle twine. They did not seem to have so much of the skin disease we had been seeing in Dakai and Patitpi but one of the babies was very sickly with dreadful tropical ulcers covering its tiny body. The mother offered it to me in the hope of help. Sadly I had to shake my head as its only hope was an early death.

Gradually the women warmed to me and were proud to show me their skills with spinning and making net bags with the jungle twine made from hairlike strips of bark. They would offer me sago from their fire in baskets of folded palm bark and I tried to be courteous and swallow yet another piece of the awful stuff. My fellow travellers had decided there was not much point in trying to communicate but I felt well rewarded for my efforts and even had one of the men demonstrate his skills with his bow and arrow and how he caught fish in a bark scoop. I also took a good look around, and bumped my head on the jawbone of a pig hanging from the ceiling. There was a frame suspended across the six central fires and this acted as storage for food but certainly not from the cockroaches. The fires were on a bed of clay sunk into the wood floor and there were wooden pallets circling each fire which were used as beds. One or two were still occupied by the children. I noticed that they were smoking a two piece bamboo pipe, which was passed freely between the men and women.

Jim confirmed its contents were probably hallucinatory when he had a puff the night before and advised us not to try it.

When we climbed down to leave at about 8.00 a.m., the women and children ventured out onto the verandah and responded to our cheery waves, and so I felt we left them feeling comfortable with our visit. They would naturally be anxious that we would not give away their whereabouts to the government officials and we had asked our guide to reassure them of that. It seemed a pretty grim existence in the gloom of that treehouse, but it was still better than the squalid life in Patipi.

PATIPI TO SENGGO

Our return to the river over the logs was just as difficult and one could never become skilled in big hiking boots. We took only four hours for the return down the river to Patipi, stopping on the way for a jolly good wash of our clothes and ourselves. There was no sign of the motorized dugout, and the teacher's wife and children waited hopefully by the river landing until nightfall. We were anxious too as our food sacks were empty. Dinner was plain rice with our last can of sardines on top.

Next morning there was still no sign of a boat. We were getting anxious as our plane out of Senggo was scheduled in two days and we could not make it in time without a motorized canoe. No one would sell us a dugout, so we could only wait and hope that Jean would have us rescued. Our breakfast was sago and three small bantam eggs between us which we scrounged from the villagers. We were very hungry and already I could see that I had shed many pounds more than I would have liked.

I spent a great deal of time by the river watching the women washing their babies and filling their bamboo water carriers, when one young girl came up to me with a smile. She held her arm against mine to compare the colour and then she opened my shirt and pulled out my breasts, which she delightedly "flapped" at the other women and they all chattered excitedly. Obviously, as I was dressed in long pants, boots, shirt and hat the same as the men, they were uncertain if I could be a woman and wanted some proof. Again I admired their babies, which is always a good opening gesture, and tried to indicate that I too had babies and, goodness, we were all girls together. I gave them the last of my embroidery threads and in turn picked up some barbed head hunting arrows for which they no longer had any use and had stored in the rafters of their houses. In one house I tripped over a moving bundle in a sack which turned out to be a tiny tree kangaroo which they had tried to conceal from me. Perhaps they thought I might want to eat it. Perhaps they were right. It certainly looked tasty when compared to sago grubs.

About ten thirty we heard an engine and a stranger in a hard hat appeared and shouted "Senggo?" It was music to our ears. We established that he was an Indonesian storekeeper from the mission whom Jean had paid to come up the river and pick us up, as she didn't think we could depend on the teacher. We were all packed up in a jiffy and underway in his big dugout making ten knots downriver. The river was high and fast and it seemed a cracking pace after the paddlers. I was able to use my binoculars and spotted parrots, ibis, egrets, cranes, bee eaters, hornbill, kites and a multitude of sulphur crested white cockatoos. The banks were steep and muddy and the vegetation lush, with the high canopy of trees towering a hundred feet above.

At the first village we came to, we met the Patipi teacher on his way home. He had a box of food for us and we immediately dived in and found a note Jean had included explaining who our rescuer was. We stopped at a couple more villages we passed that afternoon and played balloons with the children and I traded salt for some more head hunting arrows. Jim was also buying shields as we now had entered Asmat country, which is the only area in Irian Jaya where the natives show any artistic development with their skilled wood carvings. This was the territory of the Citak tribes and again the women wore bark bikinis whilst the men wore ragged shorts or bottomless Y fronts.

We tied up at Brubis, just before the confluence of the Brazza with the Eilander River, and took a break to have a cooked supper in this abandoned village. We were surprised to find an English speaking Indonesian there who was travelling through the area as a crocodile trader. He paid the natives 30 cents a centimetre of length and then sold the skins to Japan for $60.00 per inch of width, which was a nice mark up. So far I had not seen one crocodile but apparently there are plenty still around. As we continued our journey to Senggo down the huge Eilander River in the pitch dark, with the help of only a dim flashlight, we saw many boats out crocodile hunting near the banks. Fortunately our boatman knew the river well and, after turning upstream into the Becking River, it was midnight when we negotiated some narrow bayous. We were on the final approach to Senggo as it lies a few kilometres from the main river.

With one dim flashlight between us we had to find the path into town and when we all became embedded in deep mud, and Big Jim's big sandals disappeared completely from his feet, we all dissolved in laughter. Perhaps it was partly hysterical relief at our safe arrival. There was no sign of human habitation and our boatman, his charter completed, had just disappeared. We were all laden with our gear, which we had never really packed properly and we staggered along, Jim in his socks, till we realized we were on a runway. We walked its full length before we finally spotted a building. It was about one o'clock in the morning. As it had an open shelter attached at the side and no one seemed to be about, we decided to drop everything there until daybreak when we could get our bearings. However we had hit the jackpot as a sleepy Jean appeared out of the main door of the building to see what all the noise was about and was delighted to see we had arrived. No one had ever imagined we would continue on the river after dark and did not expect to see us till the next day at the earliest.

What a wonderful welcome we received from the group the next morning as obviously they had had doubts that they would ever see us again, and we were spoiled with omelette and toast for breakfast and gallons of tea and coffee. We hadn't even so much as a tea bag in our rations for the past three days. They were envious of our successful visit to Sepanna, if not of our limited diet, as Senggo did not have much to offer in entertainment.

It was certainly a well run mission station of approximately a thousand natives, neatly housed in western style cabins on metre high stilts and comprising three separate village areas. There were both Catholic and Protestant churches, a Presbyterian doctor, and a Mosque for the Indonesian police and government officials. There were almost another nine thousand natives in the surrounding Citak-Mitak tribal region and this supported a large middle high school in the town, the principal of which was a Moluccan by the name of Gusty Billy. He and his wife kindly gave us the use of their kitchen and living room so that we could enjoy our meals in comfort and in turn they enjoyed our company. That afternoon, after I had been to the police station to report and have my visa checked, Gusty Billy offered to take me on a silent dugout trip through the bayous to birdwatch and collect some rare orchids for his small garden. Wally and Bob came too, and we had an ethereal glide through the jungle swamps.

Our tents were set up inside, what turned out to be, the Catholic schoolhouse. For some reason it was not in use and we were made most welcome, even the luxury of a paraffin lamp brought to us at dusk. There were large rain barrels outside with plenty of clean water to wash and launder our very smelly clothes. Unfortunately, when we were returning in our dugout, we were drenched by a sudden thunderstorm. By the time I got back to camp, not only was I soaked yet again but so was all my nice clean washing on the line. It was obviously a punishment for thinking that I could beat the elements this time and for once have a set of dry clothes. So I gave up and continued to be happy in my damp clothes and squelching boots. My rule of washing out socks and boots every night had paid off by avoiding the horrors of foot rot that had plagued some of the others..

The natives of Senggo seemed happy and healthy and obviously having a doctor and a large clinic made a difference to their quality of life. However it was much too civilized compared to what we had just experienced and I was glad we were going to be flying out the following day.

At breakfast Gusty Billy presented me with a bundle of head hunting arrows as I had expressed an interest in taking some home for my toxophilite son. They all had bamboo shafts, but the heads were either of wood or cassowary bone carved with one to three rows of jagged teeth. The teeth were sometimes reversed so that the arrow could not be withdrawn through the flesh and often the base of the barb was weakened so that it would break off inside the wound. An additional irritant was a thread of fibre from the woody ground orchid which was sometimes tied loosely round the arrowhead and, when the arrow was withdrawn, it also would remain inside the wound and set up infection. The heads were bound to the bamboo shafts with fine threads of vine roots, some displaying intricate woven patterns, and there was neither a notch nor any flights at the end of the shaft. The bows of hardwood were of very basic shape tapered at both ends, not particularly long, and the string was a substantial piece of coarse rattan. But in the demonstrations that some of the river villagers had given, despite the unsophisticated design, they were extremely accurate. However it was not often that a victim died as the result of a direct hit, but more likely from the infection that the wound would create. As there are no large mammals on the island, hunting is limited to pigs and birds. The former are shot with an arrowhead of flat sharply edged pointed bamboo and the thin round wooden bird arrows often show detailed carving leading up to its finely pointed tip. As the natives no longer have any use for their head hunting arrows, I felt I was not exploiting them by buying them as souvenirs.

FAREWELLS TO IRIAN JAYA

SENGGO TO THE BALIEM VALLEY

Our chartered Twin Otter came to pick us up at ten and, as we were so overweight with the various carvings and shields that some of the other members of the group had been collecting, the pilot declared that we would have to leave two people behind. I thought it would be more appropriate to leave some carvings behind but I was not in charge. So Henke and Scorpio were told that they would have to wait for the scheduled flight in three days. However, after we took off, I looked around and there was Scorpio who had snuck on when no one was looking. Poor Henke did not have the same initiative and we never saw him again. I was glad I had gifted my rain jacket to him that morning when I was packing. I had decided the Rain Gods were going to get me one way or the other and I would admit defeat.

It took us only forty-five minutes to fly back to Wamena over the route that had taken two weeks to hike and canoe and we had a good look at the impassable looking mountain ridges that we had managed to conquer. The pilot's charts showed a huge blank area over the mountains as these had never been mapped, and Big Jim's altimeter and compass notes were a wise plan if he ever led another expedition over The Mountain Wall. However he reckoned that, after what we had experienced, there was considerable doubt as to his hope that he could promote this route as a future tourist trek.

We were back in Wamena and established once again at the Baliem cottages in plenty of time for a welcome back lunch at Sam's, our trek's provisioner. Later that afternoon we cadged a ride out to the Sunday market at Jiwika for lots of photo opportunities. Many of the Dani were all dressed up in their very best headdresses, shell bibs and pig's tusk nose pieces and were strutting about for all to admire. The women, as usual, were doing all the market trading.

Our Wamena guide, Sam II, spread the word that we would be visiting the village of Seroba the next morning. Alan had met its headman, Kain Aloro, on the road three weeks before and promised him that, when and if he returned from the Lowlands, he would swap his telescopic hiking pole for Aloro's walking stick. Aloro was a crippled warrior photographed and mentioned in Peter Mathiessen's book. As it would be our last day in the Baliem, Alan, Jeannie, Wally and I took a taxi part way to Seroba. Nevada Jim and Kevin had decided to hike from Wamena south towards the mountain wall rather than join us for the cane exchange ceremony. The rest of the group chose to take the morning plane down to Jayapura a day ahead of schedule.

On our way we came across a group of women in a roadside ditch smearing themselves with yellow clay. Sam told us that the chief of their village had died the day before and the yellow clay was a sign of mourning. From the road it was about a mile to walk across the hiperi fields and we had shaky legs negotiating the long narrow suspension bridge over the River Aike. When we came to the village of Seroba we were disappointed to find no one there to greet us. Sam dispatched some small boys to spread the word in the fields and the woods and before long Aloro came limping along the path and there were embraces all round. He was tickled pink with his new cane which could be fixed to any length and had a large rubber knob to grip. Alan did not fare so well with a rather ragged stick that had a red plastic bottle top on the tip.

Dani woman in mourning wearing traditional skirt

Aloro walked proudly back to the main road with us and on our way we climbed the small hill called Anelarok where we had a panoramic vista of the Dani's warring area described in "Under the Mountain Wall". To the south, across the rough swampy ground of the Tokolik, was the small ridge of hills called the Waraba. This was where Aloro and his fellow Kurelu tribesmen would form their front line when they went to war against their neighbours, the Wittaia, who were stationed several hundred yards away on a small cone shaped rise called the Siobara. East and behind us were the Aike River and the stony ridge of land called the Turaba which hid the village of Seroba from view. To our right, westwards, was the flat area of the Liberek where the victory dances were held to celebrate the death of an enemy and beyond, nestled under the steep slope of the mountain wall, was Wuperaima, the central village in the documentary book.

It was from here that the little boy who had presented me with his bracelet almost three weeks before heard that I had returned and came running across the fields to meet me again. He seemed overwhelmed to find that I was still wearing his gift with pride. It was a very touching moment and I thought a very fitting conclusion to what had been very much a trip back in time. In our lifestyles we may be as far apart as thousands of years from these Stone Age people but our basic feelings and emotions are no different.

WAMENA TO JAYAPURA TO BIAK

After the one hour flight in a Hawker Siddeley 748 from Wamena to Jayapura Airport at Sentani, (during which the steward tried in vain to buy my straw solar topee), we met up with the others at the Sentani Inn. We had the whole day to spend in the area, so we took a taxi, first to the Museum at Annapura, and then on to the University of Jayapura, both of which housed excellent exhibitions of Asmat art. I am not one for souvenirs, but I felt compelled to buy one of these artistic and primitive carvings as a memory of this incredible journey. It is an 18" carving of an Asmat warrior standing over his kneeling conquest.

Yet again another dawn flight, this time from Sentani Airport to Biak Island's International Airport. I was seated next to an anthropologist and her linguist husband. They confirmed that much of Irian Jaya was still a paradise for them with so many isolated indigenous groups not yet contacted by the outside world and more than likely still practising cannibalism.

As a safe container for the delicate, sharp heads of my precious bundle of head-hunting arrows I had used a large plastic water bottle with the neck cut off. Also, I decided my pack was too dreadful and abandoned it for a matched set of garbage bags to carry home what personal items remained. I got some weird looks at L.A. Customs! I had given away most of my clothes and my trusty folding umbrella I gave to our taxi driver at Biak Airport. We had had some hours to wait till our evening flights back to the real world and had requested he take us to a deserted white sand beach. There we soaked in the shallows of the warm Pacific Ocean all afternoon.

We all assembled for a farewell supper of Gado Gado, a very substantial Indonesian salad, and a debrief of our unique and successful exploratory trek. These were early years of Tourist Adventure Travel and I have since seen tours on offer to the Baliem Valley and also to the upper Asmat to visit the Treehouse tribes. As for the climb over the mountains, it was unanimously agreed that an easier route would have to be found for any future attempts. When our head guide was interviewed later about the one woman who completed this first successful expedition to climb over the Mountain Wall to the Asmat lowlands, he apparently replied,

"OH, SHE'S JUST AN ORDINARY HOUSEWIFE!".

I took it as a compliment but also chalked one up for housewives.

Diane Jones

Floating village at Tanjung Isuy

Ronyam my porter

Extraordinary Travels of an Ordinary Housewife

KALIMANTAN

EXPEDITION - August 1994

THE WILDER SIDE OF BORNEO

"Tracking the Dayaks"

It had been mid afternoon when I finally met up with our expedition group in Samarinda, provincial capital of Eastern Kalimantan, exactly sixty hours after I had left Toronto. I had been told I would be met at Samarinda Airport, but when I stepped off the tiny Twin otter that had brought me on my final leg from Balikpapan, 120 km to the south, nobody seemed anxious to claim me. The looks from the few locals hanging around the wooden shack which, with an old pair of weigh scales, pretended to be an airport terminal, suggested I had just landed from the moon.

This may have been partly due to the fact that I was wearing my entire wardrobe of two shirts, a tee shirt, shorts and long skirt anchored at the bottom by my hiking boots and topped off by my straw solar topi. As I had had six plane changes on this journey, I was sure my backpack and I would be parted, perhaps for my entire trip, so I determined that all essentials would have to travel on me or else as part of my cabin baggage. There seemed to be much arguing and sniggering about who would help this apparition from outer space, but when I held up the equivalent of $5 in rupiah and shouted out the name of the hotel where I was to meet up with the English contingent, it was quickly snatched from my hand and I was courteously delivered by dilapidated taxi to an equally dilapidated hotel in downtown Samarinda.

Richard Hii's business base is in Sarawak, the Malaysian State that along with Sabah constitute the northern third of the Island of Borneo. He lives in Miri part of the year, and the rest with his Canadian wife Lehanna in Vancouver. He acts as a wholesaler to various adventure tour operators all over the world by planning adventure treks in various parts of Borneo, but first finds out if they are feasible, practical and profitable by running a "research" expedition such as this one. Yes six of us were actually paying to be the guinea pigs, but the opportunity to be the first to explore an area, to continually cope with the unexpected, and be flexible enough to be unfazed by sudden changes of itinerary made it an exciting challenge and offered an experience that would be difficult to repeat.

The other five "guinea pigs" were all English and in their late twenties or thirties. Hilary and John, I suspect, were anticipating a naughty romantic holiday and fortunately didn't know that between bouts of sunstroke and tummy bugs, they were going to spend more time in bed than they had bargained for. My roommate Joy, a lawyer, was to prove to be a swell companion and a jolly good sport. Mike, a refined and well informed civil servant, had a droll sense of humour which balanced out the antics of his roommate, Nigel, a high earning recent graduate who had finally broken from his mother's apron strings. Nigel was full of fun, with an enthusiasm for this his first real adventure, but it came as a bit of a shock when he realized he was going to be spending the next three weeks keeping close company with a woman even older than his mother.

The most important member of our group was to prove to be Chris, our local Indonesian guide. He was himself a Dayak of the Benauq tribe from the area. He was the one who was responsible for getting us from A to B each day, acting as our interpreter, and finding us food and shelter each night. Not normally being presented with a female trekker of such advanced years he instinctively addressed me as "Madame" (an old hangover from Dutch colonial days). The rest of the gang thought this was such a giggle that they adopted it too, and so I was Madame for the entire trip. I don't know if it earned me much respect, but it certainly guaranteed me a seat on local transport!

Our plan for the first week was to explore the longhouse communities of the native Dayak in the middle reaches of the Mahakam River. It was now the dry season and water levels would be too low to go further into the Apo Kayan Highlands and so we would then return downriver to Samarinda and consider the possibility of accessing, to the north, the half million acres of Kutai National Park. This conserves one of the largest lowland primal rainforests in the world. If we proved lucky enough to encounter wild orangutans in Kutai, we would probably decide to abort the planned trip to the Orangutan Rehabilitation Centre at Camp Leakey in Central Kalimantan. We had been invited to visit the centre by the Canadian, Birute Galdikas, who had been in charge of the research team for many years. However we learned that she had just recently been dismissed by the government and declared persona non grata. She had, it seemed, spoken out once too often against Indonesian logging and resource practices in Kalimantan. Instead, we would spend our final week exploring the tribes of the mountainous region north of the city of Banjarmasin in the southernmost area of the country.

With only a couple of daylight hours left to explore this early 18th century port, now sitting many miles inland from the mangrove delta of the Mahakam River, we headed for the market. The streets were clogged with motorbikes and bemos (the communal taxi cum bus service), and only mad dogs and Englishmen like us would have been stupid enough to walk. Samarinda is just below the Equator with mean temperatures in the nineties which, when combined with very high humidity, makes for a very disagreeable climate. Where one would have expected sidewalks there were instead moulded concrete open sewers on both sides of each street. It was difficult to keep the sweat out of my eyes, my feet out of the sewer, the foul smell from my nostrils, and my rear end from the front wheel of a motor bike. At the market I best remember an exotic array of fruit and vegetables interspersed with fly ridden meat stalls. Specials of the day seemed to be a whole leg of water buffalo with hide, hair and hoof attached, and boil-in-the-bag fish so fresh the bags were squirming all over the place. I made a mental note to remember never again to wear sandals when exploring food markets.

THE MAHAKAM RIVER

"Not catfish again!"

To save a day and a half's journey on the meandering lower reaches of the Mahakam River, we caught the public bus that gets to the same point on the river, Kota Bangun, in just three and a half hours. Well that's what the schedule said and it would have been the case without the breakdowns! These must be a very common occurrence as the bus carried a full set of tools and replacement parts and the driver was either very good at mechanical repairs or very poor at mechanical maintenance.

Public buses in Kalimantan are never full. There is always room for one more passenger. In fact the bus departure time is determined by whether every seat is occupied, every inch of roof space and floor space covered with backpacks, parcels, cardboard boxes, nursing mothers, baskets of produce, and even sacks of live chickens. The standing-room-only passengers then board and perch as best they can on the mounds of belongings cramming the centre aisle. Only then does the bus leave the depot. This could, in fact, be half an hour earlier than the scheduled departure time and so, to be certain of catching a particular bus, we were required to show up at the depot at least one hour before ETD and make sure of a seat by claiming squatter's rights.

The road surfaces were not exactly autobahn quality, so speeding was not a problem. Potholes and landslides were individually assessed before proceeding. Unfortunately, when speeds could be maintained, the wheels sent up such a stour of dust that the natural air-conditioning vents of open windows, doors, and roof hatches funnelled a thick dust storm into the bus. This explained why the experienced travellers had snaffled all the plastic barf bags. (This is an item, very much in use, that hung in bundles from the ceiling grab rail.) These they pulled over their hair and wrapped 'kerchiefs cowboy-style to cover their faces. When we encountered a tropical downpour en route, other survival tactics had to be adopted. Not only would the rain slosh through the ill-fitting windows, but also the bodywork was so rusted out that the roof sieved water from above, and it also seeped up through the floor. At these times we had to resort to squatting on the seat under an umbrella. The chickens under the seats did not fare so well.

Kota Bangun consisted of one main sandy street that stretched for three miles along the bank of the Mahakam. The prime properties, including the one and only losman (inn) where we were to be accommodated, were on the riverside, and each individual house had its own private bathroom on a raft anchored to shore by a narrow sagging gangplank. The raft size was determined by the proximity of the neighbours and was seldom more than three square metres. Not much privacy in one's privy which was a three sided cubicle, (occasionally with a door), fastened precariously over a cutout section of the raft's deck. The wake from passing vessels would often slosh up through this hole, which made the boards, around where you were required to anchor your feet, very slippery indeed. However, the Kaltese take their ablutions very seriously and spend a great deal of their daily life on their riverside rafts. There's twice daily bathing, dishwashing, fish gutting, laundry, recreational swimming and diving, garbage disposal, and a whole host of other riverside activities.

Modesty is important in an Islamic culture, and this is achieved by the use of a sarong by both men and women, although the display of little brown bums on prepubescent children was quite in order. We realized that it would be appropriate for us to follow this custom, and so after we had released some of the road grit from our teeth with copious cups of tea, we went off to purchase same. It is important for you to remember at this point that the sarong I selected was shocking pink with a purple stripe.

It was a great relief to find that our losman, which could be described generously as extremely basic, did have an inside mandi. This is a small cupboard with a squat toilet set into the floor. And where does the S bend go? One neither knows nor cares! The only other fixture is a large tank of water with a plastic pot floating in it. The plastic pot has a dual function. Firstly, to flush the toilet by pouring water into it from a great height and with maximum speed, and secondly, if you haven't already soaked yourself, to pour water over your body after a bit of a lather-up. A drain in the floor takes care of the overflow but thick-soled thong sandals are a must.

The furnishings in the wood planked cubicle bedrooms consisted of two rough hewn bed frames with dubious kapok mattresses, separated by a small table that held "A FAN!" This immediately elevated this establishment to super deluxe, especially when the village electricity supply actually kicked in at dusk and the blades began to spin. With earplugs to mute both the muezzin and noisy riverboats, sleep looked promising.

The river was perhaps only 100 m wide at this point and abuzz with constant water traffic. Cargo barges, log rafts, and passenger boats held to midstream whilst the rest of the river swarmed with small local craft. The village's main industry was the building of small-planked fishing boats. These were similar to the water taxis or klotoks that transported villagers, at dizzying speeds, using an outboard with a very long extended propeller that allowed the boat to manoeuvre in very shallow waters. Some had canopied roofs to protect passengers from the elements and side curtains to deflect the spray. Such boats are very common in S.E. Asia.

We rented a couple of these klotoks in the late afternoon to visit Danau Semayang, an oxbow lake that could be accessed from the Mahakam a few miles down river. The big attraction was hopefully to see the freshwater pink dolphins that live in its warm shallow waters and are very active at sunset. Unfortunately, they didn't perform for us and all we saw were the palm oil and cacao plantations as well as some herons and kingfishers. (I did finally see several of these pink dolphins when I was on a cruise up the Amazon River in 2020.) We stopped to buy some fresh fish to have for dinner by pulling into one of the little personal privy rafts. We were somewhat aghast to find that not only did it serve as the toilet facility for the home but also suspended from the raft, and accessed through a trapdoor, was a fish cage where fish could be stored alive with a never-ending supply of human waste to fatten them up. Chris had the owner reach down and pull up several huge black catfish before he was satisfied with the size and the price and was very excited that he was going to be able to serve us such a wonderful delicacy for supper. Boiled catfish and rice! I made little noises about not being a great fish lover and tucked my portion, which seemed to be all skin, bone and whiskers, under my leftover rice. I pigged out on the tapioca chips instead.

Our plan was to take a riverboat all the way up to Melak, about 350 km from the coast, where we would jungle trek for a few days amongst the Dayak villages. But first of all, we would take a two-day trip by klotok across the vast shallow lake of Danau Jempang to the south of the main river. The area and depth of this lake varies considerably between wet and dry seasons and, to adapt to the ever-changing water levels, the fishing villages are built entirely on floating platforms. The lake is about 25 km in diameter and as the water was very shallow, as this was the end of the dry season, the fish were so concentrated that it was a breeze to collect them in bamboo fish traps and then corral them in circular compounds shaded by floating water hyacinths. They could then be shipped to market at leisure.

As we scooted across the glassy surface, we passed countless fishing boats tending the traps, or using cast or dip nets. The water was often so shallow that the fisherman just hopped out and waded with seine nets stretched between them. It wasn't long before we found out how shallow it really was, and it was everyone overboard to shove. It seemed strange to be aground with nothing but water all the way to the horizon. We had misread the vague bamboo poles marking the channel across the lake to the main settlement of Tanjung Isuy.

Tanjung Isuy village was on the only bit of high ground at the south end of the lake. At this time of year the village dock was about twenty feet above the water level, and it was a shaky climb up a very shaky ladder. A very unpleasant odour wafting up our nostrils met us at the top, which turned out to be slabs of raw rubber awaiting shipment.

If Kalimantan has any tourist attractions Tanjung Isuy, is it. The Indonesian government has taken over the two abandoned longhouses in the village and turned one into a losman for visitors and the other into a craft market. And yes, horror upon horror, there were tourists. Fortunately, only about half a dozen Dutch and Germans and they were easily lost amongst the local villagers who are Benauq, the same tribespeople as Chris, our guide. The Benauq are talented artists and there was a wonderful display of wood carvings, masks, baskets, wall hangings, blowguns etc that they were anxious to sell to us. Unfortunately, we knew that we had three weeks still to go with all our worldly goods on our backs, but fortunately the European tourists made up for any shortfall.

The Benauq are one of the Dayak tribes who, in the past, practiced the art of piercing and stretching the earlobes. Missionaries have stopped the practice and had them trim their ears on conversion, and so we only found one "Long-ears" as they still proudly call themselves. She was our losman landlady!

The village was several sandy streets deep, with neat houses surrounded by neat picket fences. Some homes had pet monkeys tethered in the garden, and exotic birds in bamboo cages. I watched as soft shelled turtles were weighed on hand scales and sold door to door. The losman was spotlessly clean, (no doubt as demanded by past European tourists), and we were able to buy some Barking Deer for a cook-your-own venison stew. Both Richard and Chris shared all the cooking chores in the communal kitchen.

As our three privately rented klotoks were moored at the dock, we decided to use them for the afternoon to explore the Manjung River, which entered the lake a little to the west. Here the vegetation was lush and formed a canopy over our heads, as we struggled to manoeuvre past fallen logs in the shallow water. We were lucky to see black monkeys, grey monkeys and a few of the rarer proboscis monkeys, plus lots of hornbills, fish eagles, herons and large exotic kingfishers. We were to see these birds continually on our river travels. The smaller tropical birds were more difficult to spot amongst the thick vegetation.

That evening a special healing ceremony was performed in our honour by the village shaman and his four apprentices. We realized this was what they told all the tourist groups but, at least, we were the only guests invited that evening to the headman's house for a display of whirly, twirly dancing around a central decorated post. The shamans were all male in this particular village and wore long full white skirts, colourfully appliqued, and on their heads crowns of woven dried palm leaf with streaming strands of dried grass. Gongs, drums, a primitive xylophone and a flute accompanied them. Offerings of sticky rice and eggs were made to appease the spirits, and burning sticks of vine substituted for candles. The two "victims", a couple of young boys about ten years old, looked as though they were suffering from a dose of mumps. Once the head shaman had whirled himself into dizzy oblivion, he fell into a trance and was covered by his wife with a blanket to hold in the good spirit that had entered him. He lay on top of each boy in turn, both covered by the blanket so that you couldn't see what jiggery pokery was going on, and thereby transferred the good spirit into their bodies. The good spirit chased the evil mumps spirit out from the boys and into a clump of dried grasses that the shaman swished over them. He wrung out the grass into an imaginary bowl that his wife dutifully emptied out of the window. The boys then stood up and walked away, not looking any the better I may say, but rather embarrassed by the whole episode. Afterwards it was our turn to be dressed up and to whirl and twirl around the room, after which we were served tea and sweet sticky rice balls and relieved of 5,000 rupiah per head. I am not sure why, but I know I would rather give 5,000 rupiah not to have to participate. I always feel uncomfortable at such "staged" shows where the clothes and choreography seem to be a modern interpretation of the real thing. We would, in fact, be present when genuine healing ceremonies were taking place when we stayed overnight in other longhouses.

Next morning we were given a conducted tour of the graveyards in the village. The dead are laid to rest, for three to five years, in a gaudily painted and carved wooden casket on top of a couple of six foot posts. When the insects have picked the bones clean another funeral is then held, with appropriate celebrations, as this is the final send off to the spirit world. At this ceremony the bones are consigned to the family stone urn, or wooden spirit house, depending on the tribe. This is a fairly general treatment of the dead amongst all the Kalimantan tribes. Fortunately I don't think any of the wooden coffins were very recent as they were not exactly airtight, and there must have been a bit of a stench for the first few weeks.

After a lunch of deep fried chunks of taro and tapioca, we took the klotoks back across Lake Jempang to the Mahakam River and the town of Muara Muntai where, that evening, we would catch the overnight passenger boat up to Melak. Muara Muntai is a town built entirely on stilts. Its streets are wide boardwalks, lined with houses, open fronted stores, cafes, and workshops which form a solid built-up area of several blocks, all raised four to six feet above ground. It's quite a feat of engineering. In this case the floating ferry dock was about thirty feet below street level down an almost sheer riverbank. To get up to the town one had to negotiate one of those narrow sagging gangplanks from the dock to the muddy bank, then haul oneself up the sheerest and steepest set of wooden steps. We left our packs down on the dock!

It was a very picturesque place, with lots of bougainvillea squeezing up through the planked sidewalks and creating a host of colour. As with most of these riverside towns it was a Muslim community and the women's flowing robes were brilliantly coloured in yellows and pinks. This simply added to the charm. There was no English spoken, but I negotiated with an elderly distinguished looking gentleman in a doorway to, hopefully, mail a letter back home. I showed him the airmail envelope with Canada as the address and offered him a wad of rupiah notes pointing at the area to put a stamp. (Post offices are not in evidence anywhere in Kalimantan and trying to get a message home had become a real challenge.) He nodded understandingly and relieved me of about $2.00. Obviously he had underestimated the cost of international mail and, when I visited him on my return downriver a few days later, he relieved me of another dollar with the word "express". The letter did eventually arrive, by "three week express delivery".

The floating dock was full to overflowing by 6.30 in anticipation of the 7 o'clock evening boat. It arrived at 9 o'clock! Indonesian rubber time, they call it. The passenger boats that plied the river were flat bottomed, broad beamed and about fifty feet in length. The lower deck was open along the sides and, in this case, already covered fore to aft with sleeping bodies, motor bikes, and assorted cargo. At the rear behind the engine room was a communal kitchen, and behind that were two WC cubicles protruding out the back like a poop deck. (Well, I suppose they were just that!) Planks had been cut out from the floor allowing a seagull's view to the river below, and the boards on either side of "the hole" had become a slippery catwalk. Dishwashing, hand washing, and a full body shower if you wished, were undertaken with a black snaking hose perpetually circulating muddy river water all over the floor. On the upper deck were the sleeping quarters for those quick enough to grab a mattress laid out bum to bum on a communal platform either side of the central aisle. If you were lucky enough to be near the front you could enjoy the blaring noise of a TV set which showed non-stop videos from a VCR.

When we boarded, every inch of sleeping space was already occupied, and it looked as if we might have to spend the nine hour journey in the kitchen by the poop deck. However, after another forgettable dinner of catfish and rice, Chris negotiated with the captain to lay out a piece of lino on the rear upper deck that by day was the fenced-in chicken run. Yes, we had a coop of ship's chickens on board. Presumably they were more productive than a ship's cat. The hens were all shut up in their nesting box for the night and, apart from sticking their heads through the bars of their coop and giving an odd curious cluck, they were not averse to us laying out our thermarests and trying to make short of a long night. It was really quite pleasant being fanned by a cool breeze with a clear starry sky above, that is, until the boat stopped. This it did frequently at small hamlets in inky darkness, to drop off a bundle of cable, a box of provisions, or the odd passenger and even, on one occasion, it stopped in the middle of nowhere. Apparently a fan belt had snapped and, whilst they effected a pantyhose-type repair, the deckhand had to swim ashore to fix a line to a fallen tree to stop the strong current delivering us back from whence we had come. Unfortunately, every time the boat stopped so did the breeze and we found ourselves enveloped by the most awful fowl smell. Do chickens fart?

We arrived in Melak, 350 kms upriver, just as dawn was breaking and rented a room at the local losman. This allowed us to use its standard bathroom facilities that were now beginning to look quite appealing compared to... ?? Breakfast was at an open fronted warung (cafe). We squeezed onto a bench with the locals at a long table covered with plates and jars of sweetmeats and, having experimented with a few of these and drunk bottomless cups of tea, we raised the number of fingers for the number of cakes we had each consumed. All on the honour system but very difficult to overspend at five cents a bun, and ten for all the tea.

By 8.30 a.m. we were gone from Melak, Chris having managed to beg, borrow or steal a couple of jeeps. These would take us the few hours' journey to the village of Eheng where there was a particularly interesting longhouse community. From there we planned to walk for three days through the jungle from village to village and eventually back to the Mahakam River. But first we couldn't miss a visit to the Wild Orchid Reserve. It was highlighted on every government map as a must-see for anyone who ever ventured this far. (Only orchid fanatics, I suspect.) Despite having a ranger give us a conducted tour of the sandy montane jungle we came across only one orchid in flower which fortunately was the famous, and very rare, black orchid. (It's actually green with black spots). Obviously we were not alone in our disappointment at not finding many orchids in an orchid reserve, for a recent comment in the visitors book summed it up. "Where are the bloomin' orchids?"

As we were still very much on zero degrees latitude and feeling like limp washcloths, our spirits soared when our drivers stopped at a beautiful waterfall and deep swimming hole. We were now into the foothills of the mountains and this was the first clear water we had seen. It was time for sarong christening and swimming in behind the curtain of water to sit on a cool ledge. At our breakfast warung we had arranged for packed lunches, and neat little waxed paper parcels tied with twine were passed around to be washed down with milk from fresh coconuts hacked open with Chris's parang. It didn't seem to matter that it was rice and catfish yet again. I was much more horrified to find that under my sarong I had turned beetroot red with purple stripes and, while the dye may not have been permanent on my sarong, it was certainly here to stay on my skin. The others had sensibly chosen more reserved and muted colours and didn't seem so afflicted.

We were dropped off at the Papas Eheng longhouse mid-afternoon. It was an enormous structure 65x15 metres, raised 3 metres above ground. Fifteen huge hardwood trunks supported the central length and hundreds of stilts supported the planked floor. Wooden shingles covered the roof and woven palm bark the walls. A communal gallery ran the full length and about two thirds of the width. The other third was divided into eight separate apartments with kitchens out the back in separate adjacent stilted structures reached by covered catwalks. A fire precaution?

Thirty-eight families lived in this one longhouse. Another dozen or so single dwellings were scattered along the road. Though mainly Catholics, they still maintained their animist culture with carved spirit poles which guarded the three doorways, and in the woods behind were their spirit houses with offerings of dried cornhusks and grasses. The inhabitants were members of the Tunjung tribe.

We climbed up to the main entrance by means of a notched pole with a fearsome figurehead carved at its top, and squeezed through the low doorway being careful not to step on an elderly lady lying there having her head deloused by a younger relative. Only a few elderly people squatted in the gallery weaving baskets or carving images. Most were working in the nearest town and would return on the factory bus at four o'clock.

Racks suspended from the ceiling held old dusty ceremonial structures, and water buffalo skulls (definitely not human) hung on the central posts. Against the wall I noticed an ancient treadle sewing machine and an equally ancient bicycle, obviously highly prized. Peeping inside the apartments the only furniture was a four-poster double bed with mosquito netting in each flimsily partitioned room. All the other worldly belongings were just heaped up against the walls in no particular order.

Woven rush mats were laid out for us in the gallery and even the odd dubious mattress was offered but gracefully declined. Instead we used our own Thermarests and rigged up our mosquito nets. Chris cooked a chicken and rice dinner for us inside sections of split bamboo on an open fire outside, whilst we tried to join in the evening ablutions down at the river. The factory bus had now arrived back so we had chosen a bad time and couldn't find a spot to bathe that didn't inherit someone else's grey water. Anyway I didn't want to confuse the natives with my beetroot bod when they would have expected a paler skin. Pit stops were now very much in the direction of the jungle. Except, of course, those jungle bound by all the rice!

After dinner the streetwise members of the community were not slow to offer to sell us their worldly goods: baskets, carvings, parangs, even their grandmother if the price was right. We fought them off by offering to employ them as porters to carry our gear for the next few days. I chose one with an upper set of solid gold teeth. He introduced me to his wife who had a set exactly to match and I realized that he knew how to make a few bucks when I discovered he had negotiated with Chris the exorbitant rate of fifteen dollars a day. In New Guinea I never had to pay more than three dollars. However he was worth every cent.

Things were pretty busy and noisy in the gallery that evening. Everyone gathered for a genuine healing ceremony by the village shaman, this time dressed in a dried grass skirt and headdress. Four drums and a set of gongs kept up a steady monotone beat for the hour or so it took the shaman to stamp his feet, punch and swing a raffia decorated punch bag and finally fall into a trance. The elderly woman patient was laid out for all to see on a mat, just a very sick bag of skin and bones that would appear to be beyond any medical help.

What was surprising was the response of the other members of the longhouse. They squatted around in groups chatting away, weaving their baskets, while the children ran around playing and shouting, oblivious, it seemed, to the seriousness of the occasion. Lots of bags of sweets and chips were shared around and one would have thought they were all attending a family celebration. I couldn't help noticing a couple of little girls, about five years of age, rolling their own cigarettes and lighting up each other's, whilst parents looked on. The poor patient probably had an advanced case of lung cancer.

Diane Jones

Finally in the early hours the drums were put away, the shaman gave-up, and we thought we might get some sleep. But what with hacking coughs and disgusting throat clearings from adjacent apartments, dogs wandering around sniffing and scratching, cockerels crowing and pigs grunting underneath, we were out of luck.

It was wonderful to finally escape into the jungle and follow narrow paths to who knows where. Joy and I were the only ones to blow the expense and each hire a personal porter. The others chose to carry their own packs despite the heat and humidity. The group had a third porter to carry the communal food, including a couple of live chickens for dinner.

My porter, Ronyam, (with the gold teeth), was the only one authentically dressed in navy Dayak turban and mandau (parang) strung around his waist, but the brown Y fronts definitely looked old European. (Penis gourds are not part of Borneo culture.) He was a tiny guy with no body hair, just a few whiskers under his chin and a vague moustache. He carried my pack strapped into his own large woven rattan basket, with a backboard and tumpline.

We had to cope with a river crossing where the single log bridge was partially submerged below the fast running water and, thinking we could keep our boots dry, we crossed in bare feet. We should have known that the next couple of miles would be through swampy ground and in no time we were waterlogged. The occasional leech kept us walking at a fair pace and before lunch we had arrived at the stream where it was planned we would camp overnight.

Ronyam was in charge of lighting a fire with the damp jungle wood whilst Neus and Besie, the other porters, cut down saplings and vines and in no time had built a sleeping platform over which they stretched a tarpaulin for shelter. Neus and Besie obviously forgot we were not Tunjung sized but by lying on our sides, two to a mosquito net, we were all just able to fit under the tarp and spent a very hot and sweaty night. Their table and bench were in better proportion, but their piece de resistance was our jungle john. This was a little square scaffold construction screened by some woven vegetation, with a neat pile of selected leaves to cover one's identity.

To pass the afternoon, Besie took us off to hunt pigs. Needless to say we didn't even see any, far less spear any, with the noise seven pairs of feet made crashing through the undergrowth. The Dayaks hunt with blowguns or spears and have intricate liana traps they set for pigs. The government has forbidden anyone to own a gun. Besie did find for us some black spindly mushrooms they use as an antidote for snake bite and the tree roots, that are almost solid resin, are useful fire starters. Unfortunately the chickens had not been dispatched by the time we returned, and so we had to witness them running around headless before being made into a perspiring curry.

We awoke to the sound of gibbons whooping in the high canopy and, after a breakfast of noodles and boiled eggs, we hiked all morning through beautiful primal and secondary montane forests, with a little bit of log walking through the swampy lower elevations. No leeches found us. This jungle was home to honey bears, leopards, wild boar and several species of monkey. We stopped for a bathe and a spot of laundry at a river crossing and my sarong continued to leech its beetroot dye. I resolved to give it away to Ronyam for his wife. The colour would not be so noticeable on her dark skin and it would set off her gold teeth rather nicely. These crowns must have been a valuable but weighty mouthful and I can't imagine who performed the fine dental work.

By lunchtime we were following a cart track into the village of Ekeni where Neus' family lived. This was a village of single dwellings on stilts, where we were greeted with drinks from fresh green coconuts and the use of grandma's kitchen to heat up leftover rice curry, which Chris had transported in fresh green bamboo tubes. He just stuck the tubes in the fire to warm, split them open and served. Voila, no pots to scrub. There was a very well kept graveyard as we left the village, with a recent intricately carved coffin. I sniffed cautiously but nothing malodorous!

The cart track led us shortly to the longhouse in the village of Benung. It was a very neat and tidy compound, with lines of washing stretching from the stilts of the longhouse to a couple of beautifully carved hardwood poles. These turned out to be the posts where they sacrificed buffalo when celebrating the second funeral. I gather that, in the interests of economy, it is now common for several families to share the high costs of this important ceremony. They wait till they have several skeletons awaiting their "second going" and have a really big bash to which they invite all the neighbouring villages.

We decided, as it was still early, we would press on to the next village. Disappointingly this turned out to be three or four miles along a dirt road, dodging motor bikes. We were even more dismayed to find that Gengan Danum was a large village as ugly and squalid as Benung had been perfect. Unfortunately it was too late in the day to go back.

Our porters, on Chris' instructions, had planned our three day circular route, but communication was obviously poor and we had covered two days' hiking in one day and left the charm of the jungle behind. All we were left with was an overnight stop in a flea-pit losman attached to the general store of a dowdy village and, tomorrow, the prospect of walking on a busy main road back towards Melak. The only redeeming feature of Gengan Danum was that the store sold beer. In front of the shop, slap-bang in the middle of the road were several rows of benches and we could at least relax on a couple of these as we reconsidered our unappealing surroundings. Many villagers came and joined us on the bleachers. As it turned out, we were not the attraction, but rather it was a hatch in the storefront wall. As darkness fell, a generator at the rear of our building kicked in, the hatch opened, and it was television time. We hadn't noticed the big satellite dish on the roof.

Chris had searched the village for a clean looking kitchen and arranged to have them cook a chicken stew for dinner. It was just my luck that my share from the serving bowl amounted to a piece of neck and one unmanicured chicken's foot. Apparently the latter is considered a delicacy!

The generator also meant that our night's accommodation was bathed in electric light. This might have been welcome as there were no windows in the cubicle rooms, and we had been groping our way around in the gloom. Unfortunately the naked light bulbs just highlighted the revolting state of our accommodation. When we came to put the lights out at bedtime we discovered there was no switch, the bulbs could not be removed, and we had to sleep in their glare all night till the generator was switched off at dawn. Gnawing rodents were not deterred by the floodlighting.

Next morning Chris managed to produce an old pick-up truck and driver willing to take us all back to Melak. The porters came with us and we dropped them off at Eheng en route. We were in time to catch the lunchtime boat back down to Muara Muntai, the riverside town on stilts. The eight hour trip was mostly in daylight and sitting up on the open top deck (no chickens on this boat) we had a chance to watch life on the river as it passed lazily by. Also it was a good opportunity to hang out our washing and give mildewed clothes a good airing. Occasionally we'd stop to load some fish for a market further downstream, or to haul on board a passenger's precious motor bike. This would require the strength of about six men to pass it up by hand onto the cargo space on the upper deck. Usually it was being loaded from the family's privy raft and how the owner had got it onto the raft over one of those sagging narrow gangplanks I can't imagine.

After a short night in Muara Muntai's "Holiday Inn" losman (i.e. no surprises, as by now we had seen it all) we caught a dawn boat back down to Kota Bangun in time to catch the morning bus back to Samarinda. This was a smaller ferry with only a lower deck and the ship's wheel forward on the same level. The captain must have taken a shine to me for he insisted that I sit on his wooden chair that he placed slap bang at the front of the boat for the best view. Much more comfortable than squatting on the floor with the rest of the passengers and an ideal observation point.

The dock at Kota Bangun was already occupied, so we all had to hop off at an adjacent private privy raft in a sad state of disrepair. When I saw the gap of murky water between the sagging dock and me I had to resort to my helpless female persona. The captain immediately summoned a few of those motorbike machos to help me disembark with my pack, and then inch me up three decrepit chicken ramps and four fallen tree trunks to reach dry land. This nickname of "Madame" served me well when I needed the royal treatment.

KUTAI NATIONAL PARK

"How to greet an orangutan"

Next plan was to head north by public bus to Botang and from there hire a boat for the two hour trip up the coast to the ranger station in Kutai National Park. Joy and I managed to get seats towards the front of the bus, which were less stressful on such a rough road. The plastic sick bags, hanging in bundles from the grab rail, were much in use by the locals and, when full, were just casually chucked out the window. (Glad we didn't hike that main road back to Melak!)

At Botang the bus was mobbed by drunken oil workers desperate for female company. Any woman who wears shorts in a Muslim area is considered fair game. This I already knew, and the reason I always wore a long skirt and a snooty look. We had to make a fast break for bemos to the Park Office to arrange park permits, then on to the dockside.

The only boat that would agree to take us was a replica of Humphrey Bogart's African Queen. It belched clouds of black smoke, that is, once its engine had been kicked into life. The chrome handle of an old faucet, attached to a long piece of fishing line served as the accelerator. In order to get from steering wheel to engine the owner had to climb up through the front hatch with faucet handle in his hand, onto the flimsy roof, under which we were all squashed like sardines, run over our heads and back to the engine at the rear. He would then try to kick it into life whilst pulling on the accelerator line like a remote control. No sooner would he reverse his journey and slip back through the hatch, than the engine would cut out again. It looked like we might find ourselves shipwrecked in the pirate-plagued Straits of Makassar. Fortunately, even though we were a fair distance from the coast, it looked shallow enough to wade to shore. Borneo is continually increasing in size due to the enormous amount of silt brought down by the many rivers that enter these waters. It is already the third largest island in the world, after Greenland and New Guinea.

What looked like oil platforms turned out to be bamboo structures supporting fishermen's shacks, where they lived with their families and kept their fish fresh in an ocean compound below. We hailed a few of these fishermen before

Diane Jones

we could find one willing to sell us some of his catch. We knew we had to take all our supplies into the park with us and what better than a nice bit of catfish but a nice bit of dogfish!

We were not too far out from the dock at Teluk Kaba Ranger Station when we went aground. Nothing for it but to slip over the side, hold our packs as high as possible and wade ashore. Did I mention that in 1994 Kalimantan had a maximum of fifty tourists a month, who are easy to lose in a population of five and a half million. Kutai never gets any of these tourists as it is so remote. What a shock to slosh our way up to the only two cabins at the ranger station to find one already occupied by four recently qualified Harvard law graduates.

These two couples had only arrived that morning, having obviously commandeered the only decent boat in Botang. As they had a third bedroom in their cabin, Joy and I had to share with them for the next couple of days, whilst the rest of our group squeezed into the other unit. To put it mildly, they were a pain! The girls were obviously American Princesses who had great trouble with the resident giant spiders and the other even furrier inhabitants. One excursion along one of the jungle paths was quite enough and instead they chose to stay home to paint their nails and make pillow talk. Their guys put on their big macho roles and headed off to see all the wildlife which, on hearing their Wall Street discussions in loud Brooklyn accents coming along the path, made itself scarce.

The station was manned by a lonely little guy called Suporno, who was so glad to have Chris to talk to that he would do anything for our group. He would lock himself in his little cabin when he saw the Americans coming. He shared in our cooking, and our food supplies, in the communal kitchen that stood as a separate hut, again to minimize fire risk. Apart from these buildings there were a couple of outside privies beside a genuine old-fashioned well. When a shower was required, we donned a sarong, hauled up the bucket hand over hand and doused ourselves. By now I had replaced my beetroot sarong with something a little more permanent.

Suporno was happy to guide us through some of Kutai's half million acres of protected forest. The vegetation ranges from the coastal mangrove swamps, to freshwater swamps, into heath forests and finally well drained hilly dipterocarp forests with huge hardwood trees. After dark was a good time to take a walk with a flashlight and pick out pairs of eyes in the trees staring back, or hear the odd wild pig grunting in the underbrush. We had some monkeys swing in the trees around the station clearing and some sambar deer that were very tame. Hornbills would sometimes fly over with their loud wing beats audible even before they came into view. We came across some fishermen on an isolated spit of land who seemed to be cooking turds over a fire. (Sorry, but I can think of no better description.) It was a relief to find they were only black sea cucumbers which, when boiled then smoked, fetched big bucks in Botang.

Otherwise we saw very little, even when Suporno took us on a full day's hike, hacking a path through the undergrowth with his mandau, and cutting away strands of rattan with its vicious barbs that seemed to reach out and grab one. This was called "tunggu sebentar" or the "wait-a-second plant". He carried a sharpening stone in his pack and stopped frequently to sharpen the mandau. The foliage was too thick to see birds clearly and only occasionally would we know there were monkeys above when the foliage high up in the canopy rustled. However the vegetation was lush and beautiful to walk through, and we found lots of wild fruit trees; durian, jackfruit, starfruit, mangos, wild coffee, ugli fruit and some phosphorescent fungi.

We stopped to have a picnic, which had to be eaten standing up as ants monopolized any possible seating area. Chris had thoughtfully wrapped little individual lunches in green banana leaf, tied with some pink nylon string from our food supply cartons. What do you know, it was rice and dogfish! I don't know how my package managed to slip from my hands and land in an irretrievable mess on the ground. The ants were on to it, but Suporno quickly dived down and snatched up the fish eyes, which I insisted he enjoy, as I really wasn't that hungry.

Orangutans were, of course, the main item on the agenda. We had seen lots of abandoned night nests but learned from Suporno that the biggest concentration was to be found in another section of the park. This meant coercing him into arranging for the park's decrepit 4WD vehicle to come into Teluk Kaba via an impossible road, and take us out the same way to the northernmost limits of the park. Here the ranger station at Sengatta arranged for two fishing boats from the local village to take us on the two hour trip up the Sengatta River to the Mentoko Reserve. For this we were charged an exorbitant price of U.S.$200 and it was quite obvious that every official involved was getting a cut. However it was worth it to reach an area seldom visited.

The river was only about twenty metres wide with steep banks of cane. It acted as the northern boundary of the park and so on one side was primal jungle and on the other various habitations, oil concessions, and logging terminals. Once or twice we encountered logging rafts being hauled downriver and had to squeeze tightly into the bank to let them pass. Some of these enormous hardwood logs were as much as two metres in diameter. As we neared Mentoko the river narrowed and we had thick jungle on both sides.

Diane Jones

Japanese scientists have recently been given the concession to conduct orangutan research in Mentoko, and a beautiful wooden building was under construction to house them when they eventually arrive. Unfortunately it was not sufficiently complete for us to use, so we had to make do with a grubby shack as our base. It didn't really matter as we spent every minute exploring the jungle with Baster, a park ranger who escorted us for the two days.

As this was primal jungle there was little undergrowth under the high canopy and it was not necessary to always follow paths. Baster knew which fruit trees to look for that would attract the orangutans and, within a couple of hours, we had our first sighting of a big male. As they are so high up in the canopy, and move so slowly, they are difficult to spot. But as they have no natural enemies they were unperturbed by our presence and we had unlimited time to observe them. Indeed this one was still in the same tree when we passed the next morning. When we returned to our shack by the river that evening, we found we had another one swinging lazily in a tree on the opposite bank, which gave us some twilight entertainment.

Mentoko has counted thirteen orangutans in its area: nine males, two females and two babies. Their main food source is fruit and although many of the trees come into production at different times of the year, they may be sparsely distributed through the forest. For this reason the orangutans always travel alone, as each adult requires several square kilometres of forest to support it. This makes them very difficult to find but, walking behind Baster for many hours the following day, we had another two excellent sightings.

The second male became quite annoyed at our presence 150 ft below. It was the start of the mating season and he may have been concerned that we were competition. He started by dropping half eaten fruit on us, then some leafy twigs. When we still didn't budge, he broke off some branches and flung those down at us, but we had plenty of time to take avoiding action. Finally, when grunts and branches had no effect, he peed on us! We could see the shower coming, splashing off the leaves, but had time to take cover.

Baster knew many of the healing properties of the plants in the rainforest. The first thing he did was to chop a section of prickly thick vine and get us to pour the clear sap into our eyes to improve our vision: jungle eye drops. He pointed out lots of unusual insects and we spotted gibbons, wild boar and a mouse deer. Lots of hornbills cackled overhead. Sometimes they are known as the mother-in-law bird because of their bouts of "hysterical laughter". We had many streams and steep gullies to cross, usually via a very slippery log. I would resort to crawling across on my hands and knees, rather than lose my balance and fall many feet to a muddy fate.

Some of our party missed these wonderful treks as both sunstroke and tummy upsets were taking their toll and they were glad to get back to Sengatta village and more standard accommodation. Our losman was spotless, mainly because the owner was a strict Muslim and all shoes had to be left outside. The bed linen was fresh and the mandi clean, except that the water reservoir was obviously just topped up with the brown sludgy river water. The sick ones in the party were glad to crawl under their mosquito nets for a good night's rest. My room was fairly noisy as the highly prized TV was plugged into a socket on my door jamb. This meant every time I left my room I had to step over half the village squatting in the corridor watching the soaps. We were also back in cockerel crowing and muezzin calling country. I was amused to step out my door in the morning and find the now silent TV had been concealed with a custom-made sequined velvet modesty cover.

Eating out in those villages meant a roadside stall consisting of some battered tables and benches under an old tarp, with goat, chicken or fish cooked on an open brazier. One could choose either noodles or rice and there were usually some good highly spiced soups. It was a 200 km trip by public bus back to Samarinda, which took five to six hours over very forgettable roads. We then continued south for another couple of hours to Balikpapan. These buses offered, and insisted on giving, "full music" service. The selection was not soothing to the ear. I noticed that they declared a maximum capacity of twenty-seven passengers, but I counted thirty-four plus two babies. We were squashed in the back seats and had the full effects of the locals' chain-smoking habits and maximum exposure to the frequent dust storms. Where the gritty sand could go no further it collected in drifts on those in the rear section.

Balikpapan is the centre of a recent oil industry boom and has quite a few decent hotels and even a shopping mall on three levels with a grand atrium. I had had to overnight here on my outward journey but had no time to explore. As is common in most of these rich/poor countries, these nouveau riche cities are a mix of fancy commercial buildings and shabby dwellings, the usual substandard roads and open sewers. Beggars were evident, as were unpleasant attentions from passers-by. Everything seemed either to be half constructed or half demolished. The traffic was heavy and noisy and, to help discipline the drivers, I noticed that the many traffic policemen positioned at the intersections were, in fact, very life-like plaster dummies. Our small hotel had western style toilets and even baths with showers. I was amused by a notice on the wall that asked users not to squat on the toilet with their feet on the seat. In the public lounge area there were three identical swing doors in a row. One the Gents, one the Ladies and the other the Musholla, if you needed a quick prayer rather than a quick pee. We had a grand time pigging out on some western food. I had french fries and lamb chops washed down with a beer, and rounded off with <u>two</u> ice cream cones. At this point we agreed we had had enough of public buses and rather than suffer another eighteen hours of road travel to the south coast of Kalimantan, we would gladly pay the difference and fly directly the following day.

THE SOUTHERN MOUNTAINS

"Swinging through the jungle"

To research a third possible trekking area we flew to Banjarmasin, an old sixteenth century pirate port on the southernmost tip of the island of Borneo. Being at the confluence of the Barito and Martapura Rivers it is so dependent on its waterways it is called the Venice of Indonesia. Houses on stilts line the many intersecting canals and there are floating fruit and fish markets, individual little snack bar boats, water taxis galore, all jostling for position. A constant stream of barges and cargo ships ply the rivers.

Our restaurant choice for dinner that evening had a wonderful view of the river as it was situated on the top of a multi-storey car park! Just a simple wooden-framed shelter with a bit of lino to sit on at the low tables and a counter at which a plump woman, with a beaming smile, prepared the food. Meanwhile her son cooked pigeons on a charcoal BBQ occupying a free parking spot. I'm not sure how "local" the pigeons were but they tasted pretty fresh and went well with a bowl of Banjar soup.

We planned to hike in the mountains of the Loksado area and visit some of the longhouse communities. En route we stopped our taxis at Tanuhi to arrange for the locals to build us three bamboo rafts that we would later use on our return journey. These rafts are used commercially to transport rubber and groundnuts to markets downstream, but only need to make a one way trip as the bamboo poles of the raft itself are sold when they get to town. The punters just hitch a ride back home.

We were dropped off at a shaky and sagging pedestrian suspension bridge which we crossed carefully, one at a time, before following a path along the river to the Balai Malaris. This was an unusual square longhouse (30x35 m) that housed twenty-four families of the Bukit tribe. These are animists of the Kaharingan faith and, as with the Bali Hindu religion, it is very closely tied to the peoples' cultural identity and for this reason has been sanctioned by the Indonesian government as an accepted religion. The centre of the balai had a sunken area of the floor with an enormous Laleya, a dried palm-frond structure resembling a dragon-like animal, with a house-shaped body and a small house-shape as a head. This was a relic from a very recent rice harvest ceremony. Other spiritual straw structures hung from racks or were stored by the doors of the many apartments that encompassed the common central square of the longhouse.

As the upper walls above the apartments were loosely planked or made of woven bark, sufficient daylight filtered through to let the villagers carry out their chores in the cool of this common central gallery. Groundnuts were being shelled, baskets woven and bark scraped from cinnamon wood. Dogs and cats roamed freely inside the balai, with pigs and chickens underneath the stilt supports. Man-made fish ponds in the compound, refreshed by a plentiful supply of mountain river water, were obviously carefully managed and farmed and it seemed a self-sufficient and prosperous community.

The Bukits are a monogamous people and both adultery and divorce are unacceptable. Although they are bound by Indonesian law they also have a strict code of conduct within the village, and the elected headman dispenses punishments if longhouse laws are broken. Perhaps the offender will be forbidden to enter the longhouse for a specified period, or not permitted to cut down any green vegetation, i.e. money earning crops.

As with the Mahakam River longhouse access was up a narrow notched pole to the door, but in this longhouse we accessed the main central area by a long narrow passageway, perhaps to secure privacy. Again the kitchens were separate stilted buildings at the rear of each apartment and approached by a covered walkway. As the cooking fires are open and sit only on a base of clay, accidents must be commonplace and we were told that the government had contributed to the present corrugated-iron roof of the main longhouse after too many fire accidents. Some other single dwellings surrounded the main building within the picket-fenced compound and a platform supported a hollowed log in which rice was being pounded, two women taking alternate strikes with wooden pounders.

The drum did not start its high monotonous beat until late in the evening. A young woman, in western dress, had come back from Banjarmasin for some home remedy from the village Shaman (Dokon) and his woman helpers (Belian). This time it was a much more intimate affair in a far corner of the gallery and we kept a respectful distance as the medicine man performed much stamping and whirls finally appearing to fall into a trance. Most people went off to bed in their separate bedrooms inside their apartments, except all the unmarried males who were required to sleep out in the communal gallery. They just pulled their sarongs up around their shoulders and lay down side by side in a perfect row.

We set up our sleeping mats and mosquito nets in a quiet area of the gallery and were cold for the first time on the trip. We hadn't realized that we would be sleeping at 700 m where the humidity and temperatures would be much lower at night. We had all left our sleeping bags behind with our packs in Banjarmasin, having never had need of them till now. We had to make do with wearing all our clothes and wrapping ourselves up in our sheet and sarong.

The following two days we had beautiful trekking through various types of forest and across clear mountain streams. We had several steep climbs with magnificent views and stopped off at a couple of small balai that we passed which would hold anywhere from twenty-five to fifty people. These Bukit people were happy and friendly and an old lady met us with a big smile of crimson betel nut and black teeth. In Kalimantan they chew the betel nut along with tobacco and not with powdered lime and green bean as in other countries. These communities were proudly self-sufficient. They practised slash and burn farming to grow dry rice, taro, tapioca, vegetables and fruit. They would also collect wild rubber to trade for other necessities, transporting the heavy rectangular moulds slung from a pole across their shoulder.

Our plan for our second overnight at the Balai Haratai was dismissed by the village headman who insisted he host us all in his individual dwelling which consisted of three empty rooms. No furnishings, just bundles of stuff against the walls. His wife was the village teacher who, with a few invited guests, were anxious to practise their limited English whilst they prepared a fine chicken dinner to share. Their house had running water delivered to their backyard via long bamboo pipelines supported on stakes several feet off the ground. As the village sloped downhill there was sufficient gravity to feed several dwellings from the tumbling stream.

We set out early for the small town of Loksado, whilst it was still cool, and encountered some very precarious swing bridges. Not only did they have next to no handrails but several sagged off to one side and had great gaps where planks had rotted away. They seemed to take forever to cross as we had to go one at a time, and very cautiously, to minimize the swing and bounce. We reached Loksado by lunchtime for bottomless cups of tea and 25c worth of sweetmeats. It was a Muslim village with a tin mosque and a little evangelical mission house. The houses lining the one and only street had gardens with white picket fences and shy women in colourful Muslim dress made a very picturesque collage. Instead of taking a bus to pick-up our rafts at Tanuhi, we learned there was a path across the hills and decided to hike there instead. It was a hard, hot, three hours, but amongst some beautiful hills which rose to almost 2,000 ft. There was little in the way of overnight accommodation in Tanuhi, as there was no longhouse, and so we just slept on the countertops of a few of the empty covered market stalls which, at least, kept us off the hard ground.

Our rendezvous with our rafts was at seven the next morning: four rafts, two passengers to a raft with two locals to punt and paddle. They consisted of twenty-six bamboo trunks, lashed together with rattan, and the narrow ends brought together to form a prow at the front. A raised bamboo bench had been specially made for us to sit on but generally we were awash and, unlike our experienced boatmen, we found it impossible to stand up. To avoid getting our cameras and packs wet Chris was left behind with all our belongings to figure out how to get transport and meet up with us downriver that afternoon. The water was clear and warm and the jungle scenery breathtaking with steep sugar loaf hills rising behind the tall trees. Occasional rapids and waterfalls had to be negotiated, but the rafts were so flexible and buoyant, and our paddlers so experienced and full of laughter, that it was all great fun. Our trip was over by about two in the afternoon. We hiked out to the main road and, lo and behold, Chris had managed to find a truck and driver to transport us all the way back to Banjarmasin in time for a final dinner before flying off in different directions the next day.

Despite the previous evening's celebrations, we were all up before dawn and headed for the Barito River to grab a water taxi to visit the floating market, which operates in the hours just before daybreak. Small boats, top-heavy with fruits and vegetables were paddled and punted in the misty pre-dawn light. The brilliant colours of the women's dresses topped with woven coolie hats, like giant domes, made them look almost as exotic as their wares. Tiny craft, operating as snack bars, would paddle alongside with their covered display case of sweetmeats. One could slide open the glass doors and reach in to help oneself from the dozen or so plates heaped with all kinds of cakes and wash them down with tea or coffee brewed on a little charcoal brazier between the boatman's legs. By the time the sun was a giant ball on the horizon and the river flooded with its orange light, the marketing was pretty much over for the day and the tiny craft dispersed in all directions back to their stores, restaurants, homes or farms.

As we all had various departure times I found myself with a couple of hours on my own for lunch before heading to the airport. I went back to the multi-storey car park, but no sign of its nocturnal restaurant entrepreneurs. Just lots of parked cars and cooing pigeons!

Loading the mules with our Titan bag of camping gear

Berber woman selling shawls

Extraordinary Travels of an Ordinary Housewife

MOROCCO

FOUR CITY BACKPACKING
10 DAY JEBEL SAHRO TREK

February 1996

Our Lonely Planet guidebook came up with an adequate hotel within walking distance of Casablanca's main station and the medina. (Old City and souk). We considered unravelling a ball of wool as we ventured into the maze of alleys of the souk, and came out the other side in front of one of the biggest mosques in the world, Hassan II Mosque, built in 1993 for the King's birthday. Not only is it a beautiful building with a tall green tower and huge forecourt, but it has been built out on a point of reclaimed land surrounded by the Atlantic surf. Even more impressive was that we found our way back to the hotel where we dined, a la Marocaine, on lamb and prune tagine (stew). The latter ingredient made sure we got the use of our "en suite" bathroom which was more "in suite" as it had no walls, only a flimsy curtain to separate it from the rest of the room!

It took only a couple of hours to cover all the highlights of downtown Casablanca, with its palm-lined boulevards, traffic-bound squares and French architecture. It took a little longer to find breakfast as all restaurants and snack bars were tightly shut. It was Ramadan! If you haven't eaten before sunrise, then you are out of luck till sundown. The hotel concierge finally directed us to a "rogue" restaurant where we quickly downed mint tea, a banana and a bun, before heading for the noon train to the capital, Rabat, 60 miles up the coast.

The Ville Nouvelle of Rabat has been beautifully laid out with wide boulevards fanning out from the central Royal Palace. Many of the mosaic-tiled sidewalks are cloistered or shaded from the sun by orange and fig trees. We visited the Chellah, which is what remains of the old walled Roman city of Sala Colonia, and is just outside the Rabat city walls. It is inhabited by hundreds of storks all clacking their bills from their precarious nests atop every vertical ruin. There was also an old medina to negotiate our way through and the 12th century Kasbah Des Oudaias on its far side. This fortress, with wonderful views out to the Atlantic and across the estuary to Sale, was large enough to contain a small town within its walls whose old houses are still inhabited.

Diane Jones

The following day, four hours on a fast corridor train took us up to Fez by noon. We took along our own breakfast of fruit and water. As soon as we stepped off the train we were surrounded by would-be guides, jostling and pestering us. We had already memorized the map and several possible hotels and so ignored them and pushed our way through. It was a hard slog in the heat with our backpacks as it took four attempts to find a suitable hotel, but we were determined not to be indebted to any of them or we would be landed with them as our guide with accompanying unimaginable fee.

We were in Fez Ville Nouvelle and, of course, the old walled city of Fez el Bali a mile or so away is the main attraction. The hotel told us what number bus to catch and the fare we would need, so we rushed from the lobby, past the waiting crowd of would-be guides, and jumped a bus. We had no idea where to get off, but when we were obviously well inside the walls of old Fez, we hopped off and asked a policeman, in our pidgin French. I had memorized most of the main buildings and streets of Old Fez, and drawn a basic map on a small bit of paper. This meant I could squint at it in the palm of my hand, and did not require getting out the guidebook map which drew hustlers like bees to a honeypot.

We found we were at the very end of the souk far from the usual tourist entry point, so we had to go backwards on the map. This was made even more complicated by the fact that, not only were the hilly cobbled streets named in Arabic script, but were seldom more than about six feet wide and, along with the millions of capillary alleys running off in all directions, were a solid mass of people. However, by coming into the souk from a non-tourist route we were left pretty much alone and, by good luck rather than good fortune, found our way to the main entry gate of Bab Bou Jeloud. When we saw the hordes of hustlers descend we turned and fled back the way we came, by now getting fairly blase about finding our way about. The souks are divided into areas for the different trades. There are the spice merchants, the slipper makers, the brass and foundry workers, the leather markets, the dyers, the malodorous tanneries, the herbalists, the basket makers and, of course, the carpet factories. The food stalls have their own area, selling sticky sweetmeats, tons of fruit and interesting butchers offering not just fresh live chickens but whole heads of horned goats or a bundle of hairy hooves!

Next day was Friday, and Islam's holy day, so not so many shops were open and the streets seemed a little quieter. We managed to find breakfast in another hotel and, feeling confident after yesterday's sortie, we headed back to Old Fez but this time took the route that leads through the third part of the city, Fez al Jdid, which lies between old and new. This is where the Royal Palace is situated, the Kasbah des Charards and the old Jewish area of the medina, the Mellah.

We entered Old Fez from yet another direction via the Bab Guissa gate in the north wall and, following our guidebook's instructions to keep going downhill, found ourselves some known landmarks from yesterday's orienteering. There were nothing like the swarms of people of yesterday, and we were able to wander about much more freely and peek up the picturesque little alleyways. The medinas are heavily populated, even though you can get a car no further than the outer walls of the city. Mules are the transport of the souks. The narrow-cobbled streets are dwarfed by the walls of shops and dwellings several storeys high. Some of the houses are so primitive that water is still drawn at a nearby fountain, and daily bread is baked in a community oven.

We congratulated ourselves on another day of outwitting the hustlers but Peter, finding someone else's hand in his pocket, reminded us that we couldn't afford to let down our guard. After an early supper of traditional spicy Harira soup and chicken couscous we made full use of the hot water and fine bath in our very private bathroom, as if it might be the last time we would enjoy such comforts. It was!

It was still dark when we walked to the train station at Fez to catch the Marrakech express. We had stocked up with bananas, oranges, water and a packet of biscuits for the eight-and-a-half-hour journey. The route was back to Rabat and Casablanca and on towards the High Atlas and Marrakesh. There were eight of us to a compartment but, fortunately since it was Ramadan, no one was smoking.

The coastal plains were green and fertile, and showed signs of recent flooding from the winter rains. Yuccas and prickly pear cactus formed hedges around the fields and wild spring flowers grew amongst the newly planted wheat and maize. Clumps of narcissi bulbs popped up everywhere and the ubiquitous marigolds made huge orange and yellow swathes. We identified eucalyptus, olive and citrus plantations; fields of vegetable crops with tomatoes under shade; donkeys and mules galore and the odd hobbled heifer. Shepherds were always chasing their sheep from the railway tracks where, obviously, the most succulent grasses grow thanks to the hole-in-the-floor loos on these corridor trains.

Although we had obviously climbed up from the coast onto a higher plateau there was still no sign of the Atlas Mountains when we pulled into Marrakech and the end of the line. The hustlers at the station were even worse than Fez. Thank goodness we knew which hotel we wanted to go to as it was our meeting point for the trekking group. Our tour info even told us the most we should pay for the taxi ride. The taxi drivers almost trod on us trying to grab our bags and put them in their cab. However we hung on to each other and our backpacks and survived the ordeal to reach Hotel Ali in the old part of the city. It was ideally situated as we were slap bang in the middle of the action on the Djemaa el Fna. This huge central square, just outside the walled souk, is filled with endless entertainers such as snake charmers, jugglers, escape artists, acrobats, musicians, magicians, story tellers, herbalists, traditionally costumed water sellers and, of course, every pickpocket in town. When we had to run the gauntlet of hustlers lying in wait just outside the hotel door, and when things got too hot and troublesome, we could retire back to the hotel for some mint tea. Also the hotel had a roof patio, where we could view all the activity from a safe distance, and a restaurant where they served an all-you-can-eat Moroccan buffet. This was a great opportunity to sample all sorts of different ethnic dishes and break the daily enforced Ramadan fast.

As we would join our Explore tour the next morning with a "Guided Tour of the Souk", we decided to head in the opposite direction from the medina and visit the museum. This is the only place you can admire a carpet without it being rolled, wrapped and tucked under your arm. Nearby we wandered through the Palais de la Bahia, built a couple of hundred years ago by a Grand Vizier. Apparently, it is still used by members of the royal entourage when the King comes to town and his adjacent Royal Palace is full. The Royal Palaces used by the King in Fez and Marrakech, as well as his main one in Rabat, are never open to the public and, in fact, you cannot even get close. Red uniformed guards and armed police keep you at a distance.

We ventured a little way into the souk and had a look at the snake charmers whose cobras were either doped or just sluggish because it was winter. Orange juice stands and food stalls were getting ready in the late afternoon for the six o'clock end to the day's fast and hungry looking locals were already seated at counters in anticipation. It was exasperating to be continually pestered and jostled by the locals, who would even try to insist they should be paid as, unbeknownst to you, they had just seen you safely across the road. They would speak first in French, then in English, and we got wise to pretending we understood neither language. This would confuse them and give us time to escape till we were hustled by the next one. Peter's unusual Aussie hat and my, as usual, unusual outfits made identifying our nationality difficult. No wonder we opted to stay home for dinner again.

Next morning we met our tour group: fifteen jolly Brits with an efficient twenty-five year-old English girl as guide. They all turned out to be good company and fortunately not a whiner or bad apple amongst them. The souk was not nearly as attractive as the souk in Fez and our official guide was more interested in his commission prospects by taking us into his "brother's" carpet shop, etc. etc. The only favour he did was show us around the Medersa Ben Yousef, built in 1565. This is the largest theological university in the whole of the Maghreb and, despite being restored in the 1960s, still only offers cell-like accommodation. These are clustered around courtyards beautifully adorned with carved cedar, Zellij tiles and intricate filigree stucco. It was an opportunity to see Moroccan architecture at its most magnificent.

The Jebel Sahro, where we would trek for ten days, lies 300 km east of Marrakech and on the far side of the High Atlas mountains. It is a northeasterly continuation of the Anti Atlas Range to the south, with peaks rising from 6,000 to 8,000 feet. Its scenery can be spectacular, with flat-topped mesas and buttes, steep gorges and pinnacles of conglomerates. It is volcanic desert, rough and stony with little vegetation but desert scrub. However it is fed in the spring by snow run-off from the High Atlas. These rivers feed wells and irrigate riverside oases of almond and fig trees, and gardens of vegetables and semolina wheat (couscous). There are neither roads nor telephones. Feet and mules are the only form of transport between the tiny villages that congregate by a stream or well, or to reach a Berber family in their rough tented compound where they live a nomadic existence with their herds of sheep, goats and camels. Winter days are sunny and warm, but nights are well below zero. Summer is unbearable with temperatures reaching fifty degrees. The nomadic Berbers head for the High Atlas for summer grazing.

We left on Explore's bus by seven, and within the hour were in the foothills of the High Atlas. Another two hours saw us above the snowline on the top of the Tizi n'Tichka Pass (2,262 m). It was a spectacular road with verdant valleys and terraced fields, sleepy adobe villages clinging to the hillside, plus landslides and road washouts to keep you alert! As soon as you drop down the other side of the pass you are in grey stony desert.

The bus dropped our packs and us off in El Kelaa outside a meat shop where they had just finished skinning and butchering a cow in the gutter and we tried not to step in the blood as we loaded our packs into a tiny pickup truck. We all walked the five miles cross country on a pretty path by the Dades River, infused with the fragrance of almond blossom that was to be with us for the next ten days. En route we had an official invitation to a local home for the traditional small glass of fresh mint tea, served from a lightbulb shaped silver teapot and poured from a great height.

By late afternoon we were established in the courtyard house of our head muleteer, Lahssen, with boys in one room, girls in another. A tight squeeze for the girls as there were twelve of us and only six men. However the rooms were totally devoid of any furnishings except some straw matting, so it was a question of claiming a two foot strip with your sleeping bag. There was a pretty corniced ceiling to stare at, and a picture of Jesus and his little lambs on the wall! Apparently he features quite strongly in Islam. We had a taste of dinners to come. A thick vegetable tagine with some stringy goat meat. Thank goodness we remembered the dental floss!

Our seven muleteers loaded complete rations for ten days, plus all our tents and personal packs, onto just twelve mules and secured it all with thick black goat hair ropes. My own legs buckled at the sight. Our trek officially started by 9.00 a.m. as we headed off over a rolling moonscape. It did look bleak even as the sun, which had shone on us every day so far, climbed higher and hotter in the sky. There was no real path, other than that just freshly trodden by the mules, and it was quite tricky to pick your way over the stony ground.

We surprised a Berber woman washing clothes in a little stream that flowed from a well. Further on another woman, with a baby on her back and three young children, seemed to materialize from nowhere to sell us some eggs. We couldn't imagine where they came from as there was no sign of any habitation. We would discover later in our trek, as we became more accustomed to scanning the landscape, that they either had a small steading or a low brown Berber tent tucked into a hidden dell, with a stone walled compound for their herds of sheep and goats and "shoats".

We were glad when the rolling hills became a little more challenging as we entered the true Jebel Sahro Mountains and found ourselves following hairpin paths down into canyons and up the other side. With only a light daypack to carry, we still found we were no match for these mules with their humongous loads. By early afternoon we were at our first campsite in the shadow of Mount Afoughal. It was a drywall compound cleared of stones beside a puit (well) with a running stream, banked by terraced gardens of couscous and broad beans and shaded by almond trees. The nearest habitation was a steading on a far hillside and this area of flat baked ground was obviously used as a threshing floor.

We had to find space for twelve two-man sleeping tents, a cooking tent and a big bell shaped mess tent. As soon as the sun went down, so did the temperature. Fast! That first evening we kept adding layers of clothes, till we had everything on by the time our hot supper was ready at seven. We all wore our hats, socks and woollies inside our sleeping bags. The sky was black velvet with a million diamonds. It was worth the odd shiver to dally and enjoy.

The daily routine was tents down, bowl of porridge, hot tea, mules loaded and on the trail by 8.30. We would walk anywhere from four to seven hours a day, and our altitude would range from 4,000 to 6,000 feet. If it was only a morning hike to our next campsite, we would always have the option of an afternoon hike up the nearest mountain for a panoramic view.

Today we did feel we were amongst the real mountains of the Jebel Sahro and had a few steep ups and downs that got us puffing. Some of the scrub was identified as wormwood and another resembled gorse with a similar yellow flower in bloom. Many clumps looked like the sagebrush of the U.S. southwest. All the vegetation had one thing in common: prickles. How the sheep and goats thrived on the stuff I do not know. It was a delight to find tiny spring flowers struggling for survival in the stony infertile soil. Most were nestled for protection in the leeward and shady side of a rock. This is the only brief period of the year when the desert blooms. The summer sun soon saps all moisture and scorches any tender plants.

The second night's camp turned out to be at the home of Lahssen's brother, Ali. Business is very much kept in the family if possible! Ali was obviously anticipating a roaring tourist trekking trade, as he had just built a new courtyard extension for guests. Only one room was complete and ready for habitation, so we opted to pitch a tent a ways away after clearing off the rocks. That way we avoided the snorers and were first at the well in the morning to have the pleasure of breaking the ice! After a dinner of soup and spaghetti with tuna sauce, the muleteers entertained us with a singsong accompanied by tambourine drums and a homemade fiddle whose soundboard was a squashed olive oil gallon can.

Our next night's camp was at Assaka-n-ait Ouzzine, a proper little village of flat roofed adobe houses which were adorned along the roofline by little hand-molded turrets. The roofs were slightly concave and drained to a single downspout. There were perhaps ten or fifteen family homes, linked by their animal compounds, perched on a steep slope by a fast flowing creek. We had to remember that rain falls only in December and January, and we were seeing rivers in spate that, for most of the year, are little more than a trickle. We monopolized the only flat ground which was the adjacent village threshing floor.

On the other side of the stream stood a ruined kasbah amongst the terraced gardens and almond blossom. In days gone by, when neighbouring Berbers were seldom friendly, village groups would either live entirely inside their kasbah fortress or be ready to retire to it when the need arose. They were basically square high walled keeps on defensible high ground. As adobe walls require continual restoration, it doesn't take long for these recent strongholds to melt into ruins.

Most of that day's trek had followed the course of this mountain stream and, at a point where it entered a gorge, we had to scale down the cliffs and skip back and forth across the waterfalls and pools of crystal clear cold mountain water. This gave us many opportunities to catch up on ablutions. There was

Diane Jones

considerable natural vegetation by the riverbed. Oleander and cane were common and we were beginning to see our first wild date palms. It was also easy to see how gravity-fed clay channels were diverted to irrigate the terraces.

I would like to be able to tell you about the friendly villagers, but they weren't! That is, apart from a few curious and, we suspect, light-fingered kids and a couple of women anxious to sell us some gaudy and glittery homemade shawls. They wear these shawls around their heads in a variety of ways but usually ending with a protruding topknot on their forehead, unicorn style. They had wonderfully patterned hand knitted leggings under their skirt wraps and a variety of layered old sweatshirt cast-offs on top. Diaper pins seemed to be popular brooches and feet were usually clad in cheap plastic slip-ons. The rest of the village metaphorically slammed their doors on us. They are very private people and not accustomed to visiting outsiders. I can't blame them for leaving nasty snarling watch dogs roaming around at night. With eighteen extended bladders searching for a secluded late night pee spot, the dogs certainly kept us well away from the houses.

We had a full day's trek the next day with a picnic en route under the almond blossom. The morning hike continued to follow the riverbed, criss-crossing via some often unreliable stepping stones, and then we climbed up to follow winding cliffside paths above a rocky gorge. Apart from the mule that was carrying the lunch rations, the others went on ahead. This allowed the muleteers to have all our tents erected in a neat row and mint tea and biscuits ready when we finally reached camp after a long haul over a barren mountain pass. The climb was not particularly steep, just steady under an unrelenting sun.

There was quite a substantial river between us and a scattered village of about a dozen houses, with T.V. dishes! (Satellite?) There was a little square whitewashed schoolhouse standing alone. Was this a government contribution? The muleteers had not been too careful about clearing the stones from under our tents, so we had to do a bit of scraping and poking with sticks to extract the razor edged ones and thus avoid any princess and pea sleepless nights.

We met our first dromedaries: four adults, one of whom had a yearling and a newly born. They were being herded by a little boy who was happy to line them up for the camera. We had taken a nineteen km round trip to Bab n'Ali Butte which stands alone on a high plain surrounded by steep sided mesas. It had been within sight from lunchtime the previous day. The morning sun had quickly dispersed any morning clouds that had spun off from the High Atlas and, as usual, we had brilliant blue skies to contrast the dramatic scenery.

We had backpacked our lunch, Peter being very macho by carrying the cans of luncheon meat. The daring climbed up the sloping scree base to the vertical cliffs of the butte and the even more daring Peter scrambled all the way around this big fat flat-topped tower of sandstone. Fortunately he left the Spam behind so that the rest of us could get on with lunch. Our walk back for a second night in Irhazzoun'n'Imlas was a hard slog as we returned via a dry river bed with long stretches of sinking sand.

Two days we had trekked to the south, two days to the east and now we headed north. Almost immediately we had a very steep two hour climb to the top of the Tizi'n'Taggourt (6,500 ft) plateau with panoramic views of the Tête de Chameaux and Tassigdelt Tamajgalt mesas. We were growing accustomed to spotting the low broad brown tents of the nomadic Berbers (usually just one family) and met another herd of nine camels and a bunch of baby mules. I think we saw the proud donkey dad on our way up to Bab n'Ali. We were also getting better at spotting the darting lizards and chameleons and came across a large group of Barbary ground squirrels playing by a stream.

Again we carried our lunch as the muleteers had taken the low route to Tagra and, this way, they were able to have our tents all ready to fall into when we arrived across the mountains. We dropped into a valley to eat by a little stream out of the wind, and were just as surprised as the French trekkers we bumped into who were doing likewise. They were on another route and our paths never crossed again.

We had the threshing floor again at Tagra, a village of about three houses and a dozen snarling dogs. A good sized river, that we followed for the last hour of our hike, supplied us with a satisfying wash and attempts at some laundry. However, anything hung on the line overnight was guaranteed to be a frozen board in the morning. Pegging one's smalls to one's daypack usually had them dry by lunch.

There was another day of steep climbing but towards the west. The towering cliffs of Iskabid were on our left as we followed an ever-steeper hairpin path to a saddle of land which opened out onto a plateau below the Tine Quaiyour Peak (6,900 ft). Whilst we were enjoying a rest, our guide was approached by a young shepherd boy. Apparently we were invited to tea if we wished. This was the friendliest overture yet and we were all game, even when it turned out that it was a mile or so out of our way. Sure enough there was grandpa crushing date stones, whilst mother and aunt boiled up the kettle on a tripod over a brushwood fire. There was also a younger sister and brother of the shepherd boy, and a toddler. The father and the aunt's husband were not around and in fact we passed them returning after we had left. We knew the aunt was married as she had the traditional fertility tattoo on her chin of a dark blue vertical line with dots on either side.

We had a close look at the tent which was no more than a roughly woven dark brown wool cover, supported by sticks, stretched over a four foot high stone walled compound filled with straw. It was empty, except for a vicious dog, and seemed to be only used for sleeping. A large fat goatskin water bag was propped outside and, as there did not seem to be any sign of a stream nearby, they probably used these bloated bags to transport water to the camp. There were another couple of small circular igloo style dry stone and thatch buildings, for storage perhaps, and some dry stone compounds for this Spring's new crop of lambs and kids. Their day was made and tea efforts rewarded when one of our group bought, without bargaining, a handmade wool rug, probably worth many months of labour. The shepherd probably shot off to hunt down the French group, his family having discovered how easy it is to skin the tourist. It is almost considered a cultural offence not to bargain for goods.

Our descent to our camp was down the steep gorge of a pretty stream. The rocks were shades of cream and rosy pinks, highlighted by sparkling waterfalls and banks of oleander festooned with mistletoe. From high above we could see the ruined Kasbah of Irhissi standing alone at the bottom of a valley, made even more romantic by the lone date palm by the entrance. We were surprised that the tents were not yet up as once again the mules had taken the low route. When we came out of the gorge into the open valley we knew why. It was a wind tunnel for a wind that was a real tent ripper.

Even though we all squeezed together as much as possible to enable us to shelter within the ruined walls of the kasbah, there were quite a few tent repairs required by morning. Our only problem was that the gritty sand, which this gale-force wind carried, not only lodged in our teeth but also in the teeth of our tent zipper and we had to wait, with our legs crossed, to be extricated the next morning.

On our third day of consecutive steep climbs we continued north, right over the Tizi n'Tmirhcht Pass at 6,800 feet and our highest climb so far. From the top we could look back to where we had been and, ahead, we had a magnificent view of the snow covered High Atlas beyond the remaining hills of the Jebel Sahro. It took only half a day to reach the pass and drop gently down to our camp at Tizi n'Irhioui.

No village here but some steadings of dry stone walls with thatched roofs, and the odd Berber tent on the adjacent hillsides. We even noticed some excavated cave dwellings, probably used mainly to house livestock, but there was a mattress and other signs of human habitation in one. The sandstone rock is soft and easily hollowed out. We knew we would be headed west the next day, so Peter and I continued northwards that afternoon and hiked over another saddle where we could see the great flood plain of the Dades river and the town of Boumaine du Dades in the shadow of the High Atlas. We watched Arabe, the oldest of our muleteers, bake a fresh batch of flatbread (flour, salt and water) on a griddle over an open brush fire. This would see us through till the end of our trek in two days time.

Before each meal everyone was required to wash their hands in a basin of water and bleach. After ten days this becomes torture as your hands are so dry and chapped and, as was the case most mornings, the ice in the bucket was half an inch thick and the bottle of bleach was its own sculpture.

Our route was west, mainly downhill, and followed a wide river valley. Again we were rock skipping and criss-crossing the river which eventually dried up completely. Our campsite was not far ahead on some cleared land but this was riddled with ankle breaking holes which had been prepared for seedling almond trees. I guess, with the river drying up, the farming prospects had diminished and the field abandoned. However there was a well where you could get water if you were prepared to climb down into it via a rickety ladder and scoop it up in a bowl. There was no overhead winch and bucket. It was a fun photo opportunity.

A village nearby supplied some precocious children who were not opposed to setting fire to the odd scrub bush to get your attention. These were street smart kids, used to a bit of begging, and it was obvious we were returning to the materialistic world. To catch our last sunset we climbed to the top of the mountain to our northwest and looked out to our original starting point. We were able to follow the river valley that would take us back to Ait Youl tomorrow.

It took less than three hours of following the dry river bed to reach Lahssen's house where we would spend the last night in our separate dorms. It was our first cloudy day and during the last ten minutes of the trek we had a sprinkling of sleet. After lunch we all walked the five miles to the town of El Kelaa to pass the afternoon looking around and found a cool beer in a very passable hotel. We walked the five miles back in a drizzle of rain but, at least, we had a good appetite for the final supper prepared with great effort by our muleteers. It was a spicy soup followed by chicken and couscous, washed down with a bottle of good Moroccan wine. Just time for a final singsong with the muleteers and a round of the hokey cokey for good measure. It was a tough trek but worth every step.

Ice pick and weighted boots, ready to tackle the Fox glacier

Extraordinary Travels of an Ordinary Housewife

NEW ZEALAND

BACKPACKING
Dec. 1997-Feb. 1998 and Feb.-Mar. 2003

Auckland Airport had a special arrivals booking service for backpackers and we headed off downtown with a three month pass for the Kiwi Experience backpacker bus and a booking at Auckland Central Backpackers. Here we were given a very adequate room with a double bed but nothing else, not even a peg or a chair. However the communal washrooms and kitchen areas were very clean and we soon got the hang of this lifestyle and noted with interest that the Backpackers Guidebook had certain hostels marked as "Five star". However I won't be recommending the Central Backpackers as it was to be the place where, three months later, I awoke with bed bug bites up one arm. The front desk took one look and quickly rebooked us at another hostel saying they would have to call the exterminators and had no other room to offer. I suspect they thought we had brought them with us. Certainly not, as we had been living "Five Star" all the way. We had a pleasant discovery on our first night that, when dining out or booking accommodation, you only paid the price as advertised with no tax and NO tipping. We could also take a bottle of wine to a restaurant and just pay a dollar corkage charge. Great way to go!

A Canadian friend, who was in Auckland to visit her mother, gave us the full tour of the city which straddles a narrow strip of land between the Pacific and Tasman Sea, with a harbour on both sides. Not surprisingly it is called the City of Sails as at least a fifth of its population own a boat. Almost a third of New Zealand's population of five million live in Auckland and prefer to live in an English style bungalow with a little walled front garden. This has created a vast suburban sprawl across the isthmus with most high rises centred downtown on the Pacific side. Forty-eight volcanoes, most of which are parkland, stick up like green pimples all over the city. My favourite is The Domain and its Botanic Gardens where I have returned on my many visits to Auckland, often on a cruise ship, in the past twenty years. A favourite day trip out of Auckland is to Tiri Tiri Matangi Island across the Hauraki Gulf. It is a bird sanctuary, deliberately freed of all predators, and home to many of New Zealand's rarest birds, several of which can't fly. I have also enjoyed three days of hiking on

Diane Jones

Great Barrier Island, the largest of the many islands that guard the entrance to the Hauraki Gulf.

Our Kiwi Experience three-month bus ticket was named the "Whole Kit and Caboodle" as its itinerary included all the main tourist areas as well as the more out of the way places that can be difficult to access. We could get off and on as we pleased, at any point on the route, but we had to keep going in one direction with no backtracking. Although mainly geared to the young, with loud pop music between the driver/guide's commentary, we felt we could fit in quite comfortably especially when we found that the front seats were always vacant as most passengers preferred to go to the back seats to sleep off last night's party. It was better than joining the bifocal balding bunch on the more traditional tourist transport. Added to that there was lots of laughter and good fun banter with the driver. These were mostly well educated, well informed, responsible kids in their mid twenties, who would phone ahead to make a booking for you at your backpacker hostel of choice where the bus would drop you off and pick you up again. This meant no dragging of bags between bus station and hostel at each stop. Needless to say we always picked double rooms in 5 star hostels, which cost only a little more, over two bunk beds in a noisy dorm in one of the "party" hostels. Kiwi Experience have been smart to invest in many of these backpacker hostels as they are guaranteed to have a busload of kids coming through everyday to the required overnight stops.

We had had a little taste of New Zealand's temperate rainforest when our friend took us to the Waitakere Mountain Forest on the outskirts of Auckland, but we were still surprised by the rural landscape as we drove north to Paihia and the Bay of Islands the next day. Steeply rolling pastures covered with sheep and cattle look like the Borders of Scotland except that, where you would expect to find coniferous forest, there is this amazing lush jungle. Palm trees and Giant Fern trees are mixed with subtropical Norfolk Pines and the Pohutukawa trees, covered in a mass of crimson blooms in December, are appropriately nicknamed New Zealand's Christmas trees.

That first morning, after the bus left the main road to reach a beach for swimming and horse rides, we were surprised to stop at a Goodwill store and instructed to buy a tee shirt and shorts for $1 as we were going to explore some muddy caves to look for glow worms. No flashlights allowed; instead we were each given a candle. After struggling through narrow passages on hands and knees and wading through underground streams, we all stood in the middle of a shallow underground lake and blew out our candles to find glow worms covering the ceiling of the cavern like stars. What followed was a mud slinging, water splashing free-for-all initiated by our driver. Then candles were relit and we followed a dry path straight out of the cave, having realized that we had all been had. We dropped off our muddy clothes at the driver's mother's home further up the road, where she launders and returns them to the charity shop. It was obviously going to be lots of fun travelling with Kiwi Experience.

We stayed in Paihia for five days as there is so much to explore in the Bay of Islands area. The Treaty of Waitangi between the Maoris and British was signed here in 1840 and the original capital of New Zealand, Russell, is just a ten-minute ferry ride away. We spent a day in this sleepy and unexploited old village and another at the Treaty House Museum that sits prominently on manicured lawns that stretch down to the bay. Here traditional war canoes are on display and still used for ceremonial occasions.

Tramping, or what I call hiking, is a serious passion of New Zealanders. The Department of Conservation has a little pamphlet full of information and trail maps for every possible short walk to long treks and all readily available at our hostels or the information offices. Paihia had a little ferry that took us out to Uropukapuka, one of the larger islands in the bay, for a circular scenic hike along the cliffs. This compelled us to immediately buy a NZ bird book and our twelve km hike the next day from Paihia was the start of our bird list of the country's unique birdlife. First on this list were the fearless little Fantails, Rosella parakeets, Parson Birds (called Tui) with their clerical collar, and the huge brightly coloured NZ Pigeon measuring fifty cm! We also recognized the many imports by British homesick immigrants such as Chaffinches and Yellow Hammers. Our Kiwi bus ticket entitled us to a full day trip up to Cape Reinga, the northern tip of New Zealand, visiting en route some of what's left of the old Kauri forests. Kauri trees are thick, tall, straight and highly desirable and the forests have been decimated in the past. We got to hug the fifty foot girth of Tane Mahuto, the Lord of the Forest, rising 148 ft to the sky in the west coast's Waipoua Forest. We had the thrill of driving, at 100 kilometres per hour, down the firm sand of famous 90 Mile Beach. There were occasional stops for some boogie boarding down the high dunes or to dig for tua tua (small clams) which we crushed together between our palms and ate raw. We preferred the world famous, not to be missed, fish and chips at Mangonui on the return journey to our five star Centabay Lodge in Paihia where our beautifully furnished double room even had french doors opening onto a private garden.

The scenic and hilly Coromandel Peninsula, which hugs the south eastern side of the Hauraki Gulf and to the south of Auckland, was next on our list. Kiwi Experience covers only part of the ocean side of the peninsula and we had been told not to miss the isolated northern tip. It took two local buses and two overnights in Thames and Coromandel and, finally, a three-days-a-week mini bus to reach Fletcher Bay at the northern tip of the peninsula. This scenic but very rough coastal road ended at a single campsite on the beach and a small six-person backpacker bungalow, belonging to a sheep farm, sitting high on the hill behind. Fletcher Bay is the start of the remote Coromandel Coastal Walk which clings to the steep cliffs then winds through sheep covered hillsides for seven and half kilometres to the other side of the peninsula at Stoney Bay. Here, all to be found was a deserted campsite. It was a hard slog and took three hours each way, so it was no wonder we didn't see another soul on this remote trail. I guess that is what made the scenery and the path all the more special. We were marooned in Fletcher Bay till the next bus in three days' time and enjoyed the solitude with the additional pleasure of watching the full moon roll itself up the black silhouette of the steep headland. However our three days weren't silent as 2,000 sheep were passing through the shearing shed below with the lambs calling desperately for mom.

Returning first to Coromandel town on the minibus, we caught the local bus across the mountains to Whitianga (pronounced Fitianga) on the east side of the peninsula where we were welcomed at the gate by the proud owners of this small town's award winning five-star backpackers. From this base we could take the passenger ferry across the river estuary to hike up the Shakespeare Cliffs or catch the little shuttle to Hahei village with its beautiful beach. Here you can hike along the cliffs to Cathedral Cove, so named for the natural arch in the cliffs that allows access, at mid tide, to an isolated cove. Later that afternoon, when the tide was really low, we caught the shuttle to Hot Water Beach. Here you dig a hole in the sand at the low tide mark which immediately fills with very hot water from thermal springs and, voila, you can soak in your own hot tub. As we didn't have a spade, we chose instead to wait for someone to go in for a cooling dip in the ocean and sneak a hot soak in their vacated hole.

The Kiwi bus picked us up in Whitianga and we headed south to Tauranga on the Bay of Plenty. I have visited this town frequently since on cruise ships and always choose to climb up Mount Maunganui, a steep pimple of a hill that guards the entrance to its busy harbour. From the top you have the view across the Pacific, the surfing beaches in the south and the sandbank islands to the north. We drove on to Rotorua, due south, and the start of the active thermal centre of the North Island. You can smell the city long before you reach it. We stopped on our way into town at the Whakarewarewa Thermal Area with its Maori Cultural Centre. The famous Pohutu Geyser occasionally pops up here, but not on our whirlwind tour. We did however get to see some smaller geysers, boiling mud pools, boiling water pools (used by the Maoris to boil potatoes) and, our best find, two flightless Kiwis in a nocturnal habitat display. At the Cultural Centre I saw that the Maoris' skirts are not made with hollow reeds, as I had thought, but with dried flax leaves which curl into tubes after soaking in dye then dried. The short tubes are then threaded together like a kid's straw necklace. That's what gives them that gentle rattle as they dance and the patterns of horizontal coloured stripes..

After checking in at Funky Green Backpackers, we were off to a Maori Hongi and concert. We were welcomed in an open field with the traditional Haka greeting by the chief. This amounted to much posturing and stamping of feet, threatening with a spear, and finally, as he ended his dance, by making bug eyes and sticking out his large tongue. I think it was correct to respond likewise. I did! The meal was then taken from the pit, but instead of being cooked on hot rocks, wrapped in leaves and covered with more green leaves, it was cooked on bits of rusty iron, in plastic bags and tin foil and covered with wet sacking. Hygiene regulations, we were told. However the lamb, chicken, potatoes and kumara (floury sweet potatoes) with fruit to finish were very good. I always enjoy Maori concerts with their lilting songs, tinkling skirts and twirling poi poi (pompoms) and this one, compered by a very camp elder, was a happy affair. We were glad to move on to Taupo in the morning, having almost suffocated during the night with the heavy pong of sulphur that permeates even the interior of the houses, at just about mattress level. Phew!

Taupo is an attractive town on the northern edge of the largest lake in New Zealand, Lake Taupo. We declined the Bungy Jump for Nude Couples special offer, and instead hiked along the river to Huka Falls whose turquoise waters shoot spectacularly through a narrow canyon. After another five km hike, you reach the active thermal area, Craters of the Moon. It is maintained by a charitable trust and free to anyone who has the stamina to get there. Maybe that is why it was deserted. A boardwalk takes you safely past boiling mud pools and unexpected bursts of steam from innocent vents and craters. The whole place looks as if it might blow at any moment and is much more appealing than anything Rotorua has to offer.

Of course, the main reason for staying in Taupo for a few days was to reserve a day for the Tongariro Crossing. This is billed as the finest day hike in all New Zealand. A shuttle bus picks you up in Taupo at 6:45 a.m. and deposits you at 8:30 at one end of the eighteen km trail, picking you up at 4:00 p.m. on the other side of the mountain. What a wonderful hike across Tongariro National Park and up and over the craters of Mount Tongariro (1,976m)! The Red Crater, still showing signs of activity, the Emerald and Blue Lakes, and the barren landscape combined with the inhospitable environment are what make it such a unique trek. We had a day of perfect cloudless skies and could see both east and west coasts. Mount Egmont (2,518m), a perfect iced cone, was easily seen in the distant west and we decided we must explore it someday. It is always windy at higher altitudes in Tongariro and it was sometimes an arduous hike, especially on the open cinder slopes, but we made it with time to spare and were quite elated by the whole experience. Sometimes, as many as 500 people set out on the trail each day, but we hit a quiet day, just before Christmas, and were not trampled into the ground.

Diane Jones

With good fortune, we had selected a very cosy, comfortable and friendly backpackers from Christmas Eve to Boxing Day at National Park Village. A strange name, but this is downhill ski country in the winter months and pretty much deserted in the summer. There were only five of us and the owners of Howard's Lodge had left a treat for each of us under the tree on Christmas morning. A shuttle bus from the village ferried us to the various National Park hiking trails on the lower slopes of the other two active volcanoes within the park's boundary, Mt. Ngauruhoe (2,291 m) and Mt. Ruapehu (2,797 m). We tramped over thirty kms in our two days through beech covered slopes, across tussock and alpine meadows and up to barren ground at ever higher altitudes. Our hiking boots were smouldering by the time Kiwi Experience arrived to pick us up and continue south towards the capital, Wellington.

Halfway we had to overnight at a Kiwi Experience owned backpackers on the Rangitikei River whose fast waters flow through steeply sloped bush covered hills. Nothing else for miles around, and the lodge's main attraction were white water sports. We were met with a clipboard and a price list and told to tick our choice of activities. Under "other" I put walking and bird watching. It was free to watch all the kids shooting past the lodge in rafts and kayaks, some doing involuntary eskimo rolls. There were plenty of walking trails, but access was by pulling oneself across a sagging cable whilst sitting on a trolley board, suspended above a steep chasm and over a watery grave. Not for the faint-hearted. The backpackers was surprisingly quiet that night as all the kids were exhausted. Me too, and my arms and shoulders hurt!

We had allowed ourselves two full days to see the sights of Wellington but found that we had covered most of the bases on day one. First was the view of the city from Mount Victoria which was a simple walk from our backpackers situated on one of the streets halfway to the summit. We took a tour of the Houses of Parliament and viewed City Hall, Queen's Wharf, Lambton Quay, the Anglican Cathedral, the Maritime Museum, Ascot Street with its 19th C houses, and still had time to wander through the Botanical Gardens at the top of the cable car. Next day was my birthday and I chose to take the sightseeing ferry to Somes Island Nature Reserve and, after a two hour hike around its cliffs, caught the next ferry to Days Bay and walked around the yuppie resort village of Eastbourne for a yuppie quiche lunch before catching the ferry back across the bay.

Our backpacker accommodation we chose for its reputation that "you either loathe it or love it". It was called Beethoven's, as you are awakened to the loud music of the composer plus a bit of Elgar's "Land of Hope and Glory". This is to make sure you are up in time for the compulsory communal breakfast in the garden, presided over by the owner who is a camp, fifties, Singaporean gay. The menu is standard: porridge with chopped carrot and apple, toasted cheese sandwiches, and a hot cheese roll that you have to catch as he throws one to each of the guests at random. All this whilst precariously perched on the rockery around his tiny patio. He also lists in his brochures that all birthdays are celebrated, not just his own and Beethoven's, but also those of visiting guests. Although Peter reminded him about his promised homemade birthday cake, he got a bit stressed out and boozed up whilst cooking a New Year's Eve curry for twenty-five guests. This meant he didn't get around to putting the cake in the oven till late, and finally presented it to me, with a little crowning ceremony, just before I turned fifty-seven and one day old. Most of the other guests had sensibly scurried off to the pub by now and so it was only the very polite who remained to share my cake, before they too raced for the pub before the bells. We were happy to watch the New Year celebrations on television with our host and were curious about his two Filipino transvestite friends who appeared from nowhere. However, we retired shortly to bed as we were catching the early morning ferry to the South Island.

Crossing the Cook Straits on the Inter-Islander ferry takes three hours. The first hour you must stand out on deck and watch the capital city recede to the far side of Wellington Bay before you round the headland. Then there is only time for a quick cup of coffee before you are back on deck to enjoy the voyage through the narrow fiords of the Marlborough Sounds. We had a wonderful sunny day to see it all at its best.

In Picton we settled into yet another five-star backpackers called The Villa which had won that year's New Zealand's Top Backpacker Award. No wonder, as our double room had a brass bed covered in designer linens, matching curtains and a pink fitted plush carpet, plus a washbasin and fitted closet, all for $38 per night. The communal stainless steel kitchen and loos were immaculate and there was a lovely manicured garden with lots of tables, sun umbrellas, loungers and hammocks. It was all housed in a pretty verandah-fronted villa, smothered in roses, and close to the centre of this small port.

The South Island boasts many of New Zealand's famous tramping trails, starting in Picton with the Queen Charlotte Track which runs for fifty-eight kms along the narrow ridge of land that separates Marlborough and Kenepuru Sounds. It is a spectacular path both for its scenic views and its lush forest at lower levels. Our first morning we caught a water taxi for a drop off at The Portage on Taora Bay and walked the last twenty-two kms of the track to its end at Anakiwa where the water taxi picked us up at five. Next morning we took the Dolphin Watch Tour (no luck) and visited the rare bird sanctuary of Motuara Island which is one of the few habitats of the South Island Robin (had good luck). We had arranged to be dropped off at Ships Cove, at the very northern end of the Queen Charlotte Track, where we hoped to hike another fifteen kms. But it was very hot and we were pooped from the previous day so we quit early and sought refuge at a cool lodge, which sold excellent coffee and muffins, and waited for our Dolphin Watch boat to pick us up on its return from the afternoon tour. This time we did see a school of Hector Dolphins on our way back to Picton. These are one of the smallest and rarest of dolphins.

Kiwi Experience picked us up for the mountainous ride over to Nelson with great views of the many fingers of ocean that make up the Marlborough Sounds. Further to the west, across Tasman Bay, is the famous Abel Tasman Track. We had a day off in Nelson to catch our breath as it was a pleasant bright and artsy-crafty town. Next morning our Kiwi bus to Westport scheduled a drop-off and afternoon pick-up to allow us kids to hike part of the Abel Tasman Track for a day. Included was a discount for the cruise/hike from Kaiteriteri to further up the rugged coastline and we were dropped off at Torrent Bay. There we were rowed ashore for a wet landing on the beach with hiking boots hanging round our necks. It was about ten kms north to Bark Bay where the boat picked us up and returned us to our Kiwi bus at 3:30 p.m. This was a beautiful track through lush rainforest with bonus glimpses of intimate coves, beaches of golden sands and tidal estuaries below.

When we returned to New Zealand five years later we drove from Kaiteriteri over the Abel Tasman Mountains to Golden Bay and Farewell Spit, the very north westerly point of the South Island. This meant a steep climb over Takaka Hill and Harwood Lookout Pass at 791 metres. A charming valley greets you on the other side and we stayed for two nights at The Nook, a quiet country backpackers in Pohara. From here you can access the northern end of the Abel Tasman Track and other hikes such as Wainui Falls in Abel Tasman National Park. Much quieter and less touristy and especially interesting was the drive further north and around the long beaches of Golden Bay to Farewell Spit. It is a sandy peninsula, full of migratory birds, which stretches out to sea for almost thirty kms. From here you can also access Wharariki Beach, on the ocean side, which we found wild and windy and accessed with a heads down stagger across some glistening white sand dunes. The beach is a natural break in a coastline of high cliffs and if you dare brave the strong sea breezes, kilometres of hiking trails follow close to the cliff edge and seals, penguins and seabirds can be spotted far below.

On that same driving tour we checked out Nelson Lakes National Park at St. Arnaud. There are two beautiful hikes, the first around Lake Rotoroa with an idyllic woodland trail and a steep climb to a lookout point above the treeline. The best known is the trail around Lake Rotoiti with a lengthy wade, of unknown depth, across the broad feeder river at the far end. Thankfully, with boots slung around the neck, this only involved water to just above the knee. I managed to give my middle toe a hard thwack on a rock, so the last eleven kms down the west side were more of a hobble and a moan. The beech woods and soft peaty ground make for perfect tramping trails and every corner turned can take your breath away. Needless to say, you are accompanied by birdsong and only bothered by sandflies if you stop and hang about. A good incentive to keep moving, even with a limp.

Also in 2003 we continued from Nelson Lakes to Arthur's Pass, which was the old east-west direct trade route from the West Coast to Christchurch, and settled into a little cabin at Mountain House Lodge in Arthur's Pass Village (920 m). Three days of great hiking and fine views down to the flat glaciated stony valleys of the Bealey and Taramakau Rivers. We climbed up to Temple Basin, a winter ski field where you must carry your skis for one hour up to the basic huts and rope tows. We followed the alpine meadows and tussock grass trail of the Dobson Track up at the top of the Pass, and also hiked to the top of Bealey Spur (drops on both sides of the ridge) to an old sheep musterer's hut of the 1930s. Then there were the waterfalls of the Devil's Punchbowl and Bridal Veil Falls close to the village and, to top off our final morning, we climbed up the Bealey Valley towards its glacier beginnings on Mount Rolleston (2,270 m), the hike's towering backdrop. With the sunshine, blue skies, red alpine tussock grass, dappled beech woods and crystal-clear streams, it was magic.

Going back to our Kiwi Experience in 1998, Westport was a depressed gold mining town but the start of the West Coast of the South Island or, as they say, The Wet Coast because of its high rainfall. After a forgettable side tour out to Cape Foulwind, aptly named by Captain Cook after he had a whiff of its seal colony, we had the bus drop us off at Punakaiki close to Paparoa National Park. The Beach Hostel in this tiny hamlet is opposite the famous Pancake Rocks and Blowholes where, when the tide is full, columns of water shoot skyward through chimneys in the eroded limestone rocks which resemble piles of pancakes. We had a full day of hilly hiking in Paparoa National Park which included fording two mighty rivers, one of which was at knicker wetting level. No sign of Wet Coast rain and from the hostel's sundeck we had great views of the heavy surf that batters this coastline and wonderful sunsets on the ocean's horizon.

Continuing down the coast we stopped at the Bushman's Centre to be shown the ways of the early loggers and a first encounter, and hopefully last, with some of the huge longfin eels that inhabit all of New Zealand's waterways and lakes. I had a shiver when I thought about my recent watery wades.

At an active family gold mining operation, we got to pan for gold and keep the proceeds. (I suspect the gravel is seeded with pyrite for us fools!) We were shown the old claim with its rusty cabins and wooden sludge boxes before our guides, who were a couple of real characters with lots of tall tales to tell, announced it was tucker time. This was a sausage and potato BBQ followed by billy tea and lots of laughter. We then walked down the riverbank to watch today's techniques where the gravel, vacuumed from the riverbed, is washed through more modern sludge boxes lined with astro turf which traps the heavier gold. Both these centres have reinvented themselves as successful tourist stops, guaranteed to have a Kiwi Experience busload of kids visit each day.

Arriving at Franz Josef Glacier village we were kitted out with heavy steel-toed boots with their own attached crampons, thick wool socks, and rain parka. Lastly, to give one considerable doubt about the wisdom of taking a guided walk on the glacier, an ICE AXE! At nine next morning, thirty of us were bused the five km up to the glacier car park. With our two-ton boots slung over one shoulder and a day pack with extra clothes plus lunch and our ice axe over the other, we staggered the remaining two km to the glacier's terminal cliff face. Carrying the boots was much worse than wearing them because, as soon as you got onto the ice itself, they acted like heavy magnets and made you feel very secure on the slippery surface.

It took about an hour to climb the terminal ice face on a staircase freshly cut each day by the guides. We had been divided into four groups and Peter and I chose to join two and three respectively so that we wouldn't have to see the other disappearing forever into a bottomless crevasse. I should have gone into group four, but it was for the timid, less fit and camera happy ones. The four groups fanned out in different directions and my group of six had an enthusiastic Mt. Everest rock climber type guide who wanted to give us as exciting an experience as possible by leading us through an awesome maze of rock falls, tunnels and caves. This was accomplished by placing our big hobnail boots on tiny narrow ice steps that the guide would cut as we went along, very slowly and carefully most of the time. I freaked out on quite a few occasions when presented with a jump across a bottomless crevasse, or a sideways climb up a sheer ice face with big drops below that you daren't consider. Anyway, Mr. Mt. Everest coaxed me, and a few others, over some of the worst glacial terrain I ever want to travel over again. However, when faced with an upward sloping ice ledge with an outward bulging overhang which required you to remove your backpack so that its weight wouldn't tip you over as you leant outwards, I surrendered and begged to be demoted to group four. I just wanted to enjoy the amazing ice maze with the sun and blue skies giving the ice wonderful hues and shadows. The guides said it was not only an especially good day weather wise but, because of wind conditions out on the coast, the sightseeing helicopters and planes, that normally buzz the glaciers from dawn till dusk, were grounded. At lunchtime I was rescued by the Group Four guide and from then on, till we descended at 4:30, I really enjoyed every minute and almost forgot how heavy my boots were.

The following day we took a six hour walk up a steep trail to a viewpoint on the mountain beside the glacier and looked down on the groups of flies working their way through the ice fields. It certainly put the mammoth size of these glaciers into perspective. At the viewpoint we met our first Kea, a very large and curious ground parrot that can be a real pest as they nibble on backpacks and hiking boots and are very fond of windscreen wipers.

Fox Glacier is only twenty-five km down the coast, so we were there by mid morning. However our Kiwi bus first took us to nearby Lake Matheson where, on one of the infrequent cloudless days, you can see the highest mountain in New Zealand, Mount Cook (12,317 ft), reflected in the pretty lake. We only just saw Mt. Cook, but not a ripple free reflection, before the clouds moved in and we had to get out our rain jackets. After a day of leg rest, we tackled twenty kms of trail up the side of the Fox Glacier to various viewpoints. A dirty old snowbank at the side of a wet grey shopping mall carpark could best describe it and we were so glad we had chosen the much more scenic Franz Josef for our glacier walk. Also we were very aware of the constant noise of the sightseeing flights, despite the gloomy wet weather.

We left the Wet Coast behind and headed over the Haast Pass and hopped off at Makarora for a couple of days to hike in Mt. Aspiring National Park with its wide flat bottomed valleys guarded by sheer mountains on either side. Awe inspiring indeed with mountains named Mt. Dreadful and Mt. Awful. Unfortunately it took us two and a half hours of steep climbing just to get above the tree line for the promised views. Fortunately the sunshine had returned and all the surrounding peaks were unusually clear and made the climb well worth it.

It was still a day's drive to reach the centre of New Zealand's tourist industry, Queenstown. On the way we stopped at Lake Wanaka and climbed up Mt. Iron for some 360 degree views. Lots of good farming country around this area as we were now on the eastern flanks of the Alps and just into Fiordland National Park. Queenstown did not have much to offer if one is not interested in bungy jumping, river rafting, jet boating or paragliding. We did the mandatory climb of Queenstown Hill and booked the next day's tour to Milford Sound. This requires a convoluted four-hour bus ride along Lake Wakatipu and Lake Te Anau, across the Divide through the long Homer Tunnel, a zig-zag down the Clear Air Canyons and eventually into Milford. We picked up and dropped off Milford Track trampers on the way and were glad we weren't considering this famous three-day hike, especially in wet weather, with nose to butt hikers and overnights in crowded huts. We were surprised to find that Milford Sound was only seven kms long, but it is very impressive with the many waterfalls plunging directly into the sea from the steep mountains and cliffs that flank the fiord. We were blessed with blue skies all day which is very unusual in an area that gets on average 6.8 metres of rain a year.

We had the bus drop us off at Te Anau backpackers where we were given a cosy quiet room in what had been the back garden shed. This is the walking capital of New Zealand. The famous Kepler track starts almost right in town so we took the opportunity to tackle the circular route. It starts along the shoreline of Lake Te Anau through "goblin forest" where Spanish moss hangs from the trees and the rocky ground is smothered in green mosses, ferns and lichens of every hue. However, after fourteen kms, we had failed to reach even the first viewpoint above the treeline and decided we had to return. We discovered that most day hikers cover the first ten kms in a water taxi. But then we would have missed the magical goblin forest.

We joined Kiwi Experience's Bottom Bus for a circular tour out of Te Anau which meant we could stop off for a few days on Stewart Island. First, we crossed through rolling grazing lands looking very much like Scotland with gorse, bracken ferns, thistles and heather which the Scottish settlers had brought with them. These are all now considered unwelcome invasive species to be eradicated when possible. Not surprising that our next stop was at Dunedin on the Pacific Coast, where many of its streets and suburbs are named after those in Edinburgh. It was very quiet as one third of the population were students of Otago University who had left for the summer holidays. But the city's main attraction is the Royal Albatross breeding colony on Taiaroa Head on the Otago Peninsula and the only mainland colony. We joined a backpacker nature tour and lay on the grass out on the headland and let the Albatross with their ten-foot wingspan skim over us. We followed this up with visits to remote beaches where we could watch the Little Blue penguins and Yellow Eyed penguins hobble up from the sea to feed their chicks, and also visited a rare Hooker Sea Lion colony.

The rocky coasts in the southeast are named The Catlins. Here the constant winds have made all the roadside trees lean over at an almost horizontal angle. Of course, this is excellent sheep farming country with shearing in progress and where we were recruited as fleece stuffers at our Papatowai Hilltop Backpackers. We hopped off our Kiwi bus at Invercargill, another old Scottish town. From here you take the minibus twenty-seven km to Bluff, at the very southern tip of New Zealand's South Island and catch the catamaran ferry across the notorious forty km of Foveaux Strait with fierce currents, ocean swells and strong winds. No wonder most people choose to fly! Oban, on Half Moon Bay, is the only settlement on the Island and Reubens Rooms had a self contained flat for our five-day stay. Reuben was an old geyser of eighty whose mattresses were about the same age and whose skills in the house cleaning department were somewhat short-sighted. But the view over the harbour was stunning and the weather kind, especially during our long daily hikes on Stewart Island's notoriously muddy tracks. Some of the worst of these have slippery boardwalks which have been sensibly covered in chicken wire for a firmer grip. The sun even managed to break through the mist by lunchtime on most days.

Stewart Island is about the only place where it is still possible to see Kiwi in the wild. It involved a forty-five minute late evening boat trip to a remote peninsula and a stumble in the dark across a rough track to a beach on the ocean side. This is where Kiwi often come out at night to feed on the sand hoppers along the high tide mark. We were very lucky to spot four and a half, well above the average number of sightings. The half Kiwi was a fluffy rump disappearing into the thick undergrowth. The Department of Conservation manages and limits these trips in order to avoid disturbance of this rare bird's habitat. They have been decimated in the past by feral cats and stoats and other introduced predators. Ulva Island in Paterson Inlet is predator free and, although there are no Kiwis, it has a plethora of rare parrots, including Kaka, plus many other unique New Zealand birds which were binocular friendly.

Sooty Shearwaters nest on some of the offshore islands where the Maori are still allowed to collect the chicks to roast as a dubious delicacy. It is called Mutton Bird on the local menu, but rather than resembling lamb it is more like a dose of cod liver oil, washed over a salty side of duck. No second helpings thanks! Oban is a very laid-back little settlement with a population of only 400 and no roads that go further than a few kilometres in either direction. However it did offer after-dinner live entertainment at the Gumboot Theatre. This was a zippy, one woman, very professional, half hour show with its satirical review of a day in the life of your average red-necked Stewart Islander. It was worth every cent of the $4 ticket.

Our journey back to the mainland on the Foveaux Express catamaran was much more of a thrill, even though the captain announced it was a relatively calm crossing. "Relative to what?" I said, whilst hanging on for dear life to the railing on the back deck. We met up with our Kiwi bus that afternoon and reached Riverton that night at the estuary of the mighty Waiau River which comes south from Lake Te Anau and Lake Manapouri. We were to meet this river again when we based ourselves in the small town of Manapouri. This time the pair of us were trying to row ourselves across its fast-running waters in a rented boat which seemed determined to return us to Riverton. This rite of passage is required if, like us, you want to reach the Manapouri trail system and this initial obstacle serves to keep these trails under-used and all the more appealing for their isolation. Another plus was that the goblin forest was even more attractive with the warm sunlight glinting through the trees, especially after five days of cloud and mist on Stewart Island.

Diane Jones

Remote Doubtful Sound is accessed on a day excursion from Manapouri. We blew the budget for this high expense trip as the mystic fiord has only become accessible since they recently built a twenty-two km road from Deep Cove at the head of Doubtful Sound over the Wilmot Pass to Lake Manapouri. This was to enable heavy equipment to be brought in to build a generating station two km underground at the head of Lake Manapouri with a ten km discharge tunnel to Deep Cove and the ocean. Quite an engineering feat as this was not a natural draining system for the lake and therefore a dam was not a possibility. After a one-and-a-half-hour cruise across Lake Manapouri we took a shuttle bus which, after taking us down the two km spiral tunnel into the bowels of the earth to see the seven generators in action, drove across the pass to Deep Cove. Here we boarded a tour boat for an awesome three-hour cruise forty kms out to the Tasman Sea and back. We explored some of the many finger fiords along the way and were entertained by a pod of bottlenose dolphins and the occasional seal. All this was under cloudless skies which is a very rare day in this southwest corner of New Zealand that measures rainfall in feet not inches. We had hit the jackpot again.

Our Kiwi Bottom Bus returned us full circle to Te Anau where we rejoined Kiwi Experience and continued to Queenstown and on to Christchurch across the Alps stopping first, for a couple of days, at Mount Cook Resort Village just below the Tasman Glacier. Mount Cook at 12,317 ft is the highest in New Zealand and where mountaineers like Sir Edmund Hillary (first to climb Everest) cut their teeth. The Tasman Glacier drains into the glacial blue waters of Lake Pukaki to the east. The Fox and Franz Josef Glaciers start in the same ice field but drain to the west. We tried many of the short hikes up the side of the Tasman Glacier to various viewpoints to hopefully catch a glimpse of the top peaks without the ever-present clouds and constant drizzle. Even the weather can seem like a Scottish import. We couldn't afford the five-star tourist resort hotels and had to share a seven-bed chalet dorm with the Kiwi Experience kids. With my double earplugs I didn't even hear myself snoring. As we were preparing for an early departure whilst watching the Kea parrots fighting over windscreen wipers, the sun was just rising, the clouds were rolling off the slopes and we had our Kodak moment at last with the magnificent Mount Cook against a blue blue sky.

Tekapo was a compulsory overnight stop, halfway to Christchurch. It is a pretty village at the end of glacial Lake Tekapo which is fed by the Godley Glacier from the Tasman Ice Field. This is called Mackenzie Country, with its dry rolling grazing lands for cattle and sheep, and continues into the fertile farming lands of the Canterbury Plains.

Christchurch, the main city of the South Island, is sheltered by the Akaroa Peninsula, an old French Settlement. Many of Christchurch's fine Victorian buildings and its Cathedral were demolished by the earthquake in 2010 but in 1998 it was in its heyday. All very English, from the punts on the River Avon to the schoolkids in their St. Trinians uniforms. It seems fifty years behind the times. We spent a leisurely day at the Arts Centre, Museum, Botanical Gardens and, of course, the Cathedral in the main pedestrian Square. Luckily The Wizard appeared that day to preach to anyone who would listen to his rantings. He must be getting on in years but how would you know behind his long grey beard, flowing black robes and pointy Wizard's hat. He is still fit enough to arrive carrying his own stepladder to use as his soap box.

Further up the Pacific coast there is a steep drop in the continental shelf only about one kilometre offshore. This creates a unique environment, rich in nutrients, which attracts giant Sperm Whales close to shore and all year round. Kaikoura has morphed into a major tourist destination as you are pretty much required to stay for a few nights as the Whale Watching boats have to wait for a day that is not foggy and the sea reasonably calm. We had to wait till the third day before the weather cooperated, meantime putting money into the town coffers. We occupied our time hiking around the Kaikoura Peninsula saying "Hi" to the many seals lying across the rocky shoreline path. I would like to say we were not disappointed in our whaling excursion, but we were. When these fifty-foot mammoths surface, after their forty to fifty minute dive, all you see is a bit of flat floating grey blubber spouting the occasional geyser. You had better not be looking the other way when it suddenly decides to dive and show off its enormous tail fluke. We saw only three on our two-hour trip but apparently the average is two. However, another boat boasted about seeing seven. I hate that!

Crossing back to Wellington, we walked down to the waterfront, where the newly built Te Papa Museum (Museum of the People) was soon to be officially opened. Two Maori War Canoes were rehearsing for the ceremonies but strong wind squalls were buffeting them all over the harbour and, at times, seemed near to capsizing. What sounded like war cries were probably more cries of alarm by the thirty to forty bare chested warriors as they tried to hold the canoes steady and avoid ramming the other as they crossed paths.

Our Kiwi bus followed the east coast route up to Napier, an upscale seaside town on Hawke Bay. The town was levelled by an earthquake in 1931 but was rebuilt in three years to become the best example in the world of Art Deco design. In the 1980s the town realized what a treasure they had and the buildings were all restored and repainted in authentic pastels colours. An Art Deco summer festival is held with 1930s jazz bands, concours d'elegance cars, vintage plane flights etc. whilst the locals dress up to match the era: striped blazers, Oxford bags, and straw boaters, slinky dresses, feather boas and cloche hats. The Criterion five star backpackers was a 1930s hotel in the pedestrian precinct where we enjoyed all the late night musical entertainment through our bedroom window.

Following the coast from Napier all the way round to the Bay of Plenty was not a Kiwi Experience route and so we included the East Cape on our car trip in 2003. Unfortunately my diary describes the weather as drizzle interspersed with sheets of rain but we did manage a few hikes in remote Urewera National Park reached by a sixty-three km road, much of which was a muddy quagmire. We decided the recommended hikes to scenic Lakes Waikaremoana and Waikareiti had not been worth the effort when faced with the major cleaning required of our rental car. From the port of Gisborne the road follows the coast of the East Cape out to Hick's Bay Pa and around to Opotiki. This is very much Maori country with each small village having their own Marae (meeting house) with intricately carved gates and gables, but everywhere seemed deserted due to the bleak weather and we chose to drive on.

Also on our 2003 car trip we couldn't miss a visit to Mount Egmont which we had seen so clearly when hiking the Tongariro Crossing. En route we visited Waiotapu Thermal Area, near Rotorua, to see its Champagne Pools and the Lady Knox geyser that is guaranteed to spout off at 10:15 each morning and have you take cover. It did and we did! The direct route from here to Mt. Egmont took us via The Forgotten World Highway. This is a narrow winding road with a knuckle whitening drive through Tangarakau Gorge and the Moto Tunnel which had a nasty curve and was a total blackout when we entered it unexpectedly whilst still wearing sunglasses. We had never thought to switch on our headlights and stalled as we came to an abrupt halt in the sudden darkness, inches from the rocky walls. It was a frantic moment feeling for the light switch praying no one was coming from the opposite direction.

Mount Egmont (2,518 m), with its white snow cap, is a perfectly shaped volcano that anchors its own National Park and creates the bulge on the North Island's western coastline. It has since been given the Maori name of Mount Taranaki. We spent a full two days hiking its many trails on the lower flanks through lovely damp cloud forest with Spanish moss hanging from every contorted beech bough of its thick montane forest. This particular goblin forest is often used as a movie set, and Tom Cruise himself was in town filming The Last Samurai. From high points above the tree line you could see far across to Tongariro National Park with Mount Ruapehu, the North Island's highest peak. Our boot soles were getting a serious work-out but, before we left on our second day, we tramped the southern section where tiny Rifleman Wrens were in abundance around Wilkies Pools and Dawson's Falls, for a new addition to our bird list. We kept just enough energy to tramp the Coastal Path at Opunake. However it was poorly maintained, overused and the views were nothing special but it allowed us to stay an extra night under Mount Egmont's guard at Wheatley Downs farmstay, a cattle ranch, where we were adopted by Wig Wig the tame piglet. This area is the centre of New Zealand's dairy industry, especially the nearby town of Hawara where one hundred milk tankers collect from 750,000 cows at 4,000 dairy farms each week for the Kiwi Co-op Dairy, the biggest in the world.

Heading south towards Wellington for a final day of hiking in the Tararua Mountain Range that comes right down to the Kapiti Coast, we stopped for lunch at Wanganui. Sitting at the estuary of the Wanganui River, this old port has beautiful early 20th century buildings which have been restored and repainted in Art Deco colours like Napier. This is the country's third longest river, whose source is in Tongariro National Park, and in 2017 the river was given special status as an indivisible and living being owing to its spiritual importance to the region's Maori culture. Not sure what all that means!

We had already covered Wellington thoroughly on our previous visits but were anxious to spend a full day at the new museum of Te Papa Tongarewa (Museum of New Zealand), that did not open till after we visited in 1998. It has a wonderful Maori exhibition in addition to its Immigration Exhibit that includes, not just Europeans, but the many south sea islanders from The Cooks, Samoa, Fiji, Tonga, Nuie and other islands I have never even heard of. It tells wonderful stories of their personal journeys to reach New Zealand and their pioneering efforts. There is also a Natural History section with an outdoor bush exhibit to wander through and we were reminded of the incredible diversity of New Zealand's flora. A Maori choir in the atrium was singing a lilting farewell song as we departed, leaving us with warm memories of our wonderful travels through this very special country.

Angel Falls, Venezuela

Extraordinary Travels of an Ordinary Housewife

SOUTH AMERICA

TUCAN OVERLAND TRUCK
Nov. 1998-Feb. 1999 & Nov.-Dec. 2002

ECUADOR

We took the tour company's instructions seriously when we exited customs at Quito Airport. "Wear your day packs on your chest, chain your luggage to your wrist then go to the taxi stand inside the arrivals hall where you will pay the fare in advance and be directed to a safe taxi." What a relief, as we were having to carry large wads of U.S. cash in our safe pockets for this fifteen week journey. I had found that long fourteen inch cotton pockets suspended from inside the waistband of our long pants proved to be a much safer alternative to money belts for all our world travels.

As we left our hotel next morning we noticed, in the elevator, evacuation procedures in the event of an eruption "at any moment" of Mt. Pichincha which is one of the several active volcanoes that ring Quito. Our suspicions that this trip might prove to be a risky venture were confirmed when we walked to the old city to enjoy the somewhat shabby Spanish Colonial architecture and survived at least one attempt (if not three) of being swarmed by little old ladies trying to pick Peter's pockets and daypack. Shouting "ladrona" and swinging my brolly at them did the trick, as just walking away quickly induced a pounding heart and a tight head at 3,000 m altitude.

It was with relief, that evening, when we joined the safety of our group, ready to depart the next morning on our Tucan 4WD truck-bus with twenty-four fellow travellers (sixteen women, eight men, twelve nationalities) and our Australian guides Moose and Valerie. Our vehicle looked like a cross between a Brinks truck and a removal van, bright blue, with bus style seating and windows on the upper deck plus two small front windows that looked out over the driver's cab. The fridge was stocked with beer and pop and there was a hidden safe under the floor for everyone's valuables. Below the seating level were copious compartments for camping gear, folding tables and stools, a pull-out stove, water tanks etc. In the rear was a shelved compartment for luggage, tents, food etc. Custom designed for this overland type of trip, it proved to be roomy, comfortable and secure. We would stay in two-star hotels in the cities and otherwise camp in two-man tents.

Sharp at 9.30 next morning our truck joined the Pan American Highway, beyond the barrios of the sprawling city, and drove south through the famous Avenue of the Volcanoes to the spa town of Banos. It nestles beneath the Tungurahua Volcano at the top of a steep canyon that drops seventy km down to the Amazon Basin.

Banos is an attractive tourist town, with good restaurants, a cyber cafe and a grossly ornate cathedral. We had dropped in altitude but were still breathless when we went on a long day hike on the lower slopes of Tungurahua to several good viewpoints. A visit to a little zoo gave us a cheat sheet of the birds and mammals we might find, including Andean Condors, jaguars, ocelots, puma, speckled bears and various monkeys. We knew we would be unlikely to see many, if any, of these when we joined our three-day Amazon excursion the following day. That evening we were fitted out with gumboots and, after an inexpensive dinner in an elegant French restaurant (sans gumboots), we snuck into a clandestine cockfight for a little more local flavour.

An old chartered bus, with some of our braver companions perched on the roof, followed a precarious road that clung to the canyon wall all the way down to Puyo where we had lunch before the last hour's drive into the jungle to our first "lodge". We had thought the most dangerous part of our drive was over until, speeding at ninety km per hour along a rough road, through thick isolated jungle, the bus went out of control and rolled sideways down a steep embankment. It was like being inside a tumble drier watching broken glass and debris float past in slow motion. We were in the front seat and so, when we finally rolled to a stop, we were lying on the ceiling looking out the open door and were the first to crawl out. It was a miracle that only three of our group were injured seriously enough to require hospitalization. Two rejoined us the following day but unfortunately our one Swede, a woman, suffered a broken collarbone, broken ribs and punctured lung and she had to be flown home. The toppling of the bus had been very much cushioned by the thick vegetation, which allowed most of us to escape with just cuts and abrasions and we all felt sufficiently unfazed that we agreed to continue the excursion. We flagged down two pick-up trucks, one to take the injured back to a Mission Hospital in Puyo, the other to take the girls on to the lodge with the packs whilst the men walked the last few kilometres.

The lodge amounted to three simple thatched bamboo walled huts, sleeping up to twelve in bunk beds with mosquito nets. There was a covered dining area and a couple of basic latrines with a fast flowing rocky stream to wash in.

Macaws and monkeys hopped around the trees above and were obviously semi-tame, the latter better than Quito pickpockets. Beers were on the house that evening, courtesy of Tucan. We only had local guides with us at this point, as Valerie went to the hospital with the injured whilst Moose had returned to Quito on business for the three days we were on this optional excursion.

We all reported for the next morning's hike, clad in the gumboots we had rescued from the bus and managed to assemble in sufficient matching pairs to fit the survivors. I had two deep punctures on my bruised shins and was advised not to do any of the waist-high river crossings in case I infected the wounds. So I went as far as the first river crossing with my group of six, which was the halfway point on our circular route, and returned the same way with another of our groups who were travelling in the opposite direction. It was steep, muddy and thick vegetation all the way, with our guide stopping to show us various flora and "insect" fauna, and a very poisonous little green/black tree snake with a frog half devoured. Peter had continued with our original little group across the river and my return group was almost back at the lodge when local guides came running out the forest, screaming hysterically.

One of the girls in Peter's group had swung on a liana vine over the river, fallen and split her head open on a rock, had a seizure, lapsed into unconsciousness, and showed no pulse. Fortunately in her group were a nurse and a vet and they started CPR and managed to get her breathing again. To cut a horrible story short, with the aid of an Israeli paramedic following behind with a totally different tour, they managed to bring her out on a litter made of wood poles and jackets, then a mattress on a pick-up truck out to the hospital in Puyo and she was flown next day to Quito for a brain drain and intensive care. She and her boyfriend had to abandon the trip and fly back to Britain. Now we had lost three after only four days of a 104 day trip. How many of us would be left by the time we reach Rio, I thought?

That afternoon we took dug-out canoes down some hair-raising rapids to our next overnight lodge. This one was a little better appointed than the first and situated on a high bank above the confluence of the Puyo and much larger Pasazi River. Both are tributaries of the Amazon, which is not so named until it reaches Iquitos in Peru. After dinner a local shaman (who looked very much like the lodge owner in disguise) entertained us. He insisted that the traumas of our previous two days would be helped if he blew cigarette smoke up some of the girl's skirts! Definitely a bit of jiggery pokery. He skipped me, as I was wearing long pants and a sceptical look.

Day three began with a hike to a lookout where we could see for many miles across the flat Amazon Basin, 3,600 kms still to go before the Atlantic. Later that day, after returning to Banos to rejoin the truck, we continued down the spine of the Andes, along precipitous roads clinging to steep volcanic mountains through breathtaking scenery. We spent a night in Cuenco, Ecuador's third largest city and possibly prettiest with its Spanish architecture. It is the centre for Panama hats so called because they were shipped to Europe from Panama but have always been made in Ecuador. True fact.

Next afternoon found us at the border with Peru, having dropped down from the high Andes to the more arid coastal mountains with banana plantations and further south to the flat arid coastal plains. Our group had bonded well due to the initial trauma and although Peter and I were by far the oldest we found them all attractive, delightful, interesting fellow travellers with ages ranging from twenty to thirty-eight. We later found we were dubbed "The Glamour Bus" by other overland trucks following the same route..

PERU

These arid coastal plains continue all the way to Chile and beyond and the low rainfall is caused by the northerly Humboldt Current which is so cold that it supports Galapagos penguins on the Equator. Over the next few days we visited the ruins of the several ancient civilizations that inhabited this coast. The Moche (200-700 AD) left us the Pyramids of the Moon and the Sun and the Tomb of the Lord of Sipan. The Chimus (1,000-1,400 AD) built the adobe city of Chan Chan, still defined but much eroded.

The oldest were the Paracas (2,000 BC to 200 AD) who considered cone shaped heads to be highly desirable. This they achieved by binding the heads of newborn babies with splints. They were also skilled at trepanning which meant removing a piece of skull and, after a bit of brain surgery to remove a tumour, or repair a battle injury, covering the hole with a silver or gold plate. Not sure what they used as an anaesthetic, but obviously not a club on the head.

The Nazca Cultures (900 BC to 600 AD) were responsible for the famous Nazca Lines. If they were not the first in space, then they must have been the first with drones to hover above the vast desert plain to allow them to etch long lines by scraping away the grey surface to reveal the lighter ground beneath. Some of these triangular shapes and mythical figures stretch for several kilometres and the only way to view them is in a light aircraft. Are they part of an astronomical calendar, extraterrestrial landing strip for aliens to visit the Paracas coneheads, or a vision for the gods above? The jury is still out on this and maybe we will never know, but the skills involved in their creation are almost beyond belief.

Lima, Peru's capital, has one third of the country's population living in its metropolis, most of whom I swear must be thieves and charlatans. Cameras were being snatched and we had now replaced our camera neck strap with a length of chain. We were even advised to chain our luggage to our hotel room furniture! Were we becoming paranoid or just sensible? Fortunately we were in a very central hotel which meant we didn't have to go far to see the sights, which are mainly Spanish colonial buildings and churches - some beautiful, some overly elaborate and few of much interest.

The museums are a must-see. The Gold Museum with all the treasures from the past 1,500 years or more is like an ornate Fort Knox. It also includes the fine textiles and pottery from early centuries A.D. to Spanish colonial times. This pottery is not only sophisticated in its moulds and decoration, but displays many realistic scenes of copulation, birth and death. Erotic pieces from the 5th to 9th centuries especially, are enough to bring an embarrassed gasp from even the most seasoned "seen-it-all-before" voyeur. The New Museum of the Nation gives a detailed overview of all the civilizations of South America up to the Incas and the 16th Century when the Spaniards took over. It also had the items discovered recently in the Lord of Sipan's tomb of the Moche Period. Riches beyond belief.

Lima, with its permanent smoggy haze, is not a city to dwell in for longer than necessary. Its chock-a-block traffic, crazy taxis, beggars and hawkers were marginally offset by helpful and friendly little cheap restaurants where one could dine well with a beer for under five dollars. We even enjoyed dinner in a nunnery! The nuns cook and serve sophisticated meals with beer, wine etc. in a beautiful high-ceilinged refectory with fancy-wancy table settings, floral arrangements etc. The only drawback is that you have to sober up and join in an Ave Maria with the staff at ten p.m. vespers.

We headed inland at Puerto Inka, the seaport for Cuzco, 240 kms and 3,400 m up in the Andes. Using relay runners and a paved path, the Incas had fresh fish on the tables of Cuzco in twenty-four hours. En route to Cuzco, from where we planned to hike the last part of the Inca's Trail to Machu Picchu, we spent a couple of days in Arequipa, Peru's second largest city. Its most attractive and outstanding tourist attraction is the Santa Catalina Convent, a small walled town of two hectares, with laneways, plazas and cloisters, fountains and potted geraniums. For 400 years nuns, despite their vows of poverty and silence, lived in grand style with beautifully furnished apartments, personal maids and cooks to serve meals with porcelain plates, silver cutlery and damask linen. We were beginning to question the wealth of the church and the poverty of the people. We also visited "Juanita", a mummy found in 1995 on top of Ampato Volcano at 6,320 m. As an Incan "chosen woman" of about twelve years old, she was honoured to climb to this high spot and be sacrificed to her Inca Gods with a swift blow to the head.

Unfortunately Arequipa is claimed to be the least safe city in Peru and we were instructed to walk in groups of no less than six. Its notoriety was confirmed when a distressed American woman came to our group's restaurant table to ask our guides for help. She had been mugged with chloroform outside the convent and awoke to find her skirt over her head and her money belt gone with all her money, passport, air tickets etc. Locals were around but seemed to turn a blind eye to these frequent events. Even our "emergency" vehicle, a mountain bike attached to the front of our truck, was stolen that night from within the security of the hotel's high walled compound. A guide, from another overland truck, had all his luggage stolen from his hotel room!

Onward, upward and over Mt. Caracora Pass at 4,800 m, our Tucan truck took it in its stride. We camped overnight on the edge of the Colca Canyon, deeper even than the Grand Canyon, to watch the Condors, the world's largest bird of prey, sweep over our heads at sunset. These were impressive at such close range with their ten foot wingspan. Sleeping at 3,650 m meant headaches and breathlessness, but we were happy in the knowledge that Condors only eat carrion.

Cuzco was the capital of the Incan Empire in the 15th century and many of its present day buildings still show Inca brickwork in their foundations. It is criss-crossed by narrow original Inca cobbled streets and anchored in the centre by the floodlit Plaza des Armas and Cathedral. It is very much a jumping off point for Machu Picchu. So there are many tourists, many touts, many thieves, but not too much to see and do.

From Cuzco you either take the train direct to Machu Picchu or you go by road through the Sacred Valley to Ollantaytambo and hike to Machu Picchu on the Inca Trail. Most of our group chose the latter and so, after spending a whole day visiting the famous Inca settlements of Sacsayhuaman (phonetic pronunciation is Sexy Woman) and Tambo Machay on the northern limits of Cuzco (and where the original Inca Trail started), we toured the extensive Inca Ruins at Pisac and Ollantaytambo in the Sacred valley to the northeast of Cuzco. The mountains are covered in Inca-built terraces, some of which are still in use. You can only marvel at their stone construction techniques. One stone in the ruins of Sacsayhuaman weighs 120 tons. They used the same methods as the Egyptians to move these huge blocks from the quarries some distance away and also used ramps to bring them up the mountainside.

Pisac at the southern end of the Sacred Valley has a colourful local market to visit on a Sunday morning. Great photo opportunities to catch the many different outfits worn by the Quechua women. Big voluminous knee length skirts and petticoats, some plain and some embroidered, were worn beneath hats of many kinds from felt bowlers to fine white straw top hats with a black band, to a flat black felt square shape from which hung brightly coloured wool fringes and often topped with fresh white roses. There was even a hat, like a shallow soup bowl in embroidered felt, held onto the head with a lace chinstrap. Covering grubby wool sweaters were the ubiquitous shawls stuffed with anything from young children to daily groceries, to souvenirs to hustle to the tourist. Bright colours everywhere for the women whilst the men were dressed only in shabby shirts and trousers with dun coloured soft bowler hats.

Our Inca Trail hike was four days and three nights and started where the road ends, about twenty km north of Ollantaytambo. Only the train tracks go on to Aguas Calientes, the station for Machu Picchu. Eighteen of our group chose to go with a more up-market outfit which meant we had our own excellent guides (two), plus cook and thirty porters to carry our tents and personal gear as well as food, cooking equipment and mess tent with tables and stools and candelabra. Three others chose to join a budget group and the two remaining decided to go by train and forget the hike.

Our first day of hiking, as with the next two, enjoyed perfect weather all the way. We were into the rainy season so rain ponchos and thick mud could have been the norm. We covered eleven kms before our first camp at the small village of Huayllabamba. From a high point en route we had looked down on the Inca Ruins of Llaqtapata, the first of many well excavated Inca towns we would visit on the trail. The Spanish, when they conquered the Inca in 1535, insisted on destroying or covering these Inca settlements, and so they are only being discovered and excavated in recent times.

Day two saw us set out at 6.30 a.m. for a hard ten km up to Dead Woman's Pass (Warmiwanusqu at 4,000 m) and the highest point on the trail. We had camped at just over 3,000 m so it was a major climb with altitude being the main problem as the trail was dry and the skies clear. Some suffered headaches, nausea and even vomiting by the side of the path. However Peter and I only suffered from racing heartbeats and lack of breath but found that with frequent stops to let our hearts return to more normal rhythms we could keep up a good pace. Peter, in fact, was the first to the top in two and a half hours and I was in the middle of the pack an hour later. We had been fed the old Inca cereal called quinoa for breakfast as it is apparently a complete food in itself and was what gave the Incas their remarkable stamina, especially those fish runners. The mess tent was all set for lunch just over the summit and then we had a steep but stepped descent to camp two in the valley below. Exhausted!

Our bowl of warm water for ablutions was outside our tent at 5.00 a.m. On day three it was a long sixteen km past the Runkurakay Ruin Lookout fort on our way up to the second pass at 3,750 m and another steep drop down to the ruins of Sayaqmarka (Dominant Town) which clings to a cliff face. We were now hiking on original rough paving and the very steep steps of the Incas, the first section of the trail having been restored and the steps lowered. Gosh, our knees were really complaining. We had a long long haul up the side of the next ridge through damp cloud forest to our lunch stop on the Phuyupatamarca Pass at 3,560 m. The views were spectacular and we could now look down to the town of Agua Calientes and the River Urubamba winding its way through the steep sided valleys.

Again there was another Inca settlement to visit before we descended to our third camp beside the ruins of Winay Wayna (Forever Young) at only 2,680 m. This was a packed campground perched precariously on old Inca terraces. It is the point at which all hikers converge to make the early morning five km trek to be at the Sun Gate above Machu Picchu by dawn.

Winay Wayna was discovered and excavated long after Machu Picchu and was probably an agricultural settlement to supply produce to Machu Picchu as there is wonderful terracing but few dwellings. This means lots of steps to view the ruins and, as we had just had an almost three hour descent from the pass down to our camp of nothing but one steep step after another, knees were very shaky. Agony in fact!

Rising at 3.30 was the norm if you wanted to get to the Sun Gate (Intipunku 2,700 m) to see the sun rise on Machu Picchu, the apparent highlight of the trek. Well, after three days of perfectly clear weather we reached the Sun Gate at 6.15 a.m. in thick cloud. It did not clear as everyone hoped so we descended the final hour on the Inca Trail in drizzle, which kept up steadily for the rest of the day. No matter, our guide, Freddie, gave us a wonderful tour of the Inca Sacred City for two hours before the crowds from the daily tourist train arrived. He had been wonderful at interpreting all the ruins from Cuzco to Machu Picchu and gave us considerable insight into the Inca civilization, after which Peter and I wandered around by ourselves, snapping photos when the cloud briefly lifted on the odd occasion. We chose to walk all the way down the steep hairpin road to Agua Calientes and caught the local train back to Ollantaytambo for a much needed shower and comfortable hostel bed.

We had been warned about pickpockets on the train and sure enough they tried Peter's as we pushed to get off the packed train. However he spun round to confront the thief and I gave the kid a quick back-hander across the chops and we got off the train and finished our Inca Trail weary but intact. However one of our bus accident victims had found the high altitude aggravated her injuries, so she peeled off and returned home. Our group was now down to twenty-two from twenty-six.

From Cuzco south to Lake Titicaca you travel across the Altiplano, a flat high inhospitable arid plain surrounded in the distance by steep, craggy, snow-capped peaks. Adobe thatched compounds house the Quenchua Indians and their flocks of llamas, alpacas, sheep and cows that graze on the sparse tussock grass.

Lake Titicaca (3,820 m) is 170 km long by 60 km wide and is shared by Peru (2/3) and Bolivia. The Peruvian town of Puno has no other merit than as a place to catch a boat to visit the floating reed Islands of Uros. These cruisers hold about twenty people and are powered by auto engines, as normal marine engines do not function well at this high altitude. This makes them extremely slow.

The Uros, who have long since intermarried with the Quechua and Aymara Indians, live on man-made islands of totara reeds which are continuously kept afloat by adding fresh layers of reeds which are found in great profusion in all the shallow areas of the lake. They build their homes and boats with totara, feed it to their cattle, use it as fuel and make flour from the roots.

Most of these islands are about a forty-minute sail from Puno and although very touristy with lots of inhabitants begging you to buy their tacky souvenirs, it is very interesting to wander through their village on this spongy surface, sometimes sinking a bit deeper than expected. The islands are a little more than half an acre and some are anchored to the shallow lake bottom with long poles. Some eventually become so densely thatched and their base so thick that they adhere to the lake bed and become solid enough to graze cattle. The reed boats vary from simple one-man canoe shapes to high-prowed six metre vessels that may have a simple reed sail.

Lake Titicaca can spawn some two metre waves when the winds are strong. We experienced some rough weather when we continued on a four-hour cruise to the hilly island of Amantani. Here the Aymara Indians have developed a semi independent co-operative community of approx. 5,000. They are almost self-supporting agriculturally and to augment their incomes they share the tourists who visit. This means they take it in turns to billet and feed these overnight visitors in their simple homes. Those whose turn it is to supply B & B, appear at the dock as the tourist boat arrives. The new arrivals are peeled off in twos, threes or fours to be led up the steep hill to a simple adobe dwelling, by a tiny little woman in Amantani costume of full woollen skirts, hand-embroidered shirt and embroidered shawl over head and back. Most likely she will be spinning wool on a drop bobbin (like a yo-yo) or knitting on four pins as she walks along. The men also are often to be seen spinning and weaving. They even weave fine woollens as gifts for their new brides.

Our room was simple and clean with a lake view. The kitchen was an adobe hut outside in the courtyard and cooking was on a wood fire with a small smoke hole in the wall behind. Lunch when we arrived was egg, chips and rice. After a walk to the Pachamamma (Mother Earth) temple on the highest hill it was back to our own little room to be served a dinner of chips, rice and egg. Needless to say, breakfast before we left was egg in a bun. (No rice or chips!) Did I mention that, in the kitchen, guinea pigs ran around the floor unable to escape over a high board at the entrance door? They are a great delicacy for special occasions and, when we returned to Puno that night, we sampled both guinea pig and alpaca steak for dinner. The guinea pig came spatchcocked with the head, including eyes and teeth, and also the legs and claws intact and very little meat. A bit like eating a bony quail, but the alpaca was to be recommended.

On our return cruise from Amantani next morning, we visited the island of Taquile which is closer to Puno and hence has more tourists. This said, it was still very unspoiled and we walked most of the way around it. Lots of little terraced fields separated by stone dykes, well tended and planted with corn, beans, quinoa and potatoes. Mostly sheep and cows grazed the fallow terraces, watched over by fat squatting women in their big skirts and head shawls, knitting or spinning. Taquile has considerable autonomy and like Amantani the inhabitants live in a co-operative community, financed very much by tourism. No wonder we were made to feel so welcome. However they will have to improve on their privies at the end of the garden. No doors and a hole to aim for no bigger than that on a golf green. Impossible!

Extraordinary Travels of an Ordinary Housewife

BOLIVIA

We skirted the western shores of Lake Titicaca to the Bolivian border at Desaguadero and continued across the vast Altiplano which widens out to hundreds of kilometres. Snow-capped high peaks of the Eastern Cordillera were visible above the clouds and soon Illimani's triple peaks (6,402 m) came into view as we approached the rim of the canyon in which nestles La Paz. It is the world's highest capital at almost four kms above sea level. When we dropped down to the city centre we found a congested polluted city with almost every inch of sidewalk staked out by Quechua or Aymari Indian vendors, selling everything imaginable, all spread out on the dirty pavement. This meant walking in the street dodging the crazy traffic and we both came to the same conclusion that the less time we had to spend in La Paz the better.

Next morning, at first light, we took an optional tour in a minibus to the Northern Yungas region and the town of Coroico. This three hour eighty km drive ended up taking five hours. The last forty kms are on "the most dangerous road in Bolivia". In this short distance you drop from a high pass in the Eastern Cordillera at 4,700 m to 1,100 m in the foothills of the Amazon Basin. The danger of the road is not from the cocaine barons who have previously controlled this coca growing area, but from the fact that the dirt road is single lane with passing places. It runs along steep hillsides on its hair-raising descent, and has many overhangs, drenching water falls, landslides and washouts to negotiate. It is also over-used by heavy trucks hauling logs and tons of fruits up from the lowlands. These are permitted to drive on the left on the way up the hills, as it keeps them into the cliff side of the road and away from the outer edge where their weight could collapse it. Trucks must be empty to descend and again drive on the wrong side, but this time on the outer edge with its kilometres of sheer drop-offs and no protective barriers. Not surprisingly they have an average of six fatalities a week, and the road is edged with many many crosses and flower adorned shrines. It certainly has earned its name.

However the scenery is breathtaking, the road an engineering marvel and, if you don't look down, a fabulous ride. Coroico has a large population of Negroes who have adopted Aymara Indian costume and much of their culture, and it is a very pretty hillside town surrounded by cleared jungle in which is grown coca, coffee, bananas and oranges. Many "gringos" from Europe and the U.S.A. have settled here and it has a continental charm. Unfortunately we only had time for lunch before we had to set out on the five hour drive back to La Paz. An unforgettable experience and "No Go" for those with vertigo.

Our second and thankfully last day in La Paz was spent walking the main thoroughfares, watching the "ten second" changing of the guard at the Palace in Pedro Domingo in Murillo Square, and visiting the Witches' Market. Here all sorts of magic charms are dispensed, including llama foetuses, by the Cholas (urban Quechua or Aymara women) in ubiquitous bowler hats and voluminous skirts.

It was two long days of driving across the Altiplano south to the dry and dusty town of Uyuni. It is the tourists' access point for the 1,200 square kilometre Salar de Uyuni, a salt flat stretching way across the horizon. 4WD vehicles take you on a day trip, first to where the salt is being scraped into piles to be picked up by truck and taken for refining. It seems no different to a huge lake of white ice, especially when you are shown holes where springs bubble to the surface. Beyond the horizon you come first to the Playa de Blanca Hotel which is built entirely of salt blocks, even the furniture and bed bases. Expensive for such discomfort! Another sixty kms beyond is the Isla del Pescadores, just like a little island in a sea of "ice". Amongst its rough, rocky lava/coral landscape sprout many tall pipe cacti, just bursting into bloom, and several bright finches that don't seem to mind their prickly perches. On the eight km return trip across the salt flat we ran out of gas and had to be towed by another 4WD. Towed until the tow-rope broke, that is! We managed to stack twelve plus driver into the other jeep and make it back to town.

We backtracked northwest on a precipitous single lane dirt road, over an arid mountain range to the old silver town of Potosi. It was an early start so that we could be there for the tour of the Real de la Moneda (Royal Mint) at 2 p.m. Potosi was the richest of cities during Colonial times when silver was greatly treasured by the Spanish. Due to the devaluation of silver and its other minerals, i.e. tin and zinc, Potosi has become a very impoverished city with little other employment to offer its considerable Quechua population. It's a wonder there are any Indians left as it is estimated eight million local Indians and immigrant African slaves, (whose descendents now live in Coroico), lost their lives in the Potosi mines during its 300 year heyday.

Behind the town sits the famous hill, the Cerro Rico. It is still very rich in minerals and riddled with both old and active mines. Realizing the potential of the tourist dollar, enterprising ex-miners have set up mine tours offering first a stop at the Miners' Market to buy "gifts" for the men at the face. These included sticks of dynamite plus ammonium nitrate, (our guide gave us a demo of how to make and discharge a bomb made of these combined items - big, big bang), fuses, cigarettes and the ubiquitous coca leaves to chew.

After the bomb experience it was obvious that safety was not a high priority. This became reality when we entered the mine and found that not only were we suddenly pinned to the wall by hurtling ore trolleys (that is if the shaft was wide enough, otherwise we had to run back to a wider spot), but many of the wooden shaft supports were sagging or broken. To add to our concerns, our carbide lamps proved unstable and gave off acetylene gas and there were obvious cave-ins in many spots. We had to crawl through some steep and narrow tunnels to reach different levels and our party became broken into several groups as some lost their nerve and headed for the surface. I turned back after we finally reached Tio, a clay sculpture of the Mine Devil, to which the miners make offerings each Friday afternoon before sharing a few or more bottles of cheap alcohol. I doubt they would, thereafter, be able to produce anything like the huge erection that Tio the Devil displayed.

This was now Saturday morning and we came across one still very drunken miner waving a stick of gelly at us. Time to get out - fast! Peter, however, was very anxious to reach the face where the miners still use hand tools to extract the ore. But his group decided to exit gracefully when they came to an electric wire that was arcing dangerously over a flooded section.

At least we were supplied with rubber boots, jackets and helmets, but we all emerged absolutely filthy and had to line up for showers back at the hotel before we left in the afternoon to head south for the Argentinean Border. We camped halfway on a village soccer field after yet another unwanted thrill of Bolivia's mountain-hugging roads causing two flat tires, and crossed the border to camp near the town of Salta in the north west corner of Argentina.

Not much to do here except find a bank and avoid the usual churches of note and religious art museums. We had had enough of the church's ostentatious wealth juxtaposed to such poverty and, anyway, we had truck cleaning duties to keep us busy. After six weeks it was in need of a good spring clean. We were looking forward to feeling less concerned about our personal safety in both Chile and Argentina; being able to relax when wandering around the town without feeling we were going to be mugged at any moment.

Later, when we walked into Salta to do some banking, we came upon a crowd at an intersection and noticed that our throats and eyes were being irritated by acrid fumes and, suspecting tear gas, we got out of the way fast. When we walked back to the campground an hour later we found the intersection cordoned off by police and could see that the acrid fumes were not tear gas but the result of a bank bombing that must have happened just before we passed by. Glad we hadn't tried to use said bank. What did I just say about shedding our fears for our personal safety?

CHILE

After our brief stop in Salta, we drove northwest and crossed the Andes at Sico Pass (4,100 m) and into Chile. Our ride down from the pass into the great salt basin of San Pedro de Atacama was an unbelievable series of vistas of stark volcanoes rising from barren desert in colours of pinks, greys, mustards, and reds, often reflected in glacial green salt edged lakes dotted with pink flamingos. A true feast for the eyes but with a rough enough road to cheat you out of some great photo ops. It was a twelve-hour drive so little free time to stop and wonder.

It was December 23, and we were to stop at the oasis town of San Pedro de Atacama for the three nights over Christmas. San Pedro itself is a pretty pueblo village with an adobe church whose rafters and ceiling are made of the dried "wood" of the huge cardon cactus that is the only vegetation of note in some of the hilly regions of the desert. Pity we were not staying in town, but four km distant along a searing hot and dusty road at a rather tacky, rundown, dirty campground with about 200 other people.

What a ghastly Christmas for those of us who did not want to get pissed out of our mind, nor deafened by very non-Christmassy music (I use the last word loosely). We parked our tent under a shady olive tree (fortunately the campground was an old olive grove and one-time horse racetrack) and read for two days with tightly fitting earplugs.

We were glad to leave early on Boxing Day not realizing that crossing the Atacama Desert would take four days. What a big desert - and the driest in the world! Our first day took us to the port city of Antofagasta where we had a quiet campsite overlooking a dirty beach. Next day took us another 500 km south to the Pan de Azucar National Park - still stony desert with cardon cacti. We had no time to explore this vast National Park as our guides were anxious to continue, early next morning, another 500 km towards La Serena and on to Vina del Mar, two rather posh beach resort towns north of Chile's main port of Valparaiso. Both campsites were near to the beach which suited the Brits in our group, always seeking to improve their all-over tan. Fat chance though with the coastal fog, called the "Camanchaca", which can make for cloudy, damp and even chilly days in Chile's summer months.

We were to reach the capital of Santiago on Hogmanay where we would leave thirteen of our group and gain seventeen for the Santiago to Rio section over the next six weeks. They were all suitable additions to our "Glamour Bus", so named by another overland truck travelling in tandem with an excess of chubby passengers who chose to call themselves "The Lard Bus". They were good fun and excellent at playing practical jokes such as filling our large cardboard bread box with three live chickens they "borrowed" from a small holding next to our campground during the night. Later that day, as they followed us down the highway, we released the contents of a feather pillow out the window.

We had two and a half days to explore Santiago. Two and a half hours is sufficient, but a bit of R & R and laundry catch-up took care of the rest. There is a famous fish market whose restaurants are a must, so we headed there for lunch to celebrate my birthday. Just as well as the centre of the city had totally shut down by mid evening so no fancy birthday dinners. Just a yummy cake and toasts for me from our fellow travellers at six before they headed off in different directions. We grabbed a fast food pizza and retired to read till midnight. When we came down to ring in the bells with the hotel lounge TV we were the only ones, except for the manager and his wife. They invited us to a top floor room where we had a fab view of the most magnificent firework display we have ever seen - a great finale to my 58th year. New Year's Day left downtown deserted. Ideal to take ourselves on a self-guided Lonely Planet tour of the city. Lovely colonial architecture, but in need of a clean and now dwarfed by skyscrapers.

Continuing south we seemed to leave behind the central fertile region of Chile with its produce and mixed farming, many orchards and vineyards. We reached the Laja Falls on our first overnight camp and continued into the forested and mountainous Lake District Region to spend three nights in the popular and smart resort town of Pucon on Lake Villarrica near the Argentinean Border.

The main attraction of Pucon is to climb the 2,847 m Villarrica Volcano before it erupts and wipes out the town. This requires being suitably outfitted with goggles, "gas-mask", windproofs, ice pick and enormous heavy boots with crampons, as most of the climb is over icy snow. All I needed to do was try on the footwear to decide there was no way I could climb 6,000 ft in these boots and I sent Peter on his way with the guided party and my blessing.

Not only was the five-hour climb to the steaming, rumbling crater rim steep and slippery and strenuous but the return was hair-raising. You sit on your bum, brake as much as you can with your ice pick and slide down a well-worn bum "luge" run. The seat of Peter's windproof pants was as worn out as he was by the time he reached the bottom. However he had had the fun of being photographed on the crater rim in the nude with some of the other much younger "Chippendales" in our tour group. I should point out that their sun hats were strategically placed.

I was glad I had chosen to spend the day hiking amongst the mountain tarns and giant Auricara trees in Huerquehue National Park. Auricara are known more popularly as Monkey Puzzle trees and this National Park is famous for one of the largest remaining stands in the world. One of our fellow Tucan trippers was a forester by trade and knew all about Auricara and where to find them. A great hike up through beech forests, over dry loamy woodland paths, and an almost fifteen km round trip by the time we finished.

Diane Jones

CRISS CROSSING CHILE AND ARGENTINA'S PATAGONIA

We crossed into Argentina just southeast of Pucon and past the ski resort area of San Martin de los Andes. Here begins the Seven Lake District. Heavily wooded with a backdrop of Andean peaks it was a cross between New Zealand's Fiordland and England's Lake District. The latter because of the prevalence of wild roses, lupins, honeysuckle and broom and New Zealand because of the Southern Hemisphere beech trees with their underbrush of bamboo and the craggy mountain backdrop.

We camped overnight at Lake Espejo and next morning reached the famous German-Swiss resort town of Bariloche on Lake Nahuel Huapi. Chocolate factories are one of its many attractions for both foreign and Argentinean vacationers. A Mr. Bustillo designed the centre of the town in 1940 and the main square is surrounded by log chalet-style municipal buildings with one side open to a magnificent view of the lake. St. Bernard dogs, complete with cognac barrels, are happy to pose for photographs and relieve the tourist of a tacky buck. Our evening entertainment was a not unexpected blow-up between three of our original Quito travellers. This resulted in the one with a drink problem leaving the group the next morning with rumours he might rejoin us in Buenos Aires. So now we are only twenty-five.

El Calafate was our next stop on our journey south. However it took two long days over 1,400 km to reach our destination. Not only were the roads unpaved for much of the way but the scenery was nothing but arid flat sheep ranches with glimpses of the Andes in the distant west. We had a scary tire blowout at ninety kilometres, with flashbacks to our bus careening off the road in the Amazon ten weeks previous. However we were delighted by sightings of guanacos, rheas and the occasional armadillo and fox that crossed our path whilst caracara (hawks) glided overhead. The jagged peaks and towers of Fitzroy National Park, 100 km by road to the west, could be seen before we dropped down to Lake Argentina with El Calafate on its southern shore.

Calafate's only redeeming feature is that it is the gateway to the Moreno Glacier in Glacier National Park. This is the largest temperate climate glacier in the world. It spawns icebergs into Lake Argentina from an ice face fifty to sixty metres high and six kilometres wide. Travelling at two metres per day it drops from 2,000 m to 800 m in thirty-five km and is continually fed by the 7,000 mm of snow that falls annually on the Southern Patagonian Icefield.

It is also easily seen at close quarters from a peninsula of land that almost divides the lake in two and even forms a bridge to the centre of the glacier in severe winters and creates an ice dam between the two arms of the lake. In brilliant sunshine it showed us its best face and obligingly calved some of itself into the lake with an echoing roar and subsequent tsunami. A great network of boardwalks at the tip of the peninsula give wonderful views of its jumble of blue tinged icy chunks, and a boat trip takes you from side to side and gives another perspective from its base. Because of its great speed, it remains very clean, with little debris on the surface and is a photographer's delight and tourist hotspot.

Our journey south to Tierra del Fuego continued across the Patagonian steppes with their huge sheep Estancias. One of 60,000 hectares would support 35,000 sheep. Nearer the Andes are the cattle ranches because there is more rainfall. Also there are more predatory puma which cattle tolerate better than sheep. However Patagonia made its past fortunes from sheep and Punta Arenas on the north side of the Magellan Strait was the home of the wool barons earlier this century. Now oil is one of the booming industries and gas burn-off pipes dotted the plains as we headed for the ferry at Punta Delgado after crossing back into Chilean territory.

Halfway down the Isla Grande de Tierra del Fuego we recrossed into Argentina again before we left the arid flat steppes behind and entered the final mountains of the Andean chain as it stretches into the South Atlantic and ends on the archipelago of mountainous islands at Cape Horn itself.

The end of the road is twenty kilometres past the fishing port and Antarctic cruise ship dock of Ushuaia. Route 3 has come all the way from Alaska to Lapataia Bay in Tierra del Fuego National Park and 500 m from Chile's border. We had a half day to hike through its gnarled and stunted beech forests and mossy bogs to little tarns and island dotted ocean bays. We were now 3,242 km south of the capital of Argentina, Buenos Aires, where we would be in less than two weeks' time after returning to Chile for five days on our return north. We had a much needed rest day in Ushuaia after some long hard days on the Tucan truck and a taste of the high cost of living when charged $24 for apple pie and coffee. (When we returned to Ushuaia on our way to Antarctica five years later the currency had collapsed and the coffee was half the price and twice as good.)

We returned on the dusty roads to the northern point of Tierra del Fuego and crossed again to Punta Delgado, but this time stayed in Chile and overnighted in Punta Arenas. It is only a day's journey, via the Chilean fiords cruise ship destination of Puerto Natales, to reach Torres del Paine National Park. Here the Andean chain rises suddenly from the rolling Patagonian steppes in a dramatic display of almost vertical granite pillars, 2,800 m high. They are the backdrop to glacier fed turquoise lakes, roaring rivers, cascading waterfalls, dense forests and abundant wildlife. There were lots of guanacos (wild members of the llama family), grey foxes, rheas and many condors in evidence.

Diane Jones

We had a beautiful treed and grassy campsite by Lake Pehoe with Los Cuernos (The Horns) of Torres del Paine in full sunset splendour.

Our first of three full days of hiking in the park turned out to be our first real day of rain on this whole trip. However we were all glad to have a long lie-in before brunch, and after a visit to the Park's Information Centre we went for a two-hour hike in our rain gear to visit the Salto Grande (Big Waterfall) that empties the glacier melt waters from Lake Nordenskjold into Lake Pehoe through an angry canyon. A good old campfire with split logs, supplied free gratis by the park campground, gave us a great blaze that allowed us to get thoroughly dry and hiking boots in good shape for the "Big Hike" on day two.

This was a three hour climb up to the base of the Torres. Not an easy dawdle as the wind was so strong that, if a gust caught you in mid-stride whilst crossing some of the open scree areas, the weight of your daypack was enough to topple you in an undignified stumble. The last hour of the 2,000 ft (600 m) climb is almost straight up a huge rock fall on all fours, after which you finally haul yourself up to the top with the help of a knotted rope. There you find yourself, sweaty and exhausted, with a stunning view across a glacial tarn, behind which the three towers (Torres del Paine) rise almost vertically another 6,700 ft (2,050 m).

The three-hour return is almost as difficult and we were glad that we had knocked off what would have been an additional fifteen kilometres of the hike by taking the expensive minibus ride to and from the base of the trail and the Ranger Office. The six-hour hike was quite enough for one day and we were glad not to be on cooking or dishwashing detail that evening.

Day three was as sunny and windy as the day before and we enjoyed exploring our picturesque campground on its little private peninsula on Lake Pehoe. We found two good hiking trails in the surrounding hills which took us near a condor's nest and up into alpine pastures to discover mountain tarns in sheltered hollows, shaded by gnarled and stunted beech trees. Every peak gained opened up yet one more Kodak vista, always with the Torres somewhere in the picture standing guard. We had looked forward to visiting this part of the world and we did not leave disappointed. It was as beautiful and dramatic as any National Geographic article could show. Our four blissful nights under our alpaca blanket, sheltered amongst beech trees, with our tent resting on long spongy grass gave us some much needed sleep catch-up. It was a bonus to awake to the screech of Austral Parakeets roosting in the branches above.

ARGENTINA

From Torres del Paine you cross almost immediately again into Patagonia, Argentina, where we headed due east to the Atlantic and a brief overnight just north of Rio Gallegos before starting the four-day long haul north to Buenos Aires. Four days of arid treeless steppes. However it had its highlights when we stopped at Camarones and visited the Magellanic Penguin Colony at Cabo dos Bahia. It was difficult not to step on the young ones, even when confined to pedestrian roped-off walkways, as the chicks were literally thick on the ground and very busy demanding food from their parents who had returned from a day's fishing. The adults were coming ashore in droves (it was about six in the evening) and waddling hundreds of yards up the beach and across the dunes to find their very own burrow. No fear of humans whatsoever (only of predatory skuas) and entertaining to watch their various social behaviours .

Another day's drive brought us up to the Valdes Peninsula where we had the chance to visit sea lion colonies and also see some elephant seals that were on the beach for their annual moult. Valdes is the only mainland area where elephant seals come ashore, so this viewing was a fortuitous first for us. As a bonus we parked by a hairy armadillo burrow and the residents obliged us with many photographic opportunities. Wild guinea pigs running about amongst the desert brush and a sighting of the Patagonian Mara was yet another bonus. The Mara is described as a large hare, but is connected more with the wild pig physiology. Lots of rheas and guanacos to complete the roll of film, and the odd Elegant Crested Tinamou, a large quail-like ground bird, wandering about. Oh and a Snowy Sheathbill, a pure white sea bird that lives entirely on excrement. Thank goodness nature made something to clean up that very smelly stuff.

Just south of the Valdes Peninsula is Puerto Madryn, a city settled by Welsh immigrants a hundred years ago and a popular holiday resort. Right whales are common in this area from September to December so whale-watching tours are a big part of the economy. But we were out of luck. We had just missed the season. Another 1,500 km and two days' hard driving towards Buenos Aires, capital of Argentina. The pampas we now travelled through were green and fertile cattle pastures and as we got further north, these divided into arable fields. One of the main crops seemed to be sunflowers and there were these vast swathes of sunflower yellow all the way to the horizon.

Hotel Orense was situated close to the centre and one day was sufficient to visit first the Congress and then Government House called the Casa Rosada with Evita's (or is it Madonna's) balcony facing out onto Plaza del Mayo. Here the "Mothers of the Disappeared", remembering the harsh Junta regime of the seventies and eighties, make their political statement by walking round the square at 3 p.m. every Thursday. Chalk body outlines on the pavement remember those missing and never traced, with dates of disappearance as recent as 1998! After this we window shopped along the pedestrian Avenue Florida, visited Plaza San Martin with its huge spreading Ombu tree and view of a tower in the image of Big Ben and ended up wandering through the posh end of the city to the Recoleta Cementerio, on the tourists' pilgrimage, to pay homage at Eva Peron's tomb. There and back we had to negotiate the main drag, the Avenida 9 de Julio which boasts twelve lanes of traffic. It makes itself more appealing by having a central grassy strip full of an explosion of blossom trees at their summer best.

We plumped for the big, expensive Dinner & Tango Show on our first night and were very surprised to get a great set dinner (falling-off-the-plate steaks of course), and a really high-class hour and a half stage show to follow. All the wine you could drink was included, so Peter made sure we got our full money's worth. Some of the younger ones in our group were quite surprised and amused to see that he could stagger back to the hotel with the best of them and demonstrate his tango steps to boot.

Buenos Aires is stretching it a bit when it describes itself as the Paris of the South, but it was the first of the capital cities we had visited where I felt I would be happy to live. It is full of wide boulevards, blossom trees, pavement cafes, sophisticated shops, attractive colonial and modern buildings, open squares and, on the whole, is very clean and safe. I have visited it three times since.

URUGUAY

We caught the international ferry from Buenos Aires across the wide River Plate to Uruguay and spent a day in the 17th century contraband city of Colonia. This is a tourists' delight with its historical centre beautifully restored and the old houses with pastel stucco and red Spanish tiles lining the cobbled streets. On later cruises we had ports of call in the capital, Monte Video, and at Punta del Este, a popular seaside resort with beautiful beaches on the Atlantic side of the promontory and the estuary of the River Plate on the other.

I was curious about the Uruguayan tradition (also in Paraguay and parts of Argentina) of carrying, throughout the day, a special tea called mate in a silver trimmed cup or calabash gourd, along with a fancy thermos flask to keep it topped up. The tea is sipped through a stainless steel bombilla (straw) with a curved sieve at the end to block the ground leaves. I dared to enquire about this habit with a young girl sitting next to me on the ferry, whereupon she kindly pulled out a spare straw and invited me to taste. I found it similar to green tea. Made from the dried and ground leaves of the Yerba mate plant (Ilex family), it is very high in antioxidants and is caffeine rich which helps maintain energy all day long. My curiosity was satisfied and my energy renewed.

We now headed west then due north from Buenos Aires, close to the Uruguay River and the border with Uruguay. We had to first cross the delta of the Rio de la Plata and its vast wetlands were full of wading birds and snail kites. But the bus was too fast to have much bird-spotting opportunity. We camped just off the road after 800 km and noticed how much thicker the vegetation and weeds were becoming and less open grazing land, sometimes even rice paddies. Very hot and humid too and our camping gear was getting that "somethin's died" odour about it. No more need for the windmill water pumps that had dotted the pampas as there was plenty of precipitation here with an average of 2,000 mm spread throughout the year. The soil was now red, like central Australia. Occasionally we caught a glimpse of a true Gaucho, with his baggy pants tucked into cowboy boots and his black "Zorro" hat. Of course he was attached to a horse, and many horses were to be seen grazing with the cattle. We also noticed the land was now covered in bumps: ant hills as far as the eye could see.

PARAGUAY

We crossed the Parana River into Paraguay at Encarnacion. Mennonites settled west Paraguay where they ranch cattle. The Jesuits dominated the area of northeast Argentina and southern Paraguay for 150 years until, in 1767, the Spanish threw them out. They had too much control over the native Guarani whom they brought to live within their missions (Reduccions). The ruins of Trinidad Reduccion, just inside the Paraguay border, was the setting for the film "The Mission" and Iguazu Falls one of the sets.

The country suffered from an odious corrupt dictatorship for twenty-five years till 1989 and the military still exert great power. I noticed that among their listed exports are contraband stolen cars and drugs!

We camped at Ypyau National Park, 150 km south of Asuncion, where we had a couple of hours the next morning to hike its jungle trails. There were warnings of poisonous snakes but all we saw were huge swarms of butterflies of many hues, including giant blue morphs. Our journey continued through flat green grasslands interspersed with palm trees and tropical woods. The country looked visibly a much poorer version of Argentina and villages looked more like those of the third world and were strewn with garbage.

Asuncion is a very shabby behind-the-times capital, still awaiting the installation of traffic lights in 1999. Even some of the central main highways were unpaved. The Government Palace looks out over the wide River Paraguay but below the palace, on the grassy riverbank, lies a grubby shantytown. Apart from the palace, where once anyone caught looking at it was shot and where I made sure to avert my eyes, the only other sites to visit are the Legislative Palace, again overlooking the riverbank shacks, and the Plaza de los Heroes. Here guards in Colonial uniforms front the Rotunda where the remains of some of Paraguay's obscure heroes rest. To me it appeared as a country searching for some pride in its past, but with little to offer. It will continue its struggle to catch up with its southern neighbours.

We were much amused by our Hotel Sahara. An ideal setting for a murder/mystery with a rabbits' warren of stairs and rooms, all half demolished or half built, live cayman in a tank by the swimming pool, three geese in a box and various caged birds, witches cauldrons, bell towers, a plethora of antiques and used car seats and dear knows what else.

BRAZIL

Brazil is surprisingly the fifth largest country in the world. It covers nearly half of South America and has five geographical zones: Amazon Basin; Guiana Highlands north of the Amazon; Brazilian Highlands south of the Amazon; Rio Plata Basin to the south; Coastal Strip of 7,400 km behind which an escarpment causes many of Brazil's rivers to flow from east to west thus feeding into the Amazon and Rio Plata Basins. The main language of its 212 million is Portuguese, not Spanish. That stumped us!

We entered Brazil at Foz de Iguacu not far from the Falls, which are on the border between Brazil and Argentina and just a little south of the southeast corner of Paraguay. The Iguazu Falls had to be one of the highlights of our whole trip and a helicopter flight was a must to appreciate the dynamics. At the head of a narrow canyon they plunge through what is called the Devil's Throat and then, on the Argentinean side, the river spreads out and drops in a series of falls from the southern edge of the canyon, whilst on the northern Brazilian side of the canyon there are no falls as the land is higher and this allows you, via a boardwalk, to view all the falls directly across the narrow canyon which is like a finger with the Devil's Throat at the tip. Not only are the falls awesome in height and sheer volume of water but they are stunningly beautiful as they are set amongst dense jungle foliage with not a single bit of commercialization to detract from their natural state. Full marks to the bordering countries for keeping them this way.

Our second day we crossed the border and viewed the falls at close range from the Argentinean side. A boardwalk takes you up to and sometimes across the tops of the many individual falls. Lots of birds to spot in the jungle, but best viewing was at the bird aviaries just outside the Falls National Park on the

Brazilian side. This complex of walk-through aviaries shows not only local but many foreign exotic birds in very natural surroundings. Also to be visited in this neck of the woods is the huge Itaipu Dam on the Parana River that divides Paraguay from Brazil. Apparently it is one of the wonders of the modern world because of its size. Yes, it was big. We had a noisy but nice campground in Foz de Iguacu, made memorable by the fact that our guides' new replacement emergency bike was stolen again during a noisy party night. More to follow!

Heading for the Atlantic Coast we drove east through verdant rolling wooded hills, partly cleared for fertile crop and pasture land with solitary palms sticking up in the middle of fields. As we headed towards Rio de Janeiro we camped at several of the pretty resorts on this beautiful coastline where the rainforest covered mountains drop directly into the sea, then pop their heads up as a series of little jungle covered off-shore islands.

Whilst our guides went up to Rio to pick-up tickets for Carnival, we had time to enjoy the old colonial town of Parati. Its cobbled streets are washed twice daily by the tide, and it is both beautifully preserved and restored. The white terraced buildings, some with fancy second story balconies and windows and doors painted in every colour imaginable, housed tiny expensive shops or bistro style restaurants. It was a delightful place to wander through at leisure, especially inside the pedestrian only central area which extended down to a beautiful pier graced by numerous old schooners. These are now motorized for the tourist trade and we, as a group, chartered one for the day to take us out and around some of the offshore islands. A bit of a booze-up and bathers bash and not much distance covered. However, we did have a great laugh when "The Lard" tour group sailed past with our stolen mountain bike strapped to the top of the mast! Their best practical joke yet.

Our final leg on the Tucan bus to Rio de Janeiro continued past the same lush dramatic scenery. Lots of trees in blossom, arum lilies by the roadside and, although we passed several villages with shack and shanty dwellings, we did notice most homes had a TV dish on the roof. We had continued to have nothing but fine weather, though very hot and humid and a good drenching from the odd thunderstorm. One morning we awoke to find most people swimming in their tents.

Rio's famous Carnival or Mardi Gras was to start on the 12th February and we were to enjoy five days of the celebration. Our Hotel Braganza was in the red light district but very central and we could walk to the main street of the city, Rio Branca, in ten minutes. I was very nervous about venturing out from the hotel as we were given many warnings of muggings in the area (not just your gentle pickpocket). Here we go again, I thought, as we put all our security measures in place. My fears were confirmed when one of our group, a tough

Ozzie guy, was beaten up and robbed not far from our hotel. However it was agreed I wouldn't be told about the incident and see his injuries till he came to say goodbye as we left for the airport and Canada. Otherwise I may never have left the hotel.

We joined in the Carnival opening and Samba singing ceremonies in the central Floriana Square the first evening and returned the following day for the big street parade down Rio Branca of the lesser known Samba Schools. The Samba music was relentless and the streets filled with drag queens strutting their stuff and lots of other weirdly dressed people consuming a great deal of booze.

A day was spent at the famous beaches of Copacabana and Ipanema. Just as expected, these were jam packed with people of all shapes and sizes in scanty attire, especially the young and beautiful in their dental floss swim-wear. We took the cable car up Sugar Loaf, the cone shaped rock that guards the entrance to Guanabara Bay, in which sits the city of Rio. It also stands at the northernmost tip of Copacabana Beach. A half day city tour on our departure day took in the other must see, the Statue of Christ, the Corcavado, that sits high above and behind the city.

But our most memorable time in Rio must be our night at the Sambadrome. On two consecutive nights the fourteen highest ranked Samba Schools compete for the honour of best parade. The Sambadrome was built in 1984 especially to accommodate the competition and is an 800 metre original street flanked by concrete stands which are packed to capacity. There are seven schools each night with a maximum time to get their parade from one end to the other in one and a half hours. If you can count, this means you are there from 8 p.m. to 6 a.m. if you want to see them all. We did!

Each school has a cast of two to four thousand, everyone dressed in the most extravagant costumes with very fine detail. If you were to take a top Las Vegas Zeigfield Follies type show and multiply it one hundred times you might get close to the sumptuous glamour of it all. They must corner the world market in ostrich plumes! A spectacle beyond belief and we were both overwhelmed and mesmerized by the imaginative talents that could create such a glorious parade. The gigantic floats with gyrating, almost nude, dancers - the huge samba bands - the kings and queens of the favelas - the hundred-strong groups of samba dancing participants with their matching costumes made a glorious finale to our 22,000 kilometres around South America on our Tucan Glamour Bus.

In 2020 we spent three weeks cruising up the coast of Brazil from Santos, to Rio de Janeiro at Carnival, and on to Recife and Fortaleza. This included eight days cruising some of the 4,000 miles of the Amazon River, tendering ashore to small towns and villages and sometimes spotting pink dolphins along the way. On our fifth day we reached the central city of Manaus, (pop. 2 million), famous for its wonderful 19th C pink Opera House. The city sits at the confluence of the muddy Amazon and the black waters of the Rio Negro, where we took a tour upstream to an indiginenous village. The government gives financial support to this tribal group to keep their thatched dwellings and meeting- house as authentic as possible and give visitors an introduction to their culture without the hoopla of souvenir shops and expected handouts. The men in loincloths and feathered headdresses, and the women wearing grass skirts and lots of beads and feathers to cover most of their bare breasts, entertained with interpretive dances and chants. It was a well presented, respectful, learning experience.

VENEZUELA

Dragoman Overland Truck

November 2002

To reach Caracas, the capital of Venezuela, from the international airport requires nerves of steel. Not only does it mean a high-speed knuckle-whitening lengthy taxi ride across a coastal mountain range on a fast motorway that shoots in and out of long tunnels, but you also have to worry about being robbed at the same time. We were warned to push past the taxi hustlers in the arrivals hall and go out to the official taxi rank, then before loading our gear, ask to see the driver's licence number and write this in biro on our wrist. Well, we made it safely, but one of our tour group members, a husky forty-year-old Australian, who arrived a couple of hours before us, was not so lucky. His so-called legitimate taxi stopped to pick up a "couple of friends" who held him up at knifepoint and robbed him of U.S.$3,000 cash before chucking him out on the street. Fortunately they also threw out his bags and passport, but he was very shaken, as were we when we heard about it. The police were not really interested as apparently it "happens all the time"! It was a scary start to our trip and I vowed that this was the last time I was going to travel in this part of the world. To add to my fears the country was experiencing the beginnings of civil unrest and we were advised to stay in our hotel as rioting with gunfire was taking place in the downtown.

As Venezuela lies just north of the Equator, the climate is hot and humid. Our itinerary would visit all five of Venezuela's different zones in three weeks. In the West is the northern tip of the Andes with Pico Bolivar the highest mountain at 5,007 m. The Caribbean Sea borders the country to the north with the coastal beaches backed by the 2,000 m Cordillera de la Costa, south of which lies the vast swampy savannah of Los Llanos. The delta of the Orinoco River, the third largest in South America, covers a huge area to the northeast. Southeast of Los Llanos and south of the Orinoco River is La Gran Sabana with flat-topped mesas called tepuis, their sheer walls rising to over 1,000 m. Here you find Angel Falls, the highest in the world and the holy grail of water falls.

Our Dragoman overland truck was even better than Tucan. A well-equipped A/C twenty-two seater, it proved very comfortable for the eleven of us (four guys, five girls and us) plus our two excellent Australian drivers/guides. We left the high-rises and barrio-covered steep hillsides of Caracas behind and headed east along a rather boring coastal road with agrarian scenery marred somewhat by oil refineries, cement works and generally shabby habitation.

We had two overnights in tents en route to our Orinoco River jungle camp. Our first night at Playa Colorado looked promising, with its palm-fringed beach, but closer inspection revealed litter-strewn sand and sharp rusty beer bottle tops lurking just beneath. We didn't actually camp on the beach for fear of overnight robbers, but inside the garden compound of the local posada (hostel). Our second overnight was in the tropical gardens of a very civilized and secure posada somewhere near Temblador. From here it was only a short drive to Uracoa, our embarkation point for a two-hour trip by motorized dugout canoe to Daktari Jungle Camp situated on one of the many arms of the Orinoco River known as the Amacuro Delta

The camp was both pretty and pretty basic. Eleven hammocks strung in a row in an open-sided thatched shelter, a general dining/lounge area and a basic toilet hut along a boardwalk. This arm of the river, known as the Manamo Canal, is quite wide, with islands of floating water hyacinths showing the speed of the current as well as the direction of the tide, although we were a long way from the coast. We saw no other lodges or tourist boats - which is always a good sign. We were in time to have a sunset birding cruise along the banks of thick jungle vegetation and spied several Scarlet Ibis and big exotic Hoatzin birds with their jaggy haircuts and alarmed expressions, plus many Oropendolas, and various parrots, toucans and macaws hanging around the camp's bird feeders.

Next morning we took the boat along the waterways to a local Warao Indian village, built entirely on stilts over the swampy riverbank, including the main street. The simple dwellings on either side were thatched huts without walls on a wooden platform with a fireplace of baked clay. Hammocks served as beds and daytime seating. Dugout canoes with paddles were the only mode of transport. They didn't seem to be troubled by tourists too often and we were more the object of curiosity. Small, dark people with big smiles of rotten teeth, they had some pretty woven basketwork and balsam wood carvings for sale.

There are about 80,000 Warao in the Delta with their own language and a culture that has been around for eight to nine hundred years. They continue to exist by hunting and fishing.

After our lunch of catfish and yucca (yucky!) back at Daktari Lodge, we were kitted out in rubber boots and taken on a forgettable guided walk through the jungle. There were the usual explanations by our guide of the food and medicinal properties of the trees and vegetation but it was slow going with us all trying to keep our boots from being sucked under or, at very least, stop the muddy slurry from pouring over the top. To make things worse it rained in sheets and the mosquitoes were unrelenting. Getting under a mosquito net in a hammock is no easy feat and my second night's attempt was no more comfortable than the first. Try to lie across the hammock diagonally were the instructions, but that is a skill that must take years of practice. We called our morning bent posture - hammock hump.

Our third day involved a silent paddle-glide through the overgrown channels in dugout canoes. I would remember to take a cushion next time to avoid all that wriggling that nearly tips the canoe. We saw many birds, Capuchin monkeys (heard Howler monkeys) and a five foot python on a tree branch just above us. A spot of piranha fishing using a bit of nylon line and a hook baited with chicken skin came next. We landed three carefully. About six inches long they looked harmless enough until you got a close-up of their rows of razor teeth. We returned in the afternoon to Uracoa to find our Dragoman truck well and truly stuck in the mud after the previous day's torrential rains. It took much head scratching and many attempts at towing to get it out and we did not reach our night's campground at Ciudad Bolivar until the early hours of the following morning.

This compound, some distance from the city, was run by a German who had built some very acceptable little individual huts with private bathrooms close to the swimming pool for those who preferred to pay a couple of dollars extra. What luxury! We were given a rest day in preparation for our three day trip to Angel Falls. Ciudad Bolivar is not a particularly attractive or safe city, and as it was a Sunday we were happy just to hang out at the pool and talk to the many tame parrots, macaws and toucans that wandered about the gardens.

I now know why most people who have seen Angel Falls have only seen it from an aeroplane. To reach the falls overland requires some endurance. First there is a flight, by a six seater Cessna, 320 kms across the soggy savannah to the Penom Indian community of Canaima. You then carry your own bags a couple of very hot kilometres along a dirt road till you reach the Rio Carrao directly above the Ucaima Falls that tumble into Canaima Lagoon. Here you are loaded into large canoes with outboard motors for a very uncomfortable seventy kms six-hour ride, with some serious soaking scrambles up some fast flowing rapids. Sometimes gunning the motor was not enough and a paddler at the prow would do some nifty prying off boulders that got in the way. At one spot the rapids are just too much for a loaded boat, so we had to get off and hike a shadeless dusty trail and hope our bags were still on board when we rejoined the canoe. Huge tablelands, or mesas, eventually came into view as we turned into the Rio Churun in the shadow of Auyantepui, the mesa that spawns Angel Falls. Its flat top is 700 square kms in area and the Falls were discovered by accident when a Jimmie Angel landed his plane in 1937 and got mired on the boggy top. It took him eleven days to find a way down off the mesa and return to civilization. It is not until you actually reach the overnight camp at Isla Ratoncita that you get your first sight of the falls, but they are still partially obscured by a shoulder of the cliff. At 979 m (3,200 ft) they are sixteen times the height of Niagara Falls, and they have an initial 807 m drop. November is the beginning of the dry season so the volume of water coming over was less than in the summer months, but it was still impressive.

It was certainly basic accommodation at Ratoncita Camp. Yes, hammocks in an open-sided hut, and toilets a puddle-strewn path off in the woods. Not just hammocks for our baker's dozen, but another group was also there so it was all a tight squeeze, and if you swung too much you hit the next bod who swung accordingly and hit the next in line. Earplugs helped ameliorate the snoring but the tropical rains on the tin roof of the hut were too much. Regardless, we were all up at dawn to take the boats across the river to the jungle path for a hot sticky one hour climb to the Mirador. Here you could view Angel Falls from very top to very bottom, except that they create so much spray and attract their own almost permanent cloud at the top that only now and again, when the clouds parted and the spray cleared for a moment, did you get a chance for the perfect photograph. Another fifteen minutes brings you to the pool at the base where we had a refreshing swim in very very cold water before returning to the camp for lunch. Indeed, it was definitely worth the journey.

By afternoon we were headed back down the rapids (I lost count after thirty). On one occasion we became well and truly stuck on an underwater rock and it was all men overboard to push us off. Peter gamely jumped in and must have found a deep hole as he disappeared for a moment. We had to spend the second night in the village of Canaima. Here the little Penom guide directed the "old couple" to a cell-like bedroom with a somewhat lopsided broken bed. They had double-booked our hammock accommodation, which was quite O.K. by us.

The next morning we were ferried across Canaima Lagoon past the base of the four thundering waterfalls that feed the Rio Carrao into the lake. It was then a short savannah hike across Anatoly Island to another set of falls, the Salto el

Sapo and its offspring the Salto el Sapito. The purpose was to follow a path that brought us back behind the roaring falls, fortunately with a guardrail, and then down to a pristine white sand beach encircling a calm shallow pool for a swim. Then it was back to Canaima for lunch and the flight back to Ciudad Bolivar and our Dragoman truck.

It was a long day's drive northwest across dry savannah ranch lands, with a stop in El Tigre to allow the cook team of the day (us) to shop from rather basic country market stalls. We had to cater for lunch, dinner, breakfast and lunch the following day, but this got our turn over in one fell swoop and we could forget about cooking chores for the rest of the trip. We drove for almost eleven hours and finally pulled off the road into a small farm steading and bushcamped (i.e. no toilet facilities). It was a very tiring and late night for us cooks, not helped by the heat and humidity. Rain overnight meant wet tents to pack up in the dark before breakfast and another long day as we headed southwest, across the Orinoco River, into the flat swampy ranchlands called Los Llanos in Apure State.

Hato Barrigo was not quite as salubrious as we had hoped. In fact, even by our lowly standards, it was a groaner. However Peter and I were again excused from hammocks and offered a cell with beds so hard we had to put our thermarests on top. Fortunately we had our own mosquito nets as the window screens had been shredded by the pet monkey. The food was pretty poor too and, although we were in beef country, those big Brahma bulls do not a tender steak make. Cattle and horses were the mainstay of these flat plains, and possibly the choice of Brahma cattle is because they do well in both high temperatures and on wet ground. In fact, Los Llanos seems more like one great big floating field, criss-crossed by meandering creeks, broad sloughs and shallow ditches. The latter were not only full of caimans but also infested with red piranha, the flesh-eating kind. We know 'cos we went fishing in a simple roadside ditch as one of the offered activities. Fortunately the caimans don't seem too interested in fishermen and we ended up eating the red piranha rather than they us. We had a boat trip along one of the tree-lined creeks to see the millions of water birds that carpet the area and fill the branches, and had the good luck to see a pod of fresh water dolphins, many turtles, caimans and luminous green iguanas.

Each afternoon we went out on a "game drive" along the flat causeway roads. This was really a search for anacondas, the world's biggest snake. Hato Barrigo's owner and his son happily volunteered to wade through the swampy vegetation, sometimes up to their waists in water, prodding the ground with their forked poles. The first thing they found was a giant anteater which they flushed out onto the road for us to have a good look. A big animal and not too happy about having his sleep disturbed and a guy haul him by his big fluffy tail.

Diane Jones

Then it was capybaras, the world's largest rodent, that we spied. They look a bit like a brown pig with a dose of the mumps. You know, head a bit too big for the body. Anyway it was really the anaconda we wanted to spy and we did. Right beside the road in a big puddle at the edge of a field. Albeit a small one, only about eighteen feet, but with a fine girth and such a sluggish nature that it didn't seem to mind being ogled and it was only after father and son had stretched it out to its full length and let us all have a cuddle, that it decided to show its strength and slither off. Apparently Los Llanos is one of its main habitats in the world and they are very common in the area. That evening we were entertained with Venezuelan style Joropo singing accompanied by a four-stringed guitar and maracas. Dancing followed for those not already reduced to a puddle on the floor with the heat and high humidity. We left big sky country early the next morning to head for the hills.

The Andes continue up into Venezuela, splitting into an Eastern and a Western Cordillera with high mountain pueblos and rocky rivers between. From the city of Barinas at the edge of the savannah you climb to almost 4,000 m on a narrow hairpin road with vertical unimpeded drops of thousands of feet. If you dared to look there were great panoramas back out to the plains. Over the pass you drop down to Merida, a substantial city of 600,000, perched on top of a mesita. It requires many twists and turns in the road and a number of bridges to reach this "island" mesa formed by the erosion of two fast flowing rivers on either side. It is a popular cool mountain holiday town and houses the Universiti de los Andes. This makes for a young, vibrant city with attractive old buildings adding to its appeal. It is also proud to boast the longest and highest cable car in the world. This Teleferico, built in the 1950s, takes you to 4,765 m and almost the top of Venezuela's highest mountain, Pico Bolivar (5,007 m). It has four separate stages where you have to change cars, and it takes almost one hour to cover the 12.6 kms.

The first stage takes you across the river canyon to the wooded foothills. The second stage is over a thick jungle ravine and the third stage, above the treeline, crosses Andean paramo covered with frailejon (native plants, many in flower) that are indigenous to this part of the high Andes. The fourth stage is an almost vertical climb of 700 m up a rock face to the Pico Espejo Cable Station where, more often than not, you are enveloped in cloud along with Pico Bolivar further along the ridge. If you are a hiker and unaffected by the altitude you are encouraged, like us, to take the cable car back down to the third station, get off and walk down across the open rocky paramo of frailejon. Every now and then, when we looked back, the wispy clouds of the peak would part and Pico Bolivar's craggy face would peep through. It was a beautiful sunny day with great views westwards across the central valleys and we dilly dallied on this section, but made sure we were down at the second station well before the last return car of the day at 2.30 p.m. Not so two other members of our tour group who thought that, in addition, they would also hike the jungle section from the second station to the first, which everyone had been advised against. They got hopelessly lost and were lucky to find their way back to the second station, but not lucky enough to be on time for the last car. They spent a hungry and very chilly night at over 4,000 m till they were rescued by the first cable car the next morning. Let that be a lesson to the foolhardy.

All sorts of thrills and spills type activities were on offer in Merida and Peter opted for one of the more sedate mountain-bike day trips. The alternatives were paragliding and river rafting or, in my case, to use the extra day to take the Teleferico all the way back up to the top again. That's when I met the "missing pair" coming down with sheepish looks on their faces. I couldn't get enough of the stunning mountain scenery.

We left the Andes and headed north to the coast with an overnight stop in the hot springs town of Las Trincheras. Who wants to soak in a scorchingly hot spring in the high humid temperatures of an equatorial country? Judging by the size of the resort's posh hotel, many Venezuelans do.

At the inland city of Maracay we took the mountain road north over the Coastal Cordillera and the Paseo Portachuelo at 1,128 m to the visitors centre for the Henri Pittier National ParVenezuela has an enormous number of bird species and many of them hang out here, especially at the feeders where they get a free meal and an opportunity to pose for the camera. All kinds of tanagers and hummingbirds, Toucanets, Chachalaca, Oropendola, Euphonias, parakeets and trogons, to mention a few. We would return for a birding-at-dawn trip a few days later.

We descended towards the coast through five different vegetation zones of cloud forest and rainforest to coastal arid and mangrove. We were headed for Playa Ocumare and the Eco-Lodge Posada where we were given a nice little cabin to ourselves with a hammock strung on the verandah outside for breezy siestas. The beach in town was the usual litter and bottle-top variety, but the lodge organised a day-trip by small boat along the coast to La Cienega Lagoon, a saltwater bay surrounded by mangroves and slivers of coral beaches with good swimming. Unfortunately it was Sunday and much used (abused) by wealthy Venezuelans in their gin-palace boats with ugly music to match. However it was pleasant to sit on little plastic folding beach chairs, under the shade of a mangrove, with your feet (and sometimes your butt) soaking in the lapping waters. A gourmet lunch and a cooler of free beer and rum were nice touches. Our last couple of nights we spent in our tents on the sands of Playa Cuyagua, a fairly remote palm backed beach at the end of the road due east of Ocumare. Overcast skies and surf that was too strong for safe swimming didn't show it at its best. For the young Brits, hoping for a last chance to up the lobster hues of their ambitious tans, it was a dull ending to the trip. For Peter and I it was a question of winding down, waiting it out, and preparing mentally for the next part of our journey: the Galapagos Islands.

THE GALAPAGOS ISLANDS

Tip Top II Cruise

December 2002

What a treat was in store for us after three and a half weeks of trucking round Venezuela. We flew to Quito from Caracas, with a plane change in Bogota, Columbia and, mindful of our previous visit in 1998, wisely bought a ticket for a bonded taxi at a booth in the arrivals hall of the international airport. It was mid-evening when our safe taxi delivered us to Hotel Fuente de Piedra II, much grander than we were used to. It was all part of our tour package which included the return flights to the Galapagos from mainland Ecuador, seven nights on board the Tip Top II, and a night in a Quito hotel at either end.

We had to be back at the airport by 7.30 the next morning to catch our flight via Guayaquil to Baltra, the small island off the northeast end of the main island of Santa Cruz, where the airport is located. There we handed over our US$100 Galapagos National Park entrance fees (per person) and were ushered onto a bus that transported us to a jetty in the bay where we found out who would be joining us on Tip Top II. Fourteen total for our boat and fortunately no children, as we were very surprised to see families with young children on the shuttle bus. Pangas (small open outboard boats) ferried us out to our tour boat and, having gained one hour in time change, we were hanging up our clothes in our deluxe cabin before the gong rang for lunch.

From then on things just got better and better starting with delicious meals. We were a mix of nationalities, three French (all scuba divers), three Germans, an Italian couple, two British and two American girls. (One American left us on the fourth day and a young Japanese couple joined us).

After lifeboat drill we sailed across to Bachus Beach on the northside of Santa Cruz and went ashore in the pangas for a wet landing. This means you hop out of the boat as close to shore as you can and before a big wave hits you. It was our first introduction to many perfect white sand beaches and black lava rock outcrops. It is a turtle and marine iguana nesting area with plenty of Blue Footed Boobies, Brown Pelicans, Great Frigate Birds, Blue Herons and Lava Gulls patrolling the shallows. Pink Flamingos and Pied Stilts littered the shallow lagoons behind the steep beach. Gaudy red and blue Sally Lightfoot crabs covered the rocks as did the marine iguanas, which were so black and well camouflaged against the lava rock that you almost trod on them. They, like all the reptiles, mammals and birds you come across in the Galapagos, have no natural enemies and are totally unfazed by humans wandering by. That is the big attraction, as well as there being many birds only found in this part of the world, some of which evolved in order to adapt to the different environments of each island. Think - Darwin's Finches!

There was time for a hot shower in your private bathroom and a cocktail before dinner at seven. The first and last nights we were introduced to the ship's crew of eight, all in their dress-white uniforms. In addition we had an excellent National Park Guide who, along with a Divemaster, accompanied us all week. Each evening, after dinner, we would have a talk about the following day's activities and what we hoped to see. Then it was off to our comfortable twin beds before the boat sailed overnight to the following day's island destination. We were 1,000 km out in the Pacific Ocean and some of the islands are fifty or more miles apart, so night sailings proved to be pretty rough on the great ocean swells. Not a problem for Peter and I as we have always been good sailors. Others looked a little green in the morning.

Not all tours go to Darwin Bay on Genovesa Island as it is a long rock and roll overnight sail to the north, but it is the one island on which to see the Red Footed Boobies, both in white and brown phases. It is a large nesting site for them as well as Masked Boobies and Great Frigate Birds. The Red Footed nest in the low Palo Santo bushes, as do the Frigate Birds whereas the Masked Boobies prefer the open ground. Red Billed Tropicbirds and Swallow Tailed Gulls were nesting on the cliffs that surround the bay, an extinct crater, and we took the pangas along the edge to Prince Philip's Steps (named after guess-who-was-here) where we were able to climb up and follow a trail through the naked branches of the Palo Santo forests. These small squat trees only come into leaf in the wet season and are the main vegetation on many of the islands. Our path was frequently monopolized by mating Masked Boobies and hungry chicks.

By next morning we had returned south to the Northwest tip of Santiago Island, to a wet landing beach called Puerto Egas. It was dull and damp which matched the black sand beach. Maybe it was the fact that it was only six o'clock in the morning that all seemed gloomy. The sea lions frolicking in the water were happy enough and again the marine iguanas ignored us. There was once a salt factory on this point of land. We ate breakfast whilst we sailed around to the east of Santiago to Bartolome Island, with its famous Pinnacle Rock. Great Frigate birds would glide along with the boat only an arm's length away. These islands are very barren and volcanic, with little vegetation. There was a snorkel tour around Pinnacle Rock, despite some intimidatingly high waves. However Peter and I managed to stay afloat and were rewarded with a brief but exciting encounter with four Galapagos penguins. They are not often seen so we considered ourselves privileged.

The afternoon saw some big cruise ships follow us into Bartolome and, like us, they were scheduled for an afternoon moonscape hike up to the viewpoint on the highest point of Bartolome with great views across to several other islands. We got an early start to avoid the traffic jams. A maximum of sixteen people with their own National Park guide are allowed on certain sections of each island trail at any given time. It is well scheduled by radio contact so you never really feel overwhelmed by the many tourists. But as some of the larger boats have up to 150 passengers, this means they have as many as ten separate guides and groups to be accommodated and sometimes several large ships congregate at the most popular sites nearer to Santa Cruz.

Tip Top II was beginning to look like one of the classiest boats of all we would see and proved to be so right to the end. Only her sister boat Tip Top III might have been in the running. We felt so lucky when we spied some rather shabby and older boats which we knew, from our brochure searches, were no cheaper and had less extensive sailing routes. Our ninety foot boat was purpose built in 1999. On the main deck were the lounge, bar and dining area and outside, at the rear of the boat, was a lower level diving platform that made it easy to board the bouncing pangas with one step only. This was much less hassle than scrambling down ladders. There was a covered sundeck and three cabins on the bridge upper level and, below, another six double cabins. Its maximum passenger load was sixteen, the perfect number for the guided shore trips. Although the cabins were small, they were very well fitted with twin beds, rather than bunks, linen sheets changed daily and a private bathroom with hot shower stall, flushing toilet and more towels than you could ever use. Throughout the interior were plush fitted carpets (no shoes whilst on board) and very tasteful furnishings. All this, combined with terrific food and excellent service, had all of us agreeing that we were the luckiest group afloat in the Galapagos that week.

Next morning found us moored in the busy bay of Puerto Ayora at the southeast corner of Santa Cruz Island. A short walk along the main tourist promenade took us to the Charles Darwin Research Station, a lovely park full of prickly pear and Opuntia cactus and other arid coastal vegetation. Here you can walk through the corrals for both the domed and saddleback giant tortoises. I didn't realise their legs were so long and that this gives them great ground clearance when walking. They reckon that Lonesome George, so called because he is the last survivor from Pinta Island and has yet to find a mate, is about 207 years old. At that age it is no wonder that he shows little interest in the females they periodically try to introduce to him. They have a tortoise-rearing programme to introduce them back into the wild on their respective islands. If you remember, seafarers of previous centuries almost brought them to extinction as they were a fine source of fresh meat on long voyages.

We were taken on a bus tour in the afternoon up into the wetter highlands of Scalesia forest and lush grasses to visit pit craters and lava tubes to remind us how volcanic these fertile islands are. Farming is mainly vegetables, coffee and fruit. We got to pull on rubber boots at a private ranch and wandered the property in search of wild tortoises. These had the domed shaped back as they are the ones that frequent the highlands, and we stumbled over several during our muddy walk. Most were sleeping in the drizzling rain and looked remarkably like big boulders hidden amongst the long grass and totally bored by our presence.

Next morning found us on South Plaza Islet, a flat rock just off the east coast of Santa Cruz. Outstanding for both the yellow and red hues of its Sesuvian (succulent) vegetation and tall treelike Opuntia cactus, the islet boasts large land iguanas whose bright yellow and orange hues compete with the colourful plants. On the top of its cliffs, on the south side, is a colony of bachelor sea lions that haven't been lucky enough to win a harem for themselves. Climbing up onto these high cliffs from the breaking surf below must be a double penance for these poor rejects.

By lunchtime we had crossed to Santa Fe Island and were snorkeling with green sea turtles and sea lions. Our national park guide always accompanied us and would point out the different marine life below and sometimes dive down to bring us up something of interest - like these horrible sea cucumbers! We had to take some avoiding action by swimming like heck when he spotted a big male sea lion on the rocks ready to do battle with us if we went any closer to his harem. That wasn't fair as the female sea lions were the ones who chose to come and play with us. When we went ashore for a walk later in the afternoon, we were all chased by a fast moving bull who didn't want to share his end of the beach. So you see the wildlife is not afraid of the tourists, but the tourists can be scared by the wildlife. As we left the island in our panga to return to Tip Top we spotted white tipped sharks in the shallows and later a shoal of eagle rays.

We awoke in the morning to find the boat moored in Gardner Bay on the east side of Espanola. This has the most wonderful strip of pristine white sand which would have been even more dramatic if the sun had been shining. However, as the plan for the morning was to hike along the beach, an overcast day was a blessing. Here, amongst the black lava rocky outcrops, were some really large exotic marine iguanas. They were a mix-match of bright reds, greens and black made even brighter when splashed by the waves at the water's edge. The saltbush behind the beach was full of the usual finches and yellow warblers whilst mockingbirds (each island has its own variant) hopped beside us on the sand. Later we took the panga to an offshore rocky islet for some snorkeling and spotted a red octopus.

That afternoon's hike at Punta Suarez at the north end of Espanola would turn out to be the highlight of the trip. The skies had cleared and when we landed on the beach we had to pick our way carefully through an army of iguanas monopolizing the beach. As usual there were also dozens of doe-eyed lovable sea lion pups with not a care in the world. Amongst the Palo Santo forests that covered this headland were colonies of Masked and Blue Footed Boobies and, when we reached the cliffs on the opposite side, we came across a Galapagos Hawk posing only a meter or so from our cameras. Then Peter spotted a Red Billed Tropicbird land and crawl under a rock down on an accessible pebble beach. We could see its two long white tail feathers sticking out and it obviously had a nest in there. It was worth the patient wait, as it finally emerged and was within a couple of feet of us, where it stopped to let us photograph it, before it flew off. As if that was not enough excitement, next we saw a Waved Albatross fly over our heads, then another. Close by was a nesting colony and, although it was late in the season, there were still some gawky chicks on nests or waddling about and we even got close up to a pair of adults sitting on a nest. We must have seen a dozen adults altogether gliding to within feet of our heads.

Our last full day was spent on Floreana Island, firstly in the morning at Cormorant Point where you cross from a brown sand beach to a white sand beach on the other side of the isthmus. In between was a big lagoon full of flamingos. A swim from the beach was not mandatory and, anyway, I was saving myself for the day's snorkeling tour of the famous Devil's Crown, a partially submerged offshore crater. Later, when I dropped over the side of the panga the first thing I saw through my mask was a big hammerhead shark. Wow! We then followed a route around the outside of the crater and entered the centre of its lagoon from a break in the far side. The crater was probably only about 100 yards in diameter but it was just a mass of fish reflected off a white coral seabed and, to top it off, we were joined by playful seals who were sunning themselves on a little strip of white sand beach. Wow again!

The afternoon was the obligatory visit to Post Office Bay. Here a group of driftwood mailboxes and old barrels covered in notes and signs was originally used by sailors to leave and collect messages since, at least, 1793. Nowadays you can leave your own mail, unstamped, and it is suggested that you take home any other mail that is from your own country and deliver it, by buying stamps, I presume. There were attempts to set up a fish processing plant here in the 1920's but only the ruins remain. A German family, the Witmers, have lived on the island for most of the last century, and it is indeed a descendent,

Rolf Witmer, who owns and operates the Tip Top boats. The three Germans we had on board were, in fact, related to the Witmers and were making a commercial photographic journal of the tour. Maybe I'll appear as the covergirl!

To finish off the day we took the pangas around some little off shore rocks to try to spot some of the elusive Galapagos Penguins. They spend most of the day out at sea feeding so late afternoon was a good opportunity to see them come ashore, and we did.

Our return flight was at lunchtime the next day, but we managed to squeeze in one more hike on North Seymour, the island just north of Baltra and the airport. This gave us the opportunity to see a Great and also a Magnificent Frigate Bird breeding colony, the former having a green sheen to its black back and the latter a purple sheen, and we were lucky to see them inflate their red neck pouches like balloons. We had seen them with their breeding pouches inflated following the wake of the boat, but we now had the opportunity to see them up close perched amongst the low branches of the leafless Palo Santo.

We were so very lucky with our trip in every way. We had visited ten out of the twenty-two Galapagos Islands. We felt we had seen the very best and we couldn't have had a better experience. It had been one part of the world that had been on our bucket list for a long long time

.

Exodus truck in the Maasai Mara

Cape Agulhas, South Africa

Extraordinary Travels of an Ordinary Housewife

AFRICA

KENYA TO CAPE TOWN
EXODUS OVERLAND TRUCK
October-December 1999

What a struggle to stuff everything into our assigned locker under the bench seats of our Exodus Truck. Neil, our guide, showed immediate signs of being past his "use-by-date". He announced that this would be his last trip and obviously had no reason, nor enthusiasm, to see that we enjoyed it. His trainee assistant, Dylan, was much more personable, but had no experience. However our eighteen fellow travellers looked like a decent and sensible lot, most in their twenties, taking Gap years and wondering why these two wrinklies were joining them.

The truck was a Mercedes Benz chassis with a custom built "people container". The bench seating ran along the sides of the truck under the "open air "windows with roll-down canvas awnings should it be too cold, too dusty or too wet. There were several exterior lockers for tents, food storage, cooking equipment and a pullout gas cooking range. Neil announced the cooking range would only be for emergencies as all cooking would be on an open charcoal fire. Was I detecting sadistic tendencies in Neil? The whole set up was nothing like the deluxe comfort we had enjoyed with the Tucan truck on our South America Overland. When we saw the heavy canvas tents we were glad we had brought our own.

It was soon discovered, with some dismay, that the food shopping, meal preparation and clean up would depend on the initiative of the members of each team. We were divided into six teams of three plus two fire lighters who had to get up before breakfast to light the fire under the large grate and then keep it going as required, and again at dinner. Peter, a confessed pyromaniac, quickly opted for this job! Apart from being assigned head of my team I was also declared banker in charge of the safe and all accounting records. Neil was not too interested in seeing that we were fed and gave little or no help with budgeting, shopping and menu planning, but always made sure he was first in line to be served. Dylan, at least, accompanied us to the open market and helped us haggle and bargain, but my first round of shopping and cooking for twenty-two was very stressful and quite exhausting. Especially when one of my three-man team arrived back late from a boozy bar long after the dinner had been prepared and cooked, and the next morning my other team member was excused duties because of a headache. (Read hangover!) Add to this the discomfort of cooking over a scorching hot charcoal fire in equatorial climes, wearing thick socks, long pants and long sleeved shirt buttoned to the neck as malaria mosquito protection. You will understand why I was almost a basket case at the end of my first three-meal duty roster. The dishwashing team was presented with fire-blackened pots after dinner which our guide insisted be mirror clean. I was having serious personal doubts about this trip.

KENYA

We headed south from Nairobi to Amboseli National Park on day one and camped under the north face of Africa's highest mountain, Kilimanjaro (5,895 m). I had camped on the very same spot in 1985 when I went to Kenya on a week's camping safari which I had booked, at the last minute, during a visit to London. We had passed many Maasai villages with their thornbush compounds and thatched huts with walls of dried cow dung. They wore traditional red checkered togas, decorative jewellery, stretched earlobe holes and carried their knobkerrie sticks with pride.

It was dark when we erected our dozen tents for the first time to find it a very "lumpy" campsite. The Maasai caretaker announced this was "due to our camp being on an elephant toilet". However, as we were the only campers about, he assured us that he would be on elephant watch all night as they had taken a liking to our camping area and usually wandered through in the small hours. The caretaker also volunteered to rustle up his pals to give us a song and dance after dinner if we would care to stump up the necessary. We did and were treated to some whooping and shuffling in the failing light of our charcoal fire. This meant we got to photograph the usually camera shy Maasai and were not trampled by elephants whilst we slept.

A game drive, early in the morning as we left the park, showed us our first of many sightings of zebra, gazelle, wildebeest, elephant, hippo, buffalo, giraffe, jackal, hyena, warthog and a lowly rabbit. No rhino or lion as yet. We had to wait till we reached the Ngorongoro Crater, two days drive away in NW Tanzania, before we got to see many lions, elusive black rhinos and a lucky sighting of a cheetah and four cubs.

TANZANIA

Our route from Amboseli to Ngorongoro was west along Kenya's southern border, then across into Tanzania at the border town of Namanga. We reached Arusha mid-way for an overnight stay at the aptly named Snake Pit Campground. This campground boasted a full selection of Africa's most dangerous reptiles, fortunately confined to solid glass display compounds. A reminder to be careful where we squatted at roadside toilet stops over the next nine weeks.

Two nights camping on the edge of the Ngorongoro Crater allowed us a full day on expedition Land Rovers to view this isolated pocket of most of the species of African wildlife. It is a collapsed caldera, approximately twenty kms in diameter, with a soda lake full of pink flamingos and several swamp areas in contrast to the dry grassland plain that covers most of the floor of the crater. Because of the steep walls encircling the crater the wildlife is geographically contained and, as a result, is both prolific and accustomed to 4WDs full of camera toting two-legged species.

It was a long fourteen hour haul east to the Fever Coast and Dar Es Salaam, the commercial capital of Tanzania, where we caught the ferry to the Spice Island of Zanzibar. Under the rule of the sultans of Oman, the island was the biggest exporter of slaves on the east coast of Africa till David "I presume" Livingston and the Brits put an end to that in 1873. After Tanganyika's independence from Britain in 1963, it joined with the island of Zanzibar to create the new Tanzania and the first president, Julius Nyerere, encouraged mixed marriages between blacks and Arabs to put to rest centuries of ethnic hatred. Stone Town, the capital, is a typical Arab souk of narrow flagstone alleys flanked by storeyed houses built of coral rag. The flat island is basically a coral reef, but it has considerable fresh ground water to maintain mahogany forests and spice plantations. Many of the women still wear their all-encompassing black abayas and the men their long white shifts and crocheted saucepan caps. While the kids went off to spend three days in search of a lobster tan at a beach resort, we enjoyed the time at a small hotel in town with forays out to visit the spice plantations and sultans' palaces where we were impressed with the number of concubine rooms with ensuite bathrooms.

Chungu is a tiny offshore island with Aldabra giant tortoises, now kept in a protective compound. It was a pretty choppy ride in a large heavy dhow with too small an outboard, but we had some entertainment on the return when we rescued a similar boat crammed with thirty-one local fishermen. (There were only four passengers in ours!) They said they had been adrift for two days, and were relieved when we threw a line and towed them back to Zanzibar's dock. In the Jozani Forest, there is the only group in the world of the Red Colobus four-fingered monkey and our guide also pointed out shy Sykes or Blue Monkeys on our jungle walk.

Our three days and four nights, with comfortable clean beds and ensuite bathroom, were a very welcome and happy respite from truck life. An early ferry got us into Dar es Salaam for a truck departure by 9.30 for a full day's drive across the dry savanna of southern Tanzania. Simple villages of thatched roofs and mud and wattle walls, with women in colourful wrap skirts and turbans, carrying backbreaking loads on their heads, were very much the picture of Africa. After the humidity of the coast, the air in the high Rift Valley was drier, but it was still very hot by midday and the windy open sides of the truck were welcome.

The main highway was paved and fast but we slowed as we crossed the Mikumi National Park with unbelievable sightings of elephant, giraffe, zebra, baboons etc. happily grazing beside the whizzing traffic. The rains were due in November but in the meantime everything was very dry and brush fires frequent. Huge fat-trunked baobab trees with their silver finger-like leafless branches stood out among the flat topped acacia trees like giant ghosts.

We pitched camp just west of the park by a waterfall and found two problems with bush camping. (a) The ground harboured countless thorns fallen from the scrubby trees and bushes and these did a quick job of puncturing the tent floor and our thermarests. Fortunately I found the problem before we suffered flat mats and rectified it by putting a thick groundsheet and two sleeping bags spread out under our thermarests. However we fell victim to (b) by pitching our tent over insect holes, either giant ants or scorpions. Anyway in the morning we found our tent floor had been chewed through in sixteen places, some holes the size of a quarter. Thank goodness for indispensable duct tape.

MALAWI

The vegetation became much lusher, with many banana plantations, as we crossed the Malawi border. Brahman cattle and goats were plentiful and the villages more prosperous and substantial with red mud brick walls and thatched or corrugated iron roofs. We camped on the football pitch of the Pentecostal Mission where the Rev. Roberts insisted his recent arrest for theft from an Overland Truck was all a misunderstanding!

The Malawi roads deteriorated and we bounced across many potholes before reaching Chitimba beach. Hot, hot at forty degrees and the campground more like a builder's yard, with two self-flush toilets and one bucket on a pulley as a shower for all of five overland trucks. We would sample three of these beach resorts as we travelled south, each offering varying degrees of comfort. Lake Malawi, at 500 kms long, looked more like an ocean than a lake, with the afternoon breeze bringing in breakers. Very, very inviting in these scorching temperatures but, unlike our fellow travellers, we wisely took the warnings about bilharzia seriously and did not take the plunge.

We took the chance to join Neil up front in the cab hoping that we could find some redeeming feature of our cheerless guide. Dylan had been dismissed having proved not to be "the right stuff". He was a serious party boy who forgot he was required to be sober and on duty early each morning. He now had to ride in the back of the truck till he could be replaced in Harare.

At last we joined a decent paved road with great views of Lake Malawi on our left and the high escarpment to our right. Slash and burn subsistence farming supported villages and family compounds of thatched pyramid-shaped roofed huts with mud and wattle walls. We noted that the compounds were very neat and tidy and demonstrated a pride and dignity we had not observed in Tanzania, although they are both impoverished countries. We stopped every other day to stock up on charcoal fuel that was sold by roadside entrepreneurs in the most out of the way places. Big-smile kids would surround the truck and we would toss them candies and sometimes a pen. Happy people, the Malawians! At Mzuzu, the north's main town, we stopped to change money and buy food. It was my turn to decide the menu for dinner but when I saw the butcher displaying his cuts of meat by nailing them to a tree trunk I opted for vegetarian.

Kandi Beach was a little more upscale with four pit toilets, but no shower. Only lake water to fill a small basin to wash both yourself and your laundry. We spent no more seconds than we had to with our skin in contact with the water, and followed up with a thorough towel dry. Needless to say the Aussies and Brits couldn't resist spending all day swimming in the lake and frying themselves afterwards on the beach. It will be weeks or months down the road before they find they have symptoms of bilharzia worms. The sand was so hot you had to wear shoes to cross it during the day. People kept saying the temperatures were in the forties. Certainly bloomin' hot, but fortunately a dry heat and not the humidity that sapped our strength in Zanzibar. Water sports were on offer, so we hired a canoe for a late afternoon bird spotting paddle along the shore.

Continuing our journey, the Flame Trees and Jacaranda were at their spring-blossom best and vegetation was very tropical with mango, papaya, banana and palm trees. The underbrush, however, was parched and awaiting the imminent summer rains. After our picnic lunch siesta on a remote beach, we found our truck well and truly stuck in soft sand. I'm surprised the truck is not still there as it required all sorts of innovative ideas in addition to everyone's brute force pulling and pushing.

Livingstone Beach was the best of our three Lake Malawi resorts with a very upscale hotel beside a neat, grassy campground. Unfortunately we arrived late in the afternoon and left early the following morning. It was the one place that would have been safe for swimming as far as bilharzia was concerned, but the surf was enormous that evening and a notice instructed that the beach must be cleared by 5 p.m. Hippos were known to come ashore for the night. They are the cause of most human deaths by wildlife in Africa. It was an early bed, as we had to be up at 4.30 a.m. to scare off the baboons that came at dawn to rob the campground of any items not in tents or locked in the truck!

We stopped en route to the Zambian Border at Lilongwe, capital of Malawi, to food shop. Fresh plucked chickens were more acceptable than the cuts of meat hanging from a tree, but I realized that the frequent tummy problems were most likely caused by other cook teams chopping chicken on the same plate as salad preparation. A bit of advice on kitchen hygiene was in order before anyone was hospitalized.

ZAMBIA

Crossing the border at 4.00 p.m. meant driving on, in the dark, to reach a "secure" campground just past Chipata. Apparently, to try to stop by the roadside and "bush camp" is a last resort in Zambia because of bandits. That surprised me as Zambia had been Britain's proud Northern Rhodesia in colonial times. The compounds of the Zambian villages we passed looked freshly swept and litter free, and the huts, with thatched conical roofs over round or square mud walls, seemed to belong to honest hard-working people. When we left at 5.00 a.m. we passed many locals walking purposefully along the road, whether to the well, the fields or the nearest town. Of course, it was only the women who were carrying a water canister, or a bundle of firewood on their heads.

Our plan was to cross Zambia in two and a half days so another thirteen hour drive took us through the rough looking capital, Lusaka, where apparently you should avoid stopping unless you wish to be mugged. We overnighted in a campground supposedly in the safety of Gwembe Crocodile Farm near Choma. Fortunately, as with the snakes at Arusha's Snake Pit campground, the crocs were well fenced in. We only had to contend with swarms of huge flying beetles, which certainly added bulk to that evening's stir fry, and had most of the Brit girls screaming, shaking their hair and running for their tents. Even I was a little put out when, after a few minutes tucked up in bed, I felt something moving about on my scalp. This hardback beetle had obviously been parked there for sometime, but now felt suffocated by my pillow and was crawling out for some air! Ugh!

Next stop was on the Zambian side of Victoria Falls at Livingstone. Dr. David was responsible for a great many towns by the name of Livingstone or Livingstonia in Central and East Africa. However I don't think he was responsible for the name Grubby's Grotto Campground. This was the unkempt garden of an old manor house and a cheap base for overland trucks visiting the falls. Grubby had arranged an "all you can drink" sunset cruise on the Zambezi River above the falls. A beautiful evening on a small double-decker barge up the shoreline of Livingstone Game Park was when we spotted two firsts: pale Thorncroft giraffes and four white rhinos which had been sent to the park for protection. White rhino's body armour is the same battleship grey as the black rhino and the "white" is a corruption of "wide" to describe their wide mouths, all the better to graze with. Black rhinos are smaller and use their snout mouths to nibble leaves and forage in the underbrush. Plenty of hippos surfaced near the boat and provided us with Kodak yawns. But never quite when you have your camera at the ready!

Needless to say all but yours truly were very drunk by the end of the cruise, despite a blotting-paper BBQ on board. It was only 7.00 p.m! Back at Grubby's Grotto a local Rasta band of drums and a wood and gourd xylophone were pounding out the beat to keep everyone going. By mid evening most garments were being ripped off and the bods thrown into a very green unhealthy swimming pool in the garden. We slipped off to our tent for safety and found our earplugs..

VICTORIA FALLS

THE SMOKE THAT THUNDERS

Think of a narrow finger-like canyon, a couple of kilometres wide, with Victoria Falls plunging into this deep chasm along its north side. The centre of the south dry side of the canyon is split in half where the Zambezi River exits via its own deep gorge which divides Zambia and Zimbabwe. This means you can look across to the falls from the dry south side in both countries. First we walked out across the Knife Edge Bridge to Pinnacle Island on the Zambian side where the Zambezi River Gorge exits. On the Zambian side there were only some stagnant green pools at the foot of the bare 107 m cliff face opposite, as it was the dry season. From Pinnacle Island we could look west up the canyon to the main falls opposite the Zimbabwe south face. Water flows all year round on this westerly half of the falls and in the wet season apparently the force of falling water is so great that the falls are obscured by a thick mist.

So I am not quite sure when the best time is to visit! We were able to walk across the dry riverbed on the north side of the falls from the Zambian river bank to Livingstone Island, about one kilometre across the total 1.7 km expanse. What an experience to walk on the flat rocks of the dried riverbed along the very edge of the 300 ft drop which, for half the year, is a raging torrent. Out on Livingstone Island we had a good side view of the main falls. The brave ones dared to wade waist deep across a fast flowing rivulet to a rocky outcrop with a plunge pool set right on the rim. Here you could wriggle out on your tummy and look over the edge. No guard rails anywhere. You can commit suicide any time you like! Imagine the Horseshoe Falls at Niagara, totally dry, with hordes of tourists teetering along the edge of the cliff face to get a sideways view of the American Falls!

We crossed the border bridge over the gorge into Zimbabwe at lunchtime to camp at the huge overused municipal campground in the centre of Victoria Falls town. There were warnings of frequent thefts by both humans and baboons. This is a one street town with some big hotels, many tour operators, banks and a few restaurants. What to do for three days (and another two days further on in the trip) if you are not into thrill-seeking activities like white water rafting, bungee jumping, microlight flights etc. etc? A shady tree with a good book was the answer. However we did spend a few hours exploring the paths on the Zimbabwe side of the chasm that looks across to The Smoke that Thunders, enjoying the shady rainforest that is a result of the constant mist created by the roaring falls.

We treated ourselves to English afternoon tea at the famous Victoria Falls Hotel. Peter's British accent, plus a shirt with a tie and me in my best dress, got us past the snooty doorman. Cucumber and smoked salmon dainty sandwiches, scones with jam and cream, and on the top layer of the three-tiered old-fashioned silver plate stand, tiny buns and cakes. All this was served with bottomless pots of tea on the back terrace of this grand old hotel, with views across the beautiful gardens to the gorge and the International Bridge. With our binoculars we could watch the bungee jumpers tumble 111 metres, the highest bungee jump in the world. We also spoiled ourselves by having dinner, two nights running, at the Ilala Hotel. Their dining terrace was canopied by two huge Indian Acacias in full bloom and overlooked some wild bush where we could watch warthogs routing, and fruit bats flying amongst the blossom trees. Apart from all that, they served great game, such as ostrich, crocodile, and antelope (tsessebe), plus two gin & tonics that cost less than a bottle of water! Fortunately the municipal campground was quieter than usual and we had fine weather (rains had not yet come) and were only kept awake, or awakened, by noisy baboons and vervet monkeys.

BOTSWANA

The Botswana border is only a short drive from Vic Falls, however you have to wipe your feet and have the truck roll through a sheep dip bath before they let you in. (Foot and mouth disease protection). A country bang in the centre of Southern Africa, Botswana, is about 1000 square kms, the south 85% being taken up by the inhospitable Kalahari Desert - home of the San people or Bushmen. (They were known as Hottentots, who talked with clicking tongues, when I went to school).

The dry, grey, dusty, flat savannah is covered with a fair sprinkling of thorny and scrubby trees. I was in charge of erecting our tent when we bush camped, which meant I had to check every square inch for thorns and scorpions. Meanwhile Peter was off searching for wood kindling for his fire and, as always, keeping a sharp lookout for snakes. We thought we were going to have a lovely quiet night under the stars, but dreadful wind gusts appeared from nowhere and battered our poor tent so badly that our centre roof pole broke in two and one of the door poles was bent into an L shape. We were both too terrified to get out in the pitch dark to try and straighten things up in case the tent blew away without us lying spread-eagled across the floor to weigh it down. We were glad when dawn appeared and we could crawl out of our semi-collapsed tent. We were not the only ones who suffered a sleepless night under a pile of tenting. Fortunately we figured out a splint for our broken pole and the truck vice straightened the rest. With our sixteen floor holes taped and waterproof, (plus another three nibbled holes we found in the roof – ants?) we still had faith in our fifteen-year-old tent and reckoned it might yet get us to the Cape. Read on!

The town of Maun is not much more than the jump-off point for the Okavango Delta, which covers most of the northerly 15% of Botswana. We didn't see much of Maun as a dust storm was blowing. Same squalls as the night before and some even formed into dust devils, like mini tornadoes.

After an overnight camp at Island Safari Lodge (cold beers and pub style chicken and chips supper – yumm), we took off at dawn in five little six-seater Cessnas, camping gear and food included, across the Okavango Delta. The Okavango River flows south from Angola, across the Namibian Caprivi Strip and, as it enters flat Botswana, it spreads out into a huge delta. It then goes nowhere as it quite simply dries up as it reaches the Kalahari Desert. This leaves a huge expanse of wetland interspersed with islands on higher ground, which supports both dry and aquatic wildlife in abundance, and an enormous variety of birdlife.

Diane Jones

Flying low over the Delta and Moremi Game Reserve we caught glimpses of elephant, giraffe, buffalo, wildebeest and herds of antelope confined to the dry delta islands, whilst the rest was a lush green swamp of thick reeds. At Serongo village we transferred to the local mode of transport, mekoros (dugout canoes), with a pole man standing at the back to punt you along, two to a canoe. The canoes were a bit of a cheat as they were moulded fiberglass, but they were the right shape and colour and we just sat on the floor and were grateful the canoe did not leak like the traditional dugout.

It was a hefty load for our poler to punt through narrow shallow channels choked with thick five ft high papyrus reeds. Sometimes they would open out into a lily covered shallow pond, and frequently, to our alarm, a hippo would suddenly pop its head up and give us a yawn. This did not necessarily mean it was drowsy, it was more a "clear off" message. We rough-camped for two nights on a piece of high ground, obviously on the territory of a resident pack of baboons who kept us all awake each night with their squabbling. We had to keep our food and garbage inside our tents, which was not a problem by the second night as the greedier airheads in our party forgot we were on slim rations and ate three days' food supply in the first two days! Also boiling sufficient swamp water that required fifteen minutes for twenty people was a major chore, and Peter and I were glad we could sneak away and use our porcelain filter to get our own safe water. These same airheads were forever taking the boiling pots off too soon, or washing the dishes in precious boiled water.

One of the polers (who set up their own camp near to us and provided wood for our fire) was an excellent birding guide, and Peter and I pretty well monopolized his services. Over ninety birds in two and a half days wasn't bad. Nearly all new to us and we would have missed or not identified most without his keen eye. The polers also took us out each day, either for a game walk on an adjacent island (nothing dangerous spotted I'm glad to say), or for a paddle through the swamp to visit some of the larger groups of hippos, but with us safely concealed in the reeds at the edge of their pond.

As we were packing to leave our bush camp in the mekoros, four huge elephants came to visit - well they were still a hundred yards away! However, instead of being able to get up close and personal, our polers suddenly insisted we scramble and leave without delay. Apparently big elephants just go where they please and it is dangerous to stand in their way.

We returned to the small native town of Serongo on the third day and, instead of flying back to Maun, we camped overnight. The local ladies kindly cooked us a traditional meal of mashed fish with water lily roots, maize "hash", cabbage and a local beer-type drink. The only edible item was the cabbage! Considering we were out of our own food rations and starving tells you just how bad it was.

Next morning we were picked up on the more open main river channel by three speedboats. For an hour and a half we "wheeched" through river channels, enclosed by high reeded banks, and had many close sightings of big crocodiles, a five ft leguaan (water monitor), fish eagles and hippos galore. We caught a brief glimpse of a shy and rare antelope, a Sitatunga. Neil picked us up at Sepupa on the west bank of the Okavango River and we continued from there south through Maun where we turned east towards Zimbabwe and had another rough camp just off the road. Thankfully the wind didn't come up after dark and, despite a scare when a herd of free-range cows plodded through at 3.00 a.m, we got caught up on food and sleep deprivation.

Botswana is a reasonably wealthy country with its recently exploited mineral resources. The roads are excellent, but the villages remain simple with modern breeze block and corrugated roofed houses, mixed in with traditional adobe thatched round huts. Some homes had both styles inside a private courtyard fenced with high bamboo stalks laced tightly together. There was little to zero cultivation, but goats, donkeys, cows and horses were plentiful and, amongst the donkey carts and pedestrians that passed, I noticed several of the women in traditional Bechuanaland dress. Long brightly coloured floral skirt and jacket, with a huge turban that presented a two foot wide stiff bow on the front. I remember them from foreign doll collections when I was a kid, and thought both the country's name and the fancy hat most exotic. We were to see similarly costumed Herero women when we passed through northern Namibia. Apparently a style copied by the native people from the Victorian missionaries' wives.

ZIMBABWE

With good roads we picked up speed, crossed Zimbabwe's western border at Plumtree and reached Bulawayo, the country's second largest city that evening. Needless to say the increased speed meant frequent stops to rescue various hats, pillows, clothing etc that flew out the open sides of the truck. The flat grey plains of Botswana became gently rolling hills with red earth and greener more fertile cultivated fields. Bulawayo still has a strong colonial air to it, with old-fashioned department stores and Victorian buildings.

By spending two nights in the municipal campground in its central park, under the care of a posse of armed guards, we had a full day to take a safari 4WD ride in Rhodes Matopos National Park. We were encouraged by the ranger to hop out of the jeeps and get up close and personal with two white rhinos, who seemed unfazed or else short sighted. I guess it was less dangerous than the municipal campground! The afternoon drive took us to the Matopos Hills area of the park where we looked at the famous 8000-year-old San Bushman paintings in the Nswagi Cave. The cave even has a rare shadow painting near the entrance. This only reveals the black stick figures of a mother and two children when something is held up to create a shadow across it. When you take the shadow away, it disappears completely. Fascinating and something I had never come across before in primitive art.

We climbed to the top of one of the stony outcrop hillocks created by the erosion of the softer rocks of ancient magma domes. This leaves huge boulders balanced at all angles on top of one another. Cecil Rhodes, the founder of Southern and Northern Rhodesia (now Zimbabwe and Zambia) chose to be buried in a tomb cut into the rock at the top of his favourite hill, called by him "The World's View". His legacy are the 100 Rhodes Scholarships awarded each year by Oxford University. There is also a huge mausoleum erected on the site in memory of the soldiers who died fighting in the native wars in the late 19th century.

The Great Zimbabwe Ruins at Masvingo was our next bit of history. This medieval city of possibly 10,000 was the centre of a vast empire stretching from Mozambique across to Botswana and down to South Africa. Hand-hewn stone blocks with wooden lintel gateways create a maze of fortifications on top of one of these eroded magma domes, and the structures incorporate the huge boulders strewn higgledy-piggledy all over the hillside, especially at the very top. There is also a ceremonial Great Enclosure on the plain below and foundations of several villages of the Shona people. These villages carved the huge soapstone Great Zimbabwe Birds that have given their name to Zimbabwe and are the country's National Symbol. The Great Enclosure, (five ft thick walls and 300 ft diameter), has a phallic stone conical tower as one of several interior structures and is considered to possibly have been the Royal Ceremonial Compound. As we camped beside the ruins we had the chance to climb to the Hilltop Complex for sunrise at 5.00 a.m. Lots of pretty birds up at that time of the morning. Needless to say feathered ones only!

Further north, near Gweru, we spent two blissful nights at Antelope Game Ranch in their new campground on the edge of a weedy waterway full of birds and, apparently, crocs! We really were getting into civilized living again. Our full day here was spent game viewing by truck or on horseback. This particular ranch also breeds lions in captivity and they have three tame one-year-olds that go for "walkies" just like dogs. We were also taken to the grand tropical garden of the main house to play with a two-month-old lion cub and visit with two shy orphaned cheetah cubs. Canoes were available for leisurely paddles through the swamp in the cool of the late afternoon.

Our first leg of the five-week trip was almost over, so we had a final dinner at the ranch followed by a Kangaroo Court. Three of our very funny Aussie truckers made each of us stand trial for all our misdemeanours during the trip. For example, Diane and Peter for wearing safari suits in Africa! The punishments were a small fine to cover the court's "wig expenses" and to down a drink in one gulp. If not, it was poured over your head. A great laugh, including the explanation of why Peter, in his Akoubra hat, had been nicknamed, Harrison Ford. Answer: Because he was "IN DIANA JONES" a lot! We were sorry to be losing seven of these fun Aussies in Harare.

Our twenty-four-hour stopover at the Selous Hotel, five blocks from downtown Harare, was bliss. Great beds, pillows, bathroom and an inexpensive penthouse restaurant for all meals served in grand colonial style. Our excellent dinner was crocodile thermidor and warthog. The suburbs were covered with red flowering Flame Trees and the centre, much like any other high-rise city, still retained some formal old-fashioned high-end department stores near its central tropical treed Africa Square. There were murmurings of President Mugabe's plans to expropriate the farms of the white colonials such as our friends at Antelope Park. Sadly it would shortly come to pass.

Six new faces joined our Exodus truck for our final four weeks. At last I had the chance to change cook teams around, so I chose a couple of Danish girls, one with good overland truck experience. Thank goodness I was able to rid myself of the two minimum effort, maximum skivers that I had had to endure for my first five weeks. We now returned to Victoria Falls for the benefit of the newcomers. We were happy to enjoy this second visit, taking another sunset cruise on the upper Zambezi, this time in a more elegant style. There was afternoon tea again at the Victoria Falls Hotel; catching up on laundry and email; trying to stay out of the blistering heat; enjoying the cocktail hour out of town at the posh Victoria Falls Safari Lodge with its own floodlit waterhole; and enjoying evening meals of eland, ostrich and wild game stroganoff.

Back into northern Botswana, this time to spend a full day of game viewing at Chobe National Park. An early morning game drive and an afternoon cruise on the Chobe River gave our new passengers good wildlife sightings including the rare endangered puku, which is similar to the impala. (There are only 200 left in Botswana and Zambia.) When we folded up our tent after two nights in Chobe, we found that our first line of defense, a double layer of polythene groundsheet, had been chewed literally into ribbons. Not a square foot of usable material remained. Must be ants with big teeth and voracious appetites.

Diane Jones

NAMIBIA

Crossing into Namibia's narrow Caprivi Strip that separates Angola from Botswana, we camped beside the Okavango River just north of where it enters Botswana to become an inland delta. Hippo grunts and the smell of hippo poop lulled us to sleep with clothes pegs on our noses. At least we had the luxury, for the first time on this trip, of pitching our tent on a sward of green grass with a picturesque view through our mosquito netting of the river rolling past.

Next night we camped beside the world's biggest known meteorite near Grootfontein. The Hoba Meteorite weighs in at fifty tons, (54,000 kilos). It is thought to be 80,0000 years old and was discovered in 1920. It is made up of 82% iron, 16% nickel, and 8% cobalt, which all adds up to more than 100%. Go figure. I can't even figure out how they weighed it!

As we crossed northern Namibia we were aware of how neat and tidy the family and village compounds were, although very few and far between as the country has a very low population density. The earth was parched, but the leaves of the trees were surprisingly green, perhaps because there was the occasional light shower as we sped along straight paved roads. We dropped in on an ostrich farm for a look-see, but a look-see of handbags at US$1,000 was enough to shorten the visit. The chicks are reared bonded to humans so they are very tame and, when mature, happy to put their head against the barrel of the dispatching shotgun. We bought some ostrich steaks for dinner. Very tender, not unlike gamey fillet steak.

Two nights were spent in separate Government lodge/campgrounds in Etosha National Park, one of Namibia's best. Both campgrounds offered swimming pools, bars and waterholes, floodlit at night for great game viewing. Black rhinos for a start! Needless to say the humans were securely fenced off from the animals. We had daily dawn and sunset game drives and saw our first gemsbok or oryx. It instantly became my favourite antelope with its dramatic black, white and grey markings and tall horns far too long in proportion to its body. Many giraffes and elephants, lions on the prowl, springbok executing vertical leaps, plus a bonus of watching a newborn zebra stagger to its feet. A sly foxy jackal came sniffing around our leftover ostrich steaks that night.

The vast park has huge salt pans and dry wooded savannah and supports a great variety of game which was concentrated round fast-disappearing waterholes. Sadly we did not get to see the elusive leopard, but just to make sure we were cheetah-ed-out we camped at a cheetah farm where they breed for zoos etc. We were introduced in the owner's garden to three mature tame specimens and a four-month baby orphan being hand reared. The wild ones were visited in their 100 acre compound on the back of a pick-up truck. I hate bouncing along whilst packed shoulder to shoulder in a ute, so I got to sit in the passenger seat along with the baby cheetah. Not as enviable a position as some may have thought, as this playful puss was into chewing: Cameras, clothes, fingers - anything it could get its little teeth and claws hooked onto.

We noticed that we were now in giant scorpion country when our assistant guide was stung as she folded up her tent. A five inch yellow job and fortunately not so toxic as the big black ones with thick tails that can be lethal. We were a little worried as our tent zipper wouldn't close properly, and we were using clothes pegs, leaving gaps for creepy crawlies which, like scorpions, are attracted to body heat. However the bug bonus was that we were now out of malaria mosquito territory and didn't have to clothe ourselves from head to toe in bug-proof clothing, especially as temperatures were beginning to rocket off the top of the thermometer.

I forgot to mention that Sue had joined us in Harare as our replacement assistant guide/driver. Dylan got a one-way ticket home. Sue was a truck driver by profession, had a surgically enhanced very shapely body and was tattooed and pierced in places where I didn't even want to look. However she was quite a character, took her new job seriously, and entertained us with many insights into her "alternative culture".

Damaraland, further to the south in Namibia, was a dry and stony desert with rocky outcrops and stunted thorn trees. From the road we saw goats, Brahman cattle and donkey carts, but no cultivation. We visited a petrified forest formed by trees washed down 260 million years ago from Angola. San (Bushman, Hottentots) petroglyphs cover a hillside of tumbled caves near Twyfelfontein. But most fascinating of all were the Welwitschia plants that survive the harsh desert conditions by continually growing their ribbon-like leaves as they die back at the tip. They spend the first twenty-five years of their lives growing nothing but roots, which is a brief time considering they live as long as 1,500 years! Yes, fifteen hundred. There are both male and female plants, cross pollinated by a particular beetle and they were currently in bloom, although with very nondescript tight cone-like brown flowers. They dot the barren desert landscape like floppy dark green wigs of disheveled tresses and are sometimes the only vegetation to be seen.

We headed west across fifty kms of flat, gravelly coastal desert to the Atlantic Ocean. Here, for a bet, we all had to plunge into the freezing cold breakers of the Benguela Current which is also the cause of a damp fog that hugs the coastline and sometimes rolls many kilometres inland to moisten those dried up Welwitschias. What a desolate land and not called the Skeleton Coast for nothing. Many wrecks have littered its beaches and shipwrecked sailors failed to find water and civilization in the barren desert beyond the shores.

We overnighted inland at Spitzkopje. This is the biggest and highest of the many kopjes, which are rocky outcrops of volcanic origin, that dot the plains. Could be Namibia's answer to Ayers Rock but its sides are so steep as to be impossible to climb. We enjoyed a beautiful primitive campsite at its base with a simple drop toilet and miles of flat ground on which to pitch our tent. It never rains in this area, except the evening we were there, when a sudden thunderstorm broke and tested our campfire on which we were trying to cook dinner. I was putting our bed together in our newly erected tent and was stranded for more than an hour as I tried to hold the broken tent zipper together and keep out the floods.

The coastal resort town of Swakopmund is very German, very modern, very clean and very comfortable for our three nights in little A-frame chalets with hot showers and a soft bed. No tent camping allowed in town! What a treat to have two and a half days to wander around, enjoying wonderful coffee, great seafood and shopping for food in spotless supermarkets. Most visitors go on thrill-seeking experiences such as sand boarding and quad biking in the dunes, and tandem skydiving over the desert. We just enjoyed the shark aquarium and the museum giving the history of the various tribes such as the Ovabimbas in the northwest. As with the Maasai in Kenya they still maintain their traditional dress (undress) and culture. The Germans came in the late 19th century and were a very strong influence in Namibia and especially Swakopmund. German almost takes precedence over Afrikaans but, as with all of the southern part of the continent, English is spoken when required.

Eastward through Namib-Naukluft National Park, we camped in the shadow of Bloedkopje, which rose like a huge pink granite boulder behind our tiny tents. Oryx, springbok and ostrich were the only other signs of life. Quiver trees, from which the bushmen make their arrow quivers, dotted the landscape like tall multi branched yuccas.

Sesriem is the campground on the edge of the famous Namib Dune Field, 100 km. from the sea. It was a sixty-five kms drive west into the National Park along a flat, dry river plain with wonderful apricot coloured dunes rising 300 m on either side. The road runs out at Sossusvlei salt pan and from the carpark you could wander off amongst the dunes, and slip and slither up and down them at will. Dry salt pans with sparse vegetation were cradled amongst them and you felt you were the only ones there. The winds were so constant that our footprints disappeared in no time at all and we were glad to have our compass to make sure we could find our way back. We visited twice, at sunset and again next morning at sunrise, as the contrasts of light and shade, curves and ripples were quite surreal. We cooked breakfast at Dune #45, the most photographed of all.

The strong winds came in squalls and one flipped our empty tent in Sesreim's flat and open campground. It whisked the plastic replacement groundsheet from underneath and sent it off, like a magic carpet, towards India and would have done likewise with our tent if it had not impaled itself on an upright water tap. I climbed inside to weigh it down whilst Peter re-pegged it with double tent pegs. Our fly suffered a large tear but we reckoned some more duct tape might resolve that. In the Namib desert rain is not a major concern, so we limped along for a few nights without it.

Our next stop was at Duwisib Castle, built by a German with high-flying schloss ideas in 1905. A bit of a Folly really, but another well appointed campground and very quiet as we were the only residents. Well, us and the all-night clicking geckos! We seemed to have shaken off the other Overland Trucks on this route.

Back westward to the coast and another Bavarian style town called Luderitz. Smaller than Swakopmund and a very active fishing port and diamond mining centre, both in the surrounding desert and off the coast. Our tent survived the town's windy campsite on Shark Island and we took an early morning sail on an old schooner to see Heavy-sided Dolphins and Jack-Ass Penguins. Then we enjoyed a guided tour of Kolmanskop, a short drive inland from Luderitz. This ghost diamond mining town has been reclaimed by the sand dunes since it outran its usefulness in 1956.

Continuing inland from Luderitz you cross the Sperrgebiet, or "Restricted Area". The notice says "Authorized diamond mining personnel only; all others shot on sight!" In the Naukluft Mountains we camped at Aus where there is a herd of feral horses and a wilderness campsite. From here we headed south for Fish River Canyon and the border with South Africa. The desert is more than a match for Arizona's famous Painted Desert, but Fish River Canyon (despite Namibia's claims) was no match for Arizona's Grand Canyon. 160 k long, twenty-seven kms wide and over half a km deep it is quite impressive, but it's dun-coloured monotones, despite being viewed at both sunset and dawn (a 5.00 a.m. expedition to the rim) were not a patch on the Grand Canyon's multi hues.

SOUTH AFRICA

We crossed into South Africa at the Orange River town of Noordoewer. The Northern Cape province was dry veld, same as Namibia, but as we drove south the vegetation became greener and the hills higher and it was very reminiscent of the Western Scottish Highlands during a very dry summer. Even Ericas were in bloom, just like Scottish heather and, if you half closed your eyes, the flatter areas between the bare granite mountains looked just like Scottish moorland.

Diane Jones

Continuing south into the Western Cape by a scenic hairpin bend and hair-raising backroad through the Cederberg Mountain Reserve, brought us into the fruit growing valleys and, further south, the vineyards of the Cape. These flat-bottomed irrigated valleys are hidden amongst the mountains and the only access is over high passes or squeezing through narrow river canyons.

Stellenbosch, although less than an hour out of Cape Town, is a very attractive university town full of Cape Dutch architecture. We spent two hot humid nights at the Stumble Inn Backpackers, and were the only pair to take advantage of a tour of the historical homes and churches of the late 18th and early 19th centuries. Not just beautiful Dutch gabled white walls, but many still with traditional thatched roofs and set-off by colourful European style gardens. Stellenbosch, before it became famous for its wineries, was an agricultural supply station for the Dutch East India Co. en route round the Cape from Europe to the Dutch East Indies. There are dozens of wineries that offer wine tastings and tours of the plant. All high-tech stuff these days, although we did visit one that still stores its best wines in a cave (Die Bergkelder) in the hillside, illuminated by candlelight.

We arrived in Cape Town the long way round, via Cape Point. The peninsula starts with Table Mountain cradling the city on its north face, and sheer mountains continue all the way south to the Cape of Good Hope. The west coast road, through the Atlantic coast suburbs of Sea Point and Clifton, Hoets Bay and Chapman's Peak, crosses over to the old naval station of Simon's Town before entering the Cape of Good Hope Nature Reserve that covers the entire southern third of the peninsula. Of course neither Cape Point nor the adjacent Cape of Good Hope are the real bottom of Africa. This is much further to the southeast at Cape Agulhas where the Atlantic and Indian Oceans meet. We headed there the following day when we picked up our rental car and said goodbye (with some relief) to the Exodus Truck.

First we had a perfect evening in Cape Town to take the new revolving cable car to the top of Table Mountain for clear views (often cloudy) before a wonderful sunset. Then back to Ashanti Backpackers in the Gardens area for a glorious nights rest in a separate little self-contained building at the far end of the garden. Once again, we two wrinklies seemed to receive a sympathetic smile and an offer of the quietest of accommodation. Next morning was more than enough time to walk through The Company Gardens, view the well maintained historic buildings along the perimeters and take in the changing of the guard and rifle drill at the Castle of Good Hope in the centre of the city.

It was great to be on the road by ourselves with no set timetable but some determined must-sees in the next six days. We stopped for our first night in Hermanus where we strolled its cliff-top paths hoping to sight some whales below. However we were a few weeks too late for in-shore sightings of the Southern Right Whales that spend their winters in this area.

Next day we went to be photographed on the rocky shore at Cape Agulhas before driving through De Hoop Nature Reserve, famous for its white silky sand dunes and antelope called Bontebok. Yet another species of game for our Kodak collection. Before we reached our second night's stop at Swellendam Backpackers, (with another empathy offer of a cute double bed in a Wendy house out in the big garden), we crossed the Breede River on the Malgas ferry. This is a pontoon, threaded to a cable across the fast flowing river, pulled manually by two or three men (black of course). They sling a chain around the cable attached to a leather shoulder cross-strap, and with big rubber overshoes to stop them slipping, haul the pontoon as far as they can, unhook the chain, run to the front, hook-up their chain and work their way up to the back again. Talk about slave labour. Fortunately stern notices forbidding passengers to assist eased one's conscience.

We left early from Swellendam to beat the coastal traffic on the Garden Route, as it was already peak summer holiday time. East of Mossel Bay was tacky beach resort country till we reached Plettenberg Bay. It was a little more upmarket and residential, with lovely beaches, lagoons, surf and best of all the Robberg Peninsula Nature Reserve. This offered beautiful wild cliff walks where we watched seals and dolphins playing in the sea below. We managed a good 10 km in a cooling sea breeze and occasional shower. Needless to say, after nine weeks of rain-free days, we had not thought of carrying rainwear. Next morning, as we took an early walk along the magnificent beach, we watched a dozen bottlenose dolphins surfing the big waves into shore along with their human playmates.

Our little car took us inland to Oudtshoorn and the Little Karoo, famous for ostrich farming and the Swartberg Pass, one of the most spectacular in Southern Africa. It happily bounced up the dirt cliff-hanging road to the top and down the even steeper faster descent to Prince Albert on the other side. You can complete the circle back to Oudtshoorn via the Meiringspoort Gorge, where you criss-cross the river thirty-two times in the twenty kms of pink granite sheer-sided canyon.

Couldn't believe it was raining when we awoke in Oudtshoorn. However by the time we had followed our route west to the scenic village of Montagu we were back to sunny weather. This is a hiking centre and we stretched ourselves to the limit on Cogman's Kloof with six kms of very precipitous steep climbs and six kms of flatter but, by now, tiring return. However, as the brochure said, the views were worth it.

Diane Jones

Back from the Karoo rugged country to the flat-bottomed fertile valleys to the west and the attractive wine-growing valley and Huguenot village of Franschhoek, we spent our last night in Africa savouring the wine and Karoo lamb. Next morning we stopped at one of the grandest of the vineyard manor houses, Boschendal, with its beautiful manicured grounds, rustic wine tasting cellars and elegant dining facilities in the old farm buildings. Even the rows and rows of vines were weed free and trussed to perfection.

We had covered 1,200 km in our week of driving, plus the 13,800 km from Nairobi on the truck for a total of 15,000 km. It had been a good way to see the best and worst of all eight countries, from the ground up as it were. Pity our truck driver/guide was a flop and half a dozen of our companions were poor participants in the sharing of responsibilities, true products of the "me generation". It was a tiring journey due to the rough living conditions and the infernal temperatures. Africa is hot! I was glad to get home to a cold white Christmas.

Hiking along the Turquoise Coast

Istanbul Food stall at the ferry dock

Extraordinary Travels of an Ordinary Housewife

TURKEY

ISTANBUL AND THE TURQUOISE COAST
BACKPACKING AND EXPLORE TOUR
February-March 2000

Istanbul, the old capital of Turkey previously known as Constantinople, sits astride the The Bosphorus Straits which connect the Sea of Marmara to the Black Sea. This means that one half of Turkey is in Europe and the other in Asia. The old walled city and the commercial centre are both on the European side but a river estuary, called The Golden Horn, also divides these areas. The old city, where our hotel was located, is dominated by the three main landmarks, Topkapi Palace, Aya Sofya Museum and the Blue Mosque which sit atop a high promontory where the Golden Horn, The Bosphorus and the Sea of Marmara meet. Ferries serve the suburbs and across the Straits to the Asian side, whilst the Galata Bridge crosses the Golden Horn to join the old city of Sultanahmet to the city's commercial centre.

Turkey is surrounded by sea on three sides, the Black Sea, the Sea of Marmara between the Bosphorus and the Dardanelles and the Aegean Mediterranean Sea. Ankara, the capital of the Turkish Republic since 1923, (after the overthrow of the Ottoman Empire, which ruled this Islamic country for 500 years) is 700 kms. to the east. Apart from the most famous ancient cities of Troy, Pergamon and Ephesus on Turkey's Aegean Coast, there are also to be found, on the southern coast, many Hellenistic, Roman and Byzantine ruins. We were to visit many of these on our Explore Tour of Turkey's Turquoise Coast.

The sun shone on our arrival and we had a full day of sightseeing including the Topkapi Palace with its many courtyards and extensive Harem. This was the grand palace of the Ottoman Sultans from the mid 16th century to mid 19th century and is full of intriguing tales of Grand Viziers, black Eunuchs imported from Egypt, an elite bodyguard called the Janissary Corps, and influential Sultanas. Riches and jewels beyond belief are on display, including the Topkapi Dagger and Spoonmaker's Diamond. There is a Moslem sacred place, the

Pavilion of the Holy Mantle, where you can view Mohammed's tooth, beard hairs and even his big footprint for goodness sake!

Next to the Topkapi Palace, and the city's most prominent landmark with its huge dome and four minarets, is the Aya Sofya. It is the oldest standing building in the world and has been both a Byzantine Christian Church and a Mosque since it was built in 532-537 AD on the foundations of a previous Christian church of 404 AD. Apart from the enormity of the structure and its remarkable dome, it is interesting to see early Christian mosaics of Madonnas and angels juxtaposed with Islamic features of worship and a mihrab niche facing Mecca.

Minarets and Mosques dominate Istanbul on its many hills within the old city walls. The most famous is next to Topkapi and Saint Sofya and is called the Blue Mosque, so named for the marvellous blue Iznik tiling on the interior walls. It's a boots-off, freezing feet and headscarf job to gain entry to the mosques so we didn't bother to go inside any of the other ones, such as Suleymaniye Mosque, which is visible from just about everywhere. We just roamed around the courtyard and counted minarets.

Another not to be missed attraction was the Yerebatan Saray (Sunken Palaces), which are the 6th century underground cisterns featured in at least one James Bond film. Adjacent to the Aya Sofya, these vast excavated caverns, with their many herringbone lofty domes supported by 336 pillars, once held 80,000 cubic metres of water to supply the city above. Fortunately there is currently only a foot of water criss-crossed by walkways. The strategic soft lighting, the lazy carp swimming about and background classical music made it both a romantic and eerie place.

It was fun just to wander about Sultanahmet, full of crowded local markets (including a great spice market) and cheery Turkish carpet hustlers who would take your firm "no" with good humour. There were few beggars, clean streets and mainly western dress, although most women wore a headscarf. Vertical braziers with kebab cones of sliced lamb were a feature of every streetside café.

Language was definitely a problem when it came to eating and we had quite a few unexpected and unidentifiable dishes. Lentil soup, flat pita style bread and seasoned bulgar wheat came with most meals, so we did not starve. So did chickpeas ad infinitum.

Rain and snow and cold limited our other days in Istanbul to searching out the warmth of the excellent Museum of Islamic Art, with its fine carpets and ethnographic displays. Then a plod (for me) round the Military Museum which came to life with a one hour musical concert by the Military College's Janissary

Corps Band dressed in the fancy hats, baggy pants and curly toed slippers of the Ottomans. Even the instruments and music were authentic.

This was in the modern northern section of the city so we walked back to Sultanahmet and our Hotel Ipek Palis, through the smart shopping area of Taksim Square, past the Galata Tower on a steep cobbled hill to the Galata Bridge lined with hopeful fishing rods. But for those unlucky fishermen, small fishing boats tied to the dock proffered fresh fish cooked to order on live coal braziers as the vessel heaved in the choppy waters. Outstretched hands passed the fish supper across the wet divide at the appropriate moment. Perhaps in the summer months the waters of the Golden Horn and the Bosphorus are calmer. Certainly not the next day when the little ferry from the Galata Bridge Terminal tossed us over to the Haydarpasa Station on the Asian side of the Bosphorus. There we joined our group on the overnight train to southern Turkey for Explore's Walking Holiday of the Turquoise Coast.

The stretch of Turkey's Mediterranean coastline from Marmaris in the west to Antalya in the east is supposed to have a microclimate producing warm sunny winters. Hard to believe when it is backed by the rugged Taurus Mountains, very much snow-covered at this time of year. The train does not go all the way to the south coast and so our group of ten (six Brits, one American girl, delightful English woman guide, plus us) had to get off at Dinar into the snow, a hundred kms north of the coast at 6.30 a.m. It was a rude awakening from a four-berth sleeper that was hot as Hades for the thirteen-hour journey. However, we were greeted by Musafer, our bus driver, with cups of steaming hot apple tea and whisked over the remaining mountains down to sunnier and much warmer climes at Antalya.

Antalya was a picturesque old walled town, with narrow hilly streets running up from a quaint port. The sun shone on us and we were blinded from the great urban touristy sprawl that stretched beyond. However it was an excellent spot to spend our first three nights and go hiking in the canyons of the Taurus Mountain backdrop. Our bus would deliver us to the "Ruin of the Day", such as Termessos, Aspendos and Selge, and a locally hired guide would give us the Lycian background of the previous three thousand years, then we would blow our brains clear with a few hours of hiking. Just as we were getting hungry or foot weary, Musafer would show up with apple tea and our luxury bus to take us back to the hotel. Almost too civilised for the likes of us.

From Antalya we drove west to the village of Cirali and the ruins of Olympos under the shadow of Mt. Olympos. This is only one of twelve Mt. Olympus's that lay claim to Olympic Games fame. Here we got to hike over a steep mountain top on part of an extensive hiking trail called the Lycian Way. (Just like Ontario's Bruce Trail, even to the rock formation which is mainly limestone). This took us past the famous Chimaera of Greek and Roman Mythology. Non-extinguishable flames burn on a hillside in two small areas. These were all that remain of the fire-breathing mythological creature, with the head and front legs of a lion, the rear of a goat and the tail of a snake, which was pummeled into the hillside forever by Bellerophon on the flying horse Pegasus. A likely story, but there is certainly no other explanation to date of why this phenomenon of natural eternal flames exists. Metamorphic gas is one suggestion!

Just up the road is Phaselis, a city of the Lycian Federation. It was built on a piece of prime real estate; a tiny promontory scalloped by three natural harbours one of which the Romans could close off completely. Emperor Hadrian must have included Phaselis on his grand tour in 129 AD as there was the usual gate in recognition of his visit. Bet Club Med would like to get their hands on this spot.

Next morning, we headed for the hills to another set of ruins at Arycanda, this time perched on a steep south facing slope, which gave its amphitheatre, odeon and hippodrome a spectacular backdrop of snowy peaks across the valley. The local guide from the village took us home with him for lunch as it was a slow tourist day, and his wife (not us) cooked up a banquet of spicy lentil soup, baked stuffed squash, zucchini and mint patties, cheese filo pastry "cigarettes" plus rice and salad. Added to this piece of local culture was a surprise camel fighting tournament we happened to come across as we passed through the inland town of Kumluca. Pity it hadn't yet begun, but we stopped for half an hour to watch highly decorated, foaming at the mouth, male camels being readied for the fight. I gather this was done by giving them a tantalising sniff of a hot-to-trot female.

We spent a night in Elmali, 1,100 m up on a high plain (where apples and sugar beet are grown) surrounded by snow covered peaks. In the morning Elmali itself was snow-covered, so instead of our planned mountain hike that day we headed back to the sunny coast.

However we did rid ourselves of the chills in Elmali by partaking of a Turkish bath at the local hamam. Our group booked the whole place to ourselves and we were duly packed into the initial hot steam room till we were good and sweaty. One by one we were beckoned out by one of the two male masseurs who slapped us onto a marble slab like a pound of liver and proceeded to scrub us down with a loofah before covering us with soap suds to aid in a slithery massage. Swimming costumes were kept on until the final rinse, sitting beside a marble basin of warm water. This the masseur sloshed all over you, even pulling out your cozzy and pouring the water down your front and back. He then held up a towel whilst you stripped to the buff, deftly wrapped it round you, without peeking, and dispatched you out the door to be dried off modestly by the turkish towel flunky in the hallway. Finally you were pushed onto a bench in line with the previous clients and given a cup of hot sweet tea. Every ten minutes or so another victim would shoot through the door ready for the public drying-off and communal recovery bench. The whole place looked as if it had been built in the first century, but the production line was very twenty-first century, priced at five million TLira plus tip (Cdn$15).

Our next three nights were spent in Kas and Kalkan, very pretty little coastal towns with narrow steep cobbled streets, red tiled roofed houses with overhanging wooden balconies, and very quiet in an out-of-season tourist way. Some major hiking was now taking place on a daily basis, often along the newly marked Lycian Way which an English woman, Kate Clow, had recently traced following some local cart tracks or, more frequently, very rugged goat paths. The foothills of the Taurus sweep straight into the sea in this area, so we were mostly hiking along the higher slopes, with some wonderful views. To give us more time on the trail, the bus would usually drop off, at some high village, those who wished to hike ten to fourteen kilometres. The less energetic would remain with the bus. It would then meet us at a similar altitude some four or five hours later. Loose gravel and steep slopes made for slow times.

The limestone foothills were rocky and barren. A few lonely homesteads of rough stone and plastic sheeted roofs were discovered, and here we would pass stony terraces of stunted crops, olive groves and flocks and flocks of silky-coated goats.

At one such humble dwelling we were invited to stop for tea, which finally turned into a delicious lunch of spinach and onion crepes. In the tiny room the matriarch was cooking huge twenty-four-inch wafer-thin flatbreads on a convex griddle that sat in the open fireplace. She had already baked a couple of huge piles of the stuff before she started to convert the next dozen efforts into those delicious filled crepes. Then, without a hiccough, she continued her dough rolling on a big circular board till a tennis ball of dough was transparently thin before laying it, for a minute or less, to cook on the fire. Dear knows who was going to eat this huge pile of flatbreads – we hadn't passed any other habitation for hours. All sign language and big smiles for communication and, as payment, we left behind our picnic items plus a monetary tip discreetly left underneath, as to pay outright would have been an insult to their unsolicited hospitality. Dad, Mum and daughter, plus hundreds of goats seemed to be the full complement.

Spring flowers were a special treat on these hikes, especially the carpets of anemones in hues of blue, pink and red, interspersed with yellow Star of Bethlehem, Asphodel and blue wild crocus. The floral "baggy pants" worn by all the peasant women just added to the picture. It seemed that long skirts on these windy hillsides were best split into baggy bloomers with a crotch well below the knee and elastic waist to accommodate very fat tums.

From the small fishing village of Ugaciz, just east of Kas, we hired a boat to take us over to Kekova Island whose ancient city has sunk below the waves only to be revealed when the captain pops the lid off the glass viewing panels in the hull of the boat. However, as we had already been advised, it was definitely not the Lost City of Atlantis and when we spotted a pod of dolphins we made chase for more exciting viewing.

The boat dropped us off at the fishing village of Kale. This was a tricky operation as the seas were running high and the boat could not tie up, so much so that we had to leap for the jetty at the precise moment. A 12th century Crusader castle dominated the tiny homes clinging to the rock face, which in turn were built on the ancient Lycian city of Simena. Yet more historical buffing before we walked back, via part of the Lycian trail, to our bus at Ugaciz.

We had a very footsore day from Kalkan to our final coastal town of Fethiye. It started with an eleven km hike to the ancient beach site of Patara, where the lazy ones met us with the bus. As the Roman amphitheatre is now full of sand, as are most of the other ruins behind a seventeen km dune beach, we gave it a cursory glance before heading inland to the Lycian cliff tombs of Pinara. This amounted to an additional six km hike up the steep hillside, but to see a high cliff covered with rectangular excavated tombs made you feel like a wimp when you thought of the physical effort put in by these 4th century BC grave-diggers. Again, the Hellenistic amphitheatre had been deliberately built to maximize the stunning backdrop of mountain peaks.

Fethiye was not a memorable coastal city, but seven kilometres up in the hills is a ghost town of 1,500 abandoned homes. This was the Greek village of Kaya Koya, deserted in the ethnic cleansings of Ataturk in 1923. The Turks, who in turn were expelled from Greece, considered it cursed and chose not to occupy it. Mind you, they pilfered all the snazzy red roof tiles and, as a result, the buildings have fast deteriorated. Only the Greek Orthodox Basilicas were in better shape to house the limb bones of the long deceased, the skulls having gone off to Greece in the luggage of the exiled. On such rocky ground graves were often used over and over again, the old excavated bones being stored inside the church. Creepy!

From here one gets to hike over the hills to Oludeniz, a picture-postcard sandy bay with a Mediterranean blue lagoon behind a sand spit. Strong surf pounded the beach and cancelled the possibility of a swim in the brilliant turquoise sea. Oludeniz is apparently the most photographed tour brochure resort in Turkey.

Fair dues! The big waves meant a storm was brewing and sure enough, having just completed the last hike of our trip, all of them under sunny skies, the heavens opened and we had a huge thunderstorm. Fortunately, by the time it broke, we were safely ensconced in a Turkish Delight factory back in Fethiye, with as many free samples as we could stuff in our cheeks. Not many for Peter and I who hate the sickly sweet stuff, but they had plenty of chocolate covered hazelnuts to please us. Turkey is a great producer of hazelnuts and pistachios too.

Next day we drove north to the inland city of Denizli where we would catch the night train to Istanbul. The four-hour drive from the coast took us over two mountain passes at just under 4,000 ft. Spectacular scenery, all with a fresh covering of snow. Tucked between the mountains were flat fertile valleys, dotted with Lombardy poplars, cypress, spruce and pines.

We spent the afternoon at our last ancient site, Hierapolis with the usual Roman amphitheatre, agora, colonnaded street, triple arched gateway and a 5th century Byzantine shrine. St Philip was martyred here in 80 AD. However it has a spooky attraction as there is, adjacent to the Temple of Apollo, a quasi-oracular grotto dedicated to Pluto, God of the Underworld, which emits gurgling sounds and hissing noxious gases. We finally found it amongst the rubble, well caged off, as two German tourists, trying to emulate the eunuch priests who could descend unharmed into the bowels of the earth, were fatally overcome by the poisonous gases. Perhaps they forgot to castrate themselves first!

The modern name for the area is Pamukkale. Its big claim to fame was its hot springs with many therapeutic bathing pools. These springs have bubbled over the cliff face for thousands of years creating hundred metre high white travertine (chalk) terraces. Pamukkale means "Cotton Castle" but the place is more like Cinderella's Castle in Disneyland.

The overnight train got us into Istanbul just in time to hop on the local ferry that takes you up The Bosphorus to the entrance to the Black Sea, stopping at all the little suburban villages en route. A beautiful sunny way to spend our last day in Turkey. 19th century Ottoman palaces, Byzantine and Genoese fortresses, and grand million-dollar homes line the banks. Huge tankers and freighters plow past. At the last stop, Andolu Kavagi, you have a three-hour break that allows time to climb up to the fortress for a commanding view out to the Black Sea before lingering over a freshly grilled fish lunch and a bottle of wine in a local restaurant overlooking the harbour.

Diane Jones

That evening the temperature dropped as did wet snow and we knew it was time to go home. We had had a sufficiency of ancient ruins, dry pita bread and hummus, sludgy Turkish coffee, and Asian squat toilets!

Backpackers' bus

Cape York trek

Extraordinary Travels of an Ordinary Housewife

AUSTRALIA

CAMPING TOURS AND BACKPACKING
June-July 1993, Oct. 2000-Jan. 2001, Mar.-Apr. 2003

WESTERN AUSTRALIA 2000

With match sticks propping our eyes open after our thirty-six hour flight, we rented a car and headed 500 kms south to Walpole on the south-west tip of Australia. Not only is this area famous for its Margaret River vineyards but also for its forests of Giant Tingle Trees. Nornalup National Forest has a forty metre high tree-top catwalk of connecting swing bridges that threads through the leafy canopy. Some of the trunks of these Tingle Trees have a twenty-four metre circumference. There are also equally huge sixty metre Karri trees in the south-west, which are used as fire lookouts. Here you are invited to climb to the top by a circular ladder of timber spikes nailed to the trunk, with a flimsy steel net cage that might hold you if you slipped. Needless to say, as we had come all this way, we tackled both vertigo-inducing experiences. Before heading back to Perth, we overnighted in Augusta to visit Cape Leeuwin, Australia's most south-westerly point. There was a great big kangaroo munching on the lawn outside our B and B!

We were back in Perth early next morning and took the shuttle train to Fremantle, the port, for a walking tour of its historical buildings of the late 1800s, followed by a seafood lunch at the famous Kailis fish market. I have since enjoyed returning to Fremantle on cruise ship itineraries. The last time I was required to spend the night in the city's jail. The cell, with en suite, was very comfortable as was the rest of this repurposed backpackers' hostel.

PERTH to DARWIN

Camping Tour by Bus Oct.-Nov. 2000

It was a full busload. Twenty-four, all Brits bar us and one other Ontario woman. Slim was our tour guide and driver of our luxury A/C coach, and Michelle our cook who, without team effort, was to produce wonderful three-course dinners and healthy breakfasts and occasional bush tucker lunches.

Diane Jones

Explore, our favourite UK tour company, had subcontracted "Connections" to run the trip and on the side of the bus it said "Holidays for 18s – 35s"! Not this trip, as almost 90% were well over the thirty-five year limit and several actually older than us. It was a good mix of jolly people and the camping equipment was excellent, with 8'x8'x6' high tents for two and comfortable foam mattresses. So no need to crawl out of your tent each morning and take half an hour to straighten up!

We headed north-east out of Perth up the Swan Valley, with its orchards, vineyards, cattle stations and wheat fields. The banksias and bottlebrush trees were in bloom, as were many wild spring flowers. We stopped in Nambung National Park to view the Pinnacles, limestone pillars protruding from the sandy ground. Some were as high as ten feet and the first of many of Australia's unusual geological features we would visit on this trip. Next day would see us stop to marvel at the "Pink Lakes", which are man-made salt ponds for the production of commercial beta carotene produced by the algae.

North of Geraldton is Kalbarri National Park with canyons cutting through the scrubby savannah. These red rock gorges are striped with creams and whites, but weren't so dramatic as the gorges of Karijini National Park further to the north that we would visit in four days' time after enjoying a couple of nights at Monkey Mia on the Shark Bay peninsula. We were treated to a little cabin on the beach and a great sunset catamaran cruise. Next day the same racing cat, under full sail, took us out into Shark Bay to view the dugong (sea cows) that are attracted to the prolific seagrass beds that grow in this sheltered bay. We also had sightings of turtles, rays and a sea snake. Dolphins were all over the place and even swam right into knee deep water at the resort to be fed by Rangers at 7.30 each morning. Shark Bay has been declared a World Heritage Area partly because of the Stromatolites found in Hamelin Pool at the south end of the bay. These are lumpy masses, consisting of calcareous material formed by the prolific growth of microbes, and are thousands of years old. Their evolutionary history spans 3.5 billion years, back to the dawn of earth. These cyano bacterial microbes are shaped like algae which photosynthesize during the day and wave around. At night they fold over and trap calcium and carbonate ions dissolved in the water. The sea is hypersaline at the inland end of Shark Bay due to the seagrass beds and sandbars that limit the tidal flow and ideal for the development of these rare stromatolites. They looked like red sandstone dumpy pillars in shallow clear water, some even rising above the water at low tide. The only other two places in the world I have seen these are at Flower's Cove in Newfoundland, where they are called Thrombolites, and on the Quebec side of the Ottawa River west of the city's Champlain Bridge.

Another day's drive up the coast brought us to Coral Bay on Ningaloo Reef Marine Park. Our camping site was a stone's throw from the beach, and we had only to swim a few metres from the sandy beach to find ourselves right over the inner edge of the reef, which stretches for 260 kms along the North West Cape. In retrospect, the variety of fish and corals I discovered on the Ningaloo Reef has made it my all-time favourite snorkeling spot in Australia, despite many visits to popular sites on the Great Barrier Reef. What a cool way to spend two scorching days. A couple of kilometre's walk along the beach was a shallow bay full of reef sharks raising their young; black shapes cruising up and down just steps from the safety of the beach.

Heading inland to Karijini National Park, the land becomes extremely arid and everything is covered in red dust. Occasional roadhouses dot the highway every few hundred kilometres. There is no sign of habitation in between. Sometimes cattle are seen, which belong to isolated cattle stations thousands of square kilometres in size. Deep bores (wells) supply water that is always warm, mostly potable but often high in salts. Six-foot termite mounds are part of the red earth landscape, and the occasional emu and kangaroo are spotted running through the low scrub, disturbed by the sudden passing of our bus. This area is known as the Pilbara and is rich in iron ore from the red rocks of the Hamersley Range that rise from the plateau as rocky outcrops.

Our first night of bush camping was at Joffre Gorge at the west end of the park. Here we had an energetic hike, rather a scramble, down into the gorge at the foot of the Joffre Waterfall and the very daring, including Peter, returned by climbing up the sheer face of the almost dry falls. I thought I had chosen the smarter way by returning on the marked path but I was not so sure when I found my way blocked by a six-foot snake basking in the evening glow. It turned out to be a Variegated Western Brown and one of Australia's handful of potentially lethal snakes. We were continually warned by our guide to be on the look-out for snakes as they were just coming into breeding season, were on the move, and more active than at other times of the year. Keeping tents closed at all times was the rule and as we continued our exploration of Karenjini I could hardly take my eyes off the path in front of my feet.

Oxers Lookout is supposed to be one of Australia's best as it looks over the conjunction of four canyons, Joffre, Hancock, Weano and Red Gorges. We climbed down into Hancock, this time with the help of a long steel ladder, then up to the plateau again before scrambling down into Weano Gorge for a swim in some of its deep pools. The last one was Handrail Pool where you descend, first by a metal handrail across a sheer sloping rock face, before dropping into the pool down a knotted rope. I chickened out at the knotted rope as I reckoned I might not be able to pull myself back up.

A short drive took us to another bush camp at the eastern end of the park where we visited the great swimming pools below and above Fortescue Falls.

Diane Jones

The latter was surrounded by thick tropical vegetation and accessed by a ladder from a boardwalk which was noisy with flocks of white Corellas and Pink Galahs (cockatoos). What a paradise! We hiked several kilometres through Dales Gorge for another cooling swim at the more isolated Circular Pool, frequently criss-crossing the river and watching out for inhospitable wildlife but our only sightings were some large goannas (monitor lizards). That night, tucked up in our tents, we heard the dingoes howling.

It is a two day, somewhat boring, drive north to Broome. The flat scrub reminded us of the endless days we spent crossing the Patagonian desert. We were now on the northwestern edge of Australia's Great Sandy Desert. It is very HOT! We had an overnight convenience stop at Pardoo Cattle Station, less memorable for its miles of grey coastal mangrove mudflats than for its dozens of kangaroos that appeared as the sun went down. The conveniences were also memorable as all the toilet bowls were inhabited by little frogs looking up expectantly at your bare bum.

We were almost two thirds of the way to Darwin when we reached the town of Broome, Australia's pearling capital. It used to supply 80% of the world's pearls until the plastic pearl button of the 1950s put an end to that. However the Japanese and Chinese were always associated with the pearling industry and have had a strong influence on the town's ethnic make-up. There is still a thriving cultured pearl farming industry and an attractive yuppie downtown supporting many pearl retailers. A couple of kilometres north of Broome is a beautiful beach, judged seventh best in the world. Cable Beach has a nudist end, which just might have been the reason for such an exaggerated rating.

Believe it or not we spent our evening at the movies. Sun Pictures was opened as a cinema in 1916 and is half open to the sky. Seating is in low slung canvas deck chairs of the period. Before they built the sea dyke, high tides would flood the main street including the cinema and old photos showed gallant men carrying their "sheilas" out of the theatre. At 11.00 o'clock in the evening the temperature was still thirty-one degrees, so cooling seawater lapping one's ankles as you flopped in a deck chair under the stars watching a pop movie, would have been a welcome addition.

Our final five days in Western Australia were spent crossing The Kimberley which, at 700 x 600 km, is five times the size of Tasmania. Remote and mostly uninhabited, it is bordered to the west and north by the Indian Ocean and Timor Sea, the south by The Great Sandy Desert and in the east by the border of the Northern Territory. Once covered by ocean, the remains of a coral reef 100 metres high, its sheer red and black limestone cliffs rising from the plateau, stretch 100 km west to east.

Rivers cut through in several spots and at Windjana Gorge you can walk along the side of the creek to the other side of the reef and at Tunnel Creek you can do the same, but by wading along an underground river. The freshwater crocodiles make themselves scarce, but snakes in Winjana were a concern and indeed, on a part of the trail overgrown with tropical vegetation, our way was blocked by a hissing fearless green tree snake, literally out of its tree. We were later glad to hear it was not poisonous, just territorial. Mind you, the reason we nearly stepped on the darn thing was because we had our eyes in the sky, fixated by the flying foxes, hundreds of them, foraging in the branches above. The smell of their guano was pungent and we were glad we were wearing our hats for protection. These huge bats are diurnal and late in the afternoon were very active before settling in to roost in the trees.

At Geikie Gorge, the Fitzroy River has cut through the ancient reef. It flows all year and, in the wet season, reaches highs of seventeen feet or more and floods the plains around. Houses are deliberately built on high ground, often man-made hillocks. A cruise up the Gorge with a National Park Ranger is very dramatic with the red (iron oxide) and black (lichen) hundred-foot high cliffs rising vertically, the first twenty feet being honeycombed cream limestone. We saw huge Red Tailed cockatoos, stunning Rainbow Bee-eaters, Sacred ibis, Jabiru storks, Darters, White Corellas (noisy cockatoos), water monitors, crocodiles (and their nests) – great stuff. This area also has many wonderful ghostly baobab trees. They were just coming into leaf and looked like a thick bulbous vase with a narrow short neck out of which was arrayed a bunch of carefully arranged leafless branches. As they are silvery white, they do look rather spooky.

The Kimberley has a large mining industry for iron ore, zinc and lead. Most of this reaches shipping ports by one to two km-long freight trains on dedicated railway lines, or by road trains made-up of two or even three trailers behind one driver's cab. Scary when these swoosh past you on the deserted highway. Also some of the areas in The Kimberley are able to support a huge cattle beef industry. By deliberately setting fire to the spinifex tufts of grass and the low scrub cover, it regenerates these plants and they immediately sprout fresh juicy shoots to make excellent grazing. Windmills pump water from deep wells into cattle troughs.

The Kimberley's biggest attraction is The Bungle Bungle Massif. The erosion of this sandstone outcrop has created a massif of spectacular beehive shaped rock towers striped like tigers with alternate bands of orange (silica) and black (lichen). Cathedral Gorge and Piccaninny Creek were two of the walks that take you in amongst these beehives. At the northern end of the Bungles there is a short hike up a slot canyon called Echidna Chasm. This was not created by water erosion, but by a fault line that split the massif at this point. A flight in an open sided "MASH" style chopper, with only a lap belt holding you in, was the very best way to view the 3,000 sq km of Purnululu National Park and the Bungle Bungle Massif, and helped one appreciate how remote, inaccessible and exciting a place it is. We had to leave our bus on the main highway and transfer to 4WD mini buses for our two-day visit. It took five hours to reach the permanent camp set-up for overnight visitors, and sleeping was under a mosquito net beneath the stars. The fear of nocturnal venomous snakes and other reptiles, that are the main inhabitants of this harsh hot dry environment, kept me from getting my beauty sleep.

The daytime temperatures got even worse when we continued up the road to Kununurra, a large-scale fruit growing area, where it was declared the hottest place in Australia that day: 43 degrees in the shade but with unbearably high humidity. We were now well into the tropics and 300 kms short of Darwin when we stopped at touristy Katherine Gorge to swim in its deep pool, reached after a very hot climb to the top of the falls. But the prognosis of an early wet season did not materialize for us except for one or two raindrops on the windscreen as we reached Darwin. We had covered 7,300 km by road.

NORTHERN TERRITORY

July 1993 and November 2000

Darwin was definitely not a city in which to waste time. In those days its cultural side was highlighted by arm wrestling and beer swilling contests, and these were the women's events! (I have since visited on a cruise ship three times since 2000 and found the city much more civilized.) Peter and I first visited Darwin briefly in July 1993 and, because it was the dry season, we had been able to take a four-day tour to Kakadu National Park with a zoologist guide.

The leaflet in 1993 had described the transport for a group of ten as "a non luxury, non-air-conditioned, not particularly comfortable 4WD troop carrier". Greg, our guide, would scream to a halt when he spotted something on the road from tiny spiders to lizards, turtles, goannas, frogs, and lots of snakes. We were given detailed info on each one and expected to handle, sniff, taste whatever. He was very keen on pythons and said there was no need to fear them till they reached fourteen feet or so! Needless to say, the death adder he picked up he did not let us handle, only stroke it well behind its head.

The 20,000 sq km of Kakadu NP supports many different types of habitat. It is bounded to the north by the Arafura Sea into which its many rivers drain. Beyond the escarpment that forms its eastern boundary lies the Aboriginal sacred reserve, Arnhem Land. You must have a permit and a very good reason to travel there. During the wet summer months the many watercourses flood and almost the entire park is under water. The winter months of June and July are an excellent time to visit the park, as there is still water in the many billabongs that support enormous numbers of birdlife and reptiles. These become more and more concentrated as the water dries up. Greg was also a very knowledgeable birder and sometimes we felt swamped by the vast numbers of different species we could see in our binoculars at any one time. He kept a very comprehensive bird list for us.

We were towing a little covered trailer with our gear and food, and at night (usually not before eleven) we would pull off some remote dirt road, head into the eucalyptus woods and collapse in haphazardly erected tents for a few hours of "rest" on the hard ground. One night it was very, very late and the moon was full, so we just all climbed into sleeping bags on the fine white sands of a dried-up creek bed. We were always up at dawn and the reason for these long hours was that most wildlife is seen in the early morning and evenings after dark. To save time we would stop for a quick evening meal at one of the tourist lodges in the park which gave us the chance to sample some kangaroo and camel steaks or barramundi fish. We also got to sample their toilets. I had almost broken my wrist trying to spade out a hole in the clay-baked soil!

Between a.m. and p.m. animal spotting, we would bounce over the roughest of tracks to visit some of the famous waterfalls that drop off the escarpment and produce vast crystal clear plunge pools at their base. Jim Jim Falls are the most famous (as seen in the Crocodile Dundee movie) but nearby Twin Falls are the most exciting. They could only be reached by swimming 600 m up a gorge, pushing lunch, cameras, boots and sunscreen all on one airbed, to which the weaker swimmers could take turns to hang on. The current was negligible so it was an easy paced swim until one spotted a croc on a rock, at which time the pace obviously quickened. We were assured that these freshwater crocs (maximum size three metres) were not dangerous. It's the big saltwater ones of the tidal rivers and briny billabongs that eat you! It was an awesome sight to swim out of the narrow gorge into a huge cliff-encircled deep pool backed by a towering waterfall and fringed on one side with a fine white sand beach and tropical vegetation. Of course, hiking boots were brought in on the lilo so that we could climb up the cliffs to the top of the falls, usually to explore some aboriginal cave paintings and get a panoramic view. So our days were not short of exercise and quite challenging for those vertigo-impaired.

Kakadu is also famous for its aboriginal rock art and we visited the two sacred sites, Nourlangie Rock and Ubirr. Apart from our quick evening repasts, this was the closest we ever got to other tourists in the park and, as we were a pretty grubby, smelly bunch by now, we had no trouble in having them keep their distance. Back in Darwin in July 1993 we left a very dirty ring around the hotel's bath.

THE RED CENTRE

Our Connections bus tour from Perth ended on 8th November 2000 and we were now itinerants. There seemed to be a great exodus of tourists from Darwin and we couldn't get on the Oz Experience backpackers bus. Instead we hopped on a plane and flew the 1,500 kms over very uninteresting arid savanna. Three days by bus would have been a big bore heading down to Alice Springs. The Red Centre is either so named because the soil is rich in terracotta or because the temperatures are red hot! We had only an evening in Alice Springs to arrange a five day "Sahara Camping Tour" departing at 6:30 next morning.

I hadn't realized that Ayers Rock (or rather Uluru to be politically correct), is 450 km from Alice and it took our group of seventeen till lunchtime to reach our private campsite where Sahara has permanent tents and "swags" for beds, plus covered kitchen and washroom facilities. This was, of course, in the newly formed tourist area of Yulara, twenty kilometres from The Rock. No more camping allowed beside Uluru because of the possibility of having dingoes snatch your baby from your tent, as in the case of Lindy Chamberlain - or was it Meryl Streep?!

Before we joined the hordes at Ayers Rock for the Sunset Photo Op at 7 o'clock and our first close-up of this curiosity, we headed further east for fifty kilometres to hike the eight kilometre "Valley of the Winds" trail in the Olgas. These red pimples were formed by the same ancient river that deposited Uluru, but being further upstream they are of a sandstone aggregate rather than the fine sandstone (which is red through oxidization) of Ayers Rock. The trail takes you in amongst these domes (about fifty in all), and up over the steep pass of Karingana Lookout. You certainly feel like Gulliver in Lilliput, even although Mt. Olga itself is only 546 m. We were lucky, as the trail is frequently closed if the temperature goes above thirty-five degrees. As it was cloudy it was only thirty degrees, but the clouds also meant no sunset to blow your mind at Uluru, as promised in the brochures. Those who had paid a fortune for the Champagne and Cocktail Sunset bus tour to see "the last rays of the sun turn Uluru into an ever-changing artist's palette" and who had probably dropped another couple of hundred to stay in one of the expensive Yulara Resort Hotels, must have been very peeved. Especially as the same hoopla was repeated at 5.50 a.m. next morning at the Sunrise Viewing Area. This time there was a steady drizzle.

Our tour leader knew the ropes and whizzed us round the perimeter road next morning, past all the disappointed Sunrisers with their plastic glasses of Bucks

Fizz. That way he made sure we got to view all the interesting and sacred places dotted around the Rock before the big tour groups arrived. He then dispatched us to walk the same 9.4 km around the base to get a better perspective of its size. We had, in fact, been game to climb to its 348 m summit, but the climb was closed due to the possibility of rain making it slippery. When we reached the starting point and saw how steep and smooth the rock was, I was rather relieved I wasn't going to have to haul myself up the chain that is your only safety prop. Apparently people regularly slip off to their surprise demise. The myth that the Aboriginals considered the actual climb an infringement of their sacred beliefs was denied when they realized the importance of the tourist dollar from the millions that visit Uluru and Kata Tjuta (The Olgas).

We moved on that afternoon to Kings Creek further to the north. This prepared us for an early start on the six kilometre hike round the rim of Kings Canyon in Watarrka National Park. It is a spectacular gorge with domes similar to the Bungle Bungles, but striped terracotta (iron oxide) and black (algae) rather than orange and black. Where the 150 m sheer, smooth red cliffs of the actual gorge have recently shed a layer, the pale cream sandstone underneath makes a dramatic contrast. We were just as impressed as we were with the Bungle Bungles, but perhaps this was because of the constant flow of Kings Creek over a high waterfall into the lower reaches of the wooded gorge. We had a refreshing dip in a beautiful swimming hole at the top of the falls, with flocks of green budgies crowding the sky. The rock formations and outcrops, to say nothing of the drop-dead drop-off views, made for a wonderful morning's hike. Many of the shots from the movie "Priscilla, Queen of the Desert" were filmed in Kings Canyon.

Our fourth and fifth days of this tour were spent exploring the gorges and canyons of the Western MacDonnell Range which runs 150 km due east to Alice Springs. Here the Heavitree Gap divides it from the Eastern MacDonnell Range that continues due east about as far again. Mt. Sonder at the Western end is 1,380 m. There were many places of interest to visit and hike in these last two days. At Palm Valley we found the rare Australian Livistona Red Cabbage Palm and at Ormiston Gorge and Glen Helen Gorge we spotted the rare black footed Rock Wallabies. We visited the Ochre Pits where the Aboriginals have dug their body paint for millennia, and had a swim at Ellery Creek Big Hole, a billabong of enormous proportions. Our final day visiting isolated Cycad Gorge meant a very rough 4WD ride of more than an hour, criss crossing the fast flowing waters (from last night's rain) of the Finke River. This is a constantly flowing river with headwaters in the MacDonnells and a disappearing estuary in the salt pan of Lake Eyre to the south. Unfortunately our vehicle failed to cross the final section and was well and truly stuck in the mud with wheels under water. It took five hours for them to bring in a backhoe to haul it out. Meantime we took off our shoes, waded to shore and completed our hike before coming back for lunch and a long wait. The final humiliation was an unexpected downpour that gave us all a good soaking and the delay meant we had to miss our final highlight of the tour which was the slot canyon of Stanley Chasm en route back to Alice. Ah well, another time.

A day to dry shoes and sort laundry in Alice Springs before setting out on the Stuart Highway south, as passengers on the Oz Experience Backpacker Bus. We were assured we would be seeing real desert now. The Red Centre had been surprisingly green which gave wonderful contrast to the red soil and the cream seed grasses of spinifex. Also dramatic black thunderclouds, especially over Gosse Bluff, north of Kings Canyon gave another perspective of this remote isolated area. It has been suggested that the comet that excavated the twenty-two km diameter Gosse Bluff Crater ended the dinosaur age 130 million years ago.

SOUTH AUSTRALIA

Oz Experience Backpacker Bus

Alice Springs to Sydney Nov.-Dec. 2000

The road is dead straight for the first seventy kilometres south of Alice Springs and only the odd road train passed us by. The parched earth is still reddish and nothing to see all the way to the 360 degree horizon but arid savanna. The Oz Experience bus is the preferred way to travel for backpackers like us, and we chose to explore the rest of Australia this way. We were allowed to stop off for a day or two at any point en route and be picked up by the next available bus coming through. The driver would book ahead our choice of accommodation, and Oz Experience deliberately included stops each day at all the main tourist attractions en route. It proved the perfect way to travel as the majority of our young fellow passengers, who liked to party all night and sleep at the back of the bus all day, were happy for us "oldies" to occupy the empty front seats. That day we lost one hour on the clock when we crossed into South Australia, a couple of hour's drive south of Alice.

Later that day the highway crossed the 5,300 km long dingo fence that keeps the northern critters away from sheep of the southern states and as we approached our first night's stop at the "Opal Capital of the World", Coober Pedy, you would have thought the land had been decimated by an atomic bomb. You might have been right, as the Woomera Atomic Testing Range is just down the road. There was barely any vegetation as far as the eye could see, just conical piles of cream sand with a deep bore hole beside each. The roadside carries frequent warnings not to wander around or you might fall down a thirty metre hole and never be seen again. Not surprisingly Coober Pedy is aboriginal for "White Man's Hole" and supplies 80% of the world's opals from the silica veins of the Stuart Range Opal Fields. It is staked by private individuals and no big consortiums are allowed to mine. So "opal fever" is still the mainstay of the town.

Many of the houses, hotels etc are actually built into the ground as was our backpackers. This makes a lot of sense as this is a scorching place (thirty-six degrees when we drove in), and underground homes maintain an even temperature of twenty-three degrees all year round. We had a great conducted tour of the mines followed by a visit with Crocodile Harry at his extensive and bizarre underground home, all chiseled out of his open faced mine by his own hand. Apparently, when excavating your home, it is not unusual to more than cover the cost with the opals that you find in the process. We didn't find the night in our underground backkpacker's cave too claustrophobic.

Another long day of driving took us south to Port Augusta at the top of the Spencer Gulf. From here we headed north-east into South Australia's only mountains, The Flinders Ranges, and crossed the Goyder Line that determines the northern limit of pastoral land in South Australia. This fact was discovered the hard way by early pioneers and there are several derelict homesteads to prove it.

We had lots of Aboriginal rock art to view in The Flinders. Most of it is found at the end of rocky paths hiked under a relentless sun. Wilpena Pound is the big tourist attraction. Its natural crater-like formation, with steep outer walls and gently rolling inner pastures, has only one opening where a creek exits through Sliding Rocks Gap. A hike through the narrow gap and up to a lookout above the ruined homestead was well rewarded, not just by the view of this natural livestock pound, but by the close encounter with a Mulga or King Brown snake, its full fat six feet sharing our downward path. It was another of those "can be lethal" varieties of nasty snakes to add to our list of near misses.

We overnighted in a dilapidated railway workers' compound from the days when Parachilna was on the Adelaide to Alice railway line. They have long since built a much better line up to Alice, and Parachilna only sees long freight trains carrying coal down to the power station at Port Augusta. So the shabby cabins have been turned into a shabby backpackers in the middle of nowhere. Nowhere to seek out better accommodation and, to add to our discomfort, a plague of locusts descended that evening, covering everything everywhere. They dropped in your beer, filled the toilet bowls and bounced off you as you ran for cover. Apparently they will eat anything green, even paint or cloth. I was wearing my green pants so I was fast off my mark.

Diane Jones

Before heading into the city of Adelaide we spent a night in the famous South Australian wine region, the Barossa Valley. We had a bit of a tipple on our way to our backpackers, housed in the Old Marananga Schoolhouse, where we were required to select our choice of school uniform to wear for dinner in the Headmaster's study. Our busload of gap year kids were lots of fun and were happy to include us two old farts in their shenanigans. We were probably even older than their grandparents.

South Australia's capital, Adelaide, we dealt with in half a day. It has a very small central core with the State's official buildings backed by the River Torrens. Full of old schoolboy rowing teams, gentrified boat-houses and landscaped parkland, there was a walkway by the river where we watched the coaches on their bikes, hollering through their megaphones and cycling madly after their team's boat. All was frightfully British. We even had time to visit the State Museum and Art Gallery.

At dawn we were off for a two day visit to Kangaroo Island. First you have to drive down the scenic Fleurieu Peninsula by coach to catch the one hour ferry ride from Jervis Bay to Penneshaw where we were met by our tour's minibus at 10 a.m. Kangaroo is about 150x50 km so no small island, but full of wildlife protected from mainland feral predators (except wild cats). In our two days with Daniel's Tours we found rare Tammar wallabies, fairy penguins in their nest, an echidna, fur seals, Rosenberg goannas, eared sea lions, koalas and babies galore. (Did you know they not only feed their babies milk but also a bit of their own poop to help wean their young onto the otherwise indigestible eucalypt leaves?) We slept in a little bungalow at the other end of the island near Flinders Chase National Park and had easy viewing of the possums that came to the compost heap after dark, and at dawn we were off to the park to spot platypus. Unfortunately they spot you from the bottom of their pond before you see them. Only their tell-tale breathing bubbles let you know they are there. Very shy animals, they sneak up to the surface for a bit of air only when you are looking the other way, so all very frustrating.

We visited and hiked around Cape du Couedic Lighthouse, Admiral's Arch and the Remarkable Rocks before dodging the western gray kangaroos as we headed to the north coast's wonderful beaches. Stokes Bay has a tunnel through the cliff to a perfect swimming rock pool and deserted beach. We caught the pelican feeding at the main island town of Kingscote before heading back to Penneshaw to catch the evening ferry, The Sealion Catamaran, across the sixteen kilometre Backstairs Passage, a notoriously rough bit of sea.

From Adelaide our Oz bus followed the coast road, crossing the great Murray River estuary at Lake Alexandrina. From here a sandspit runs down the coast for 150 km with sheltered lagoons teeming with waterfowl. It's called Coorong

National Park. We stopped to view the gigantic fiberglass lobster at Kingston (as did Bill Bryson in his book "In A Sunburned Country") and overnighted in Mt. Gambier Gaol. Fortunately it became defunct as a gaol in 1995 and has been turned into a novel backpackers. At least the toilet in our double cell was in a closet. In some four-bunk units the toilet was in the cell itself. The door locks have been reversed to now open and close from the inside, but the peephole and food slides were still present in the heavy metal doors that all opened onto an interior courtyard. Mt. Gambier is fairly near the coast and is on the slopes of an ancient volcanic crater. Its town water supply comes from the brilliant Blue Crater Lake in the centre of the cone.

VICTORIA

We crossed into Victoria and drove north, through beautiful rolling parkland pastures and dark forest plantations of the fast growing Radiata Pine. Peter did a spot of rock climbing at Mt. Arapiles, a favourite "rockies" spot in Australia. It is just a 390 m sheer tower standing in the middle of an arable plain. Not much further and you enter the Grampian Mountains. Again they just pop up from the farm fields. They are yet another unique sandstone outcrop stretching for ninety kilometres, incredibly rich in a diversity of flora and fauna, rock formations, Aboriginal rock art and great bushwalking.

We hopped off the Oz Experience bus at the central village of Halls Gap and stayed three nights at the brand new, deluxe, eco-friendly Youth Hostel. We spent the next two days following the wooded tracks and visiting all the famous scenic spots such as The Balconies, The Pinnacles and MacKenzie Falls. We only had to jump twice when we met Eastern Brown snakes crossing our paths. Fortunately they were even more scared than we were and we were beginning to feel quite at ease with yet another of Australia's dangerous snakes.

Due south of The Grampians, across flat plains of pastureland and near the coast, is Tower Hill, a volcanic crater containing contented wildlife; koalas in the trees, emus amongst the grass, and waterfowl on the lake. A very natural self-contained habitat with a drive-through circular road and several hiking trails. It is close to Warrnambool, and the start of the Great Ocean Road. All the way south east from here to Cape Otway are dramatic cliffs of limestone topped with sandstone which have weathered into unique formations of stacks, blowholes and arches. All are a photographer's delight, especially in a setting sun. The most famous formation is The Twelve Apostles. Two of these flowerpots have eroded completely and collapsed into the sea in recent times, so really only Ten Apostles by the millenium. North-east from Cape Otway to Geelong and on to Melbourne is the second half of The Great Ocean Road, but this is noted more for its surfing beaches than cliff formations.

We had checked out the highlights of Melbourne, (the Botanic Gardens being our favourite), during a 1993 visit using Qantas Airlines' special deal of "Four Cities by Air". This was when we flew to Darwin to visit Kakadu and then went on to Cairns to hike in Cape York and snorkel on the Great Barrier Reef. (More later.) We had friends to visit in both Sydney and Melbourne from our London days in the 1960s. They were happy to take us out of the backpacker culture for a few days as our Oz Experience bus passed through.

TASMANIA

The island is only about 200 km north to south and 200 km across at the widest point in the north. It is 240 km from Melbourne on the overnight ferry, "The Spirit of Tasmania", with a fare that includes your cabin, dinner and breakfast. Tasmania was settled early in the 19th century, much thanks due to the labours of the convicts of its three penal colonies in building many of its roads, and their stone bridges are still in use today on the main routes.

We had chosen a five-day backpacker bus tour of Tasmania which took us off the beaten path to lesser known scenic spots. Unfortunately our tour guide was past his use-by date and we became more and more frustrated by his tardiness and inability to keep things on track. This meant hurried meals and late check-ins at accommodation. We stopped at far too many bakeries (for snackers) and toilets (for incontinent twenty-somethings who had drunk too much pop at the bakeries). However we did get to visit many of the famous National Parks such as the Freycinet Peninsula on the east coast and the temperate rainforest of Cradle Mountain-Lake St. Clair in the Western Highlands, but our hikes were limited and frustratingly short. At least we had unusually good weather as it is often wet and the scenery obscured by cloud.

The eastern side of the island supports sheep and crop farming such as apples, hops, vineyards and opium poppies. The latter supply the pharmaceutical industry and are grown under strict government control. Apart from the odd echidna crossing the road and our first sighting of a Tiger Snake, thankfully from the safety of the bus, our wildlife experiences were limited to examining scat on the hiking trails and squished wombats, pademelons and Tasmanian devils on the roads. However we did visit a wildlife rehabilitation centre and saw all of the above and more being raised as orphans for reintroduction to the wild.

Tasmania is quite different to the mainland of Australia and perhaps more similar to New Zealand. Hobart, the capital, is very British and the walled gardens of its little bungalows were filled with English perennials and resplendent roses. Behind the city sits Mount Wellington (1,270 m) which, from its road accessible summit, has a view all the way to the Tasman

Peninsula in the far southeast where we had stayed the previous night at historic Port Arthur.

The harsh treatment of the convicts in the penal settlements of the early 1800s does not make for a pleasant story. Port Arthur was a strategically excellent site as the whole peninsula is cut off from the mainland, except for a 100 m isthmus known as Eaglehawk Neck. Here a line of ferocious dogs was all that was needed to isolate the settlement. It was known as The Dog Line. The site has been restored as an Historical Park, complete with Ghost Tours by lantern light. No giggling please. All those ghost sightings are true! We heard those chains rattling! Our YHA, just outside the grounds, was reputedly haunted, but we had a peaceful night in #7 which was the room most prone to ghost activity. We didn't choose this room. It was the only one left!

We returned on the overnight ferry and, after a pleasant lunch of lamb brains on toast with our Melbourne friends, somewhere down in dockland with giant container ships gliding by, we rejoined the OZ Experience bus at 3 p.m.

We didn't have to travel far for our overnight on Phillip Island at the YHA in Cowes. The hostel ran a modest and environmentally attuned evening bus trip out to The Noddies at the west end of the island. The highlight is the Penguin Parade, with thousands of tourists (many Asian) on bus tours from Melbourne. Stone bleachers, floodlights and commentator all waiting in anticipation of the arrival on the beach of The Little Penguins. Fairy Penguins they used to be called, till that was deemed politically incorrect. They arrive in rafts over the surf to the tide line, where they scurry about getting into marching formation as crossing an exposed beach en masse is much safer from predators. They then head up the soft sand, but when they hit the grass and underbrush they peel off individually to find their respective burrows. The young in their nests in burrows are spread all over the grassy and rocky hillside behind the beach but a maze of boardwalks keeps the humans well out of harm's way. The hundreds of visitors far outnumber the Little Penguins, but they seem to take no notice.

From Phillip Island we crossed back by the bridge and followed the coastline through farming country before branching north to Tara Bulga National Park to look for Lyrebirds in one of the last remnants of Gippsland's southern forests. No luck, but a nice hiking trail before a picnic lunch. We touched the coast briefly at Lakes Entrance before heading north into the Snowy Mountains.

Here we spent four nights at Karoonda Park, near Gelantipy. Not only is it a working stock farm, but also an Outdoor Education Centre and backpacker retreat. At almost 1,000 m in altitude and nestled below Mount Kosciuszko

(2,228 m), Australia's highest mountain, the lodge is surrounded by forested crown land and Snowy Mountain National Park. This allowed us three days of lovely bushwalking, finding in the wild, swamp wallabies, grey kangaroos, a wombat, a fox and, best of all, a koala and baby. Peter fitted in a couple of horse rides and the rest of our days were easily frittered away reading on the secluded verandah of the little cabin we had generously been given on the edge of the complex. The young 'uns had to make do with the central backpackers' lodge. Schools were on holiday and the daily Oz Experience bus pulling through was their only business. $60 a day covered us both for four course dinners and all-you-could-eat breakfast and lunch buffets, plus it included our deluxe three room en-suite cabin. I don't think they had seen such old people get off the Oz bus before and thought we might appreciate some kid glove treatment after suffering the long journey from Alice, with the young kids headbanging music and noisy evening parties. Well we had enjoyed our young fellow travellers, but we were very happy to be spoiled by the staff at Karoonda Park.

NEW SOUTH WALES

Next stop was the capital, Canberra. To reach the Australian Capital Territory (ACT), nestled on the high plains to the west of the Dividing Range, we first had to cross through the Snowy Mountains. This we did via the Barry Way, a summer only rough road that clings to the steep hillsides above the Snowy River valley and passes through three National Parks, Snowy River, Alpine and Mt. Kosciuszko where Thredbo is the centre for Australia's downhill skiers. All very scenic on this nail-biting road with unfenced sheer drops into eucalyptus forests hundreds of feet below.

Mr. Burley Griffin designed Canberra in the early nineteen hundreds around a crescent shaped manmade lake and with a highly developed road system, much parkland, bungalows in leafy suburbs and grand vistas between the important government buildings. It was easy to spend two full days exploring the city, the first with a hop-on hop-off bus pass and the second with hired bicycles. The New Parliament House, built in 1988, is a stunning piece of architecture, both inside and out. It was built into a small hill in line with the rooftops of the Old Parliament Building and the vista continues over these rooftops, across the lake and up the wide Anzac Boulevard to the War Memorial many kilometres away. The architect first removed the top of the rounded hill, built the main building within it, and then put the grassy top back on the roof with a four legged giant flagpole to top it all off. Atriums and walls that are accessed on four sides of the hill provide plenty of daylight. One of the loveliest modern buildings I have seen.

Another highlight was the ANZAC War Memorial with an amazing Historical Museum covering, in detail, all the wars of the 20th Century involving Australian and New Zealand troops. We spent about four hours altogether over the two days, being immersed in its very informative audiovisual displays.

We rejoined the Oz Experience bus that took us from Canberra east across the Great Dividing Range of mountains which run the length of Australia's eastern coast and joined the coastal road just south of Batemans Bay. Fortunately we were able to spend a few days with our Sydney friends, who were spending the Christmas vacation in this area. This meant the chance to enjoy all the wonderful beaches, especially Booderee National Park at Jervis Bay, where we were outnumbered by the colourful Crimson Rosellas, Rainbow Lorikeets and King Parrots. On other days we hiked at Morton National Park and Kangaroo Valley, nestled between dramatic limestone gorges. Further inland, at the Wombeyan Cave, we took a guided 800 m tour of impressive Wollondilly Cave with five steep ladders and 520 rough-hewn steps to raise your heart rate. Not quite tuckered out, we continued with our guide along forested paths spotting several new bird species and, best of all, we had a sleek Black Red Bellied snake cross our path! Even the guide leaped out of its way and confirmed the identification.

If we added the Tiger snake, which we watched from the safety of our minibus, to the Death Adder, Western Brown, Mulga, Eastern Brown and Red Bellied which we had met up close and personal on our hikes, we had now met six out of Australia's ten lethal snakes. We were missing the Inland and Coastal Taipans, the Copperhead and the Small Eyed Snake. However, we were more than happy to just stick with the six. I haven't yet mentioned the deadly spiders, but our Sydney friends had Red Bellied ones and Funnel Webs living in their city backyard and insisted we take their spider stick to swiff in front of you when taking the overgrown path to the swimming pool. Then, of course, there are the lethal Box Jellyfish! More to follow on those!.

Sydney, with its magnificent harbour anchored by The Bridge and Opera House, is a city I have always enjoyed visiting, the first time in 1993 on our "Four Cities by Air" deal and several times since on cruise ships. It has a wonderful Zoo reached by the little ferries that speed you to all the suburbs around Sydney Harbour, glorious Botanic Gardens by the Opera House, famous ocean beaches at Bondi and Manly and miles of bayside walking trails. Of course, just beyond the city's western boundaries lie the Blue Mountains and a must see visit to the Three Sisters outcrop at Katoomba. You can drive to the outstanding vistas on the edge of the cliffs and look down to the many hiking trails in the steep forested canyons below.

Diane Jones

We said farewell to our Oz Experience bus and headed north to Queensland in a little Daewoo Rental Car. We had chosen the scenic inland route north through the Hunter Valley wine growing area and up the spine of the Coastal Dividing Mountain Range and found that, in the thirty degree heat, we had to turn off the AC if we wanted to crest some of the steeper hills. For some silly reason we walked up Burning Mountain in the noonday sun with its continually burning natural coal seam spewing out hot gases from vents along the way. It has been burning for thousands of years, so although it is thirty m underground, it's had long enough to build up quite a furnace blast.

From the university city of Armidale, halfway between Sydney and Queensland, we took WaterFall Way east to Coffs Harbour to spend Christmas Day on the beach. Needless to say lots of waterfalls to stop and view from all angles, followed by a seven kilometre hike in the dense rainforest of Dorrigo National Park perched on the edge of the coastal escarpment. We had our first sighting of Australia's Bush Turkeys wandering wild in the forest, quite at ease. They obviously knew they were not on the Australian Christmas dinner menu 'cos Aussies prefer a seafood "Barbie" on the beach on Christmas Day and even go to the length of bringing Xmas decorations to personalize their picnic shelters. Also of note, Santa in sunglasses and surfing shorts! Dinner for us was a cold BBQ chicken with salad, purchased at the supermarket the night before, and walks along the beach at dawn and dusk of this popular resort.

Boxing Day we headed inland again across the mountains to Lismore and on through to Nimbin. This is the centre of Australia's "Alternative Culture" and is stuck in a 1970s hippie time warp. Gaudy murals on the shopfronts, spaced out druggies ignored by the authorities, bare feet and earth mother clothes, and weird and wonderful artistically arranged rubbish calling itself The Nimbin Museum. We felt we looked quite out of place so we had a laugh and fled on up to Mount Warning National Park. Here we spotted our first duckbill platypus foraging in a pool on the River Tweed. They were a binocular distance away from our bridge stance and looked much like small beaver when they swam briefly on the surface, except they looked as if they had a beaver tail at both ends!

Next morning we joined a ranger-escorted hike up the 1,157 metres of Mount Warning. This is a steep climb with a 200 metre hand-over-hand haul up a chain at the final ascent, which took five hours to complete. The 360 degree view was worth it, as was our chance meeting with a seven foot carpet python basking on the path. No fangs, but a serious hugger if you dare to pick it up.

Extraordinary Travels of an Ordinary Housewife

QUEENSLAND

Heading into Queensland we gained an hour in time change as we headed north on the Pacific Highway through rich tropical fruit-growing country with bananas and macadamia nut plantations and, of course, sugar cane. The latter supplies the famous Rum Distillery at Bundaberg. We stopped just to sample its coffee!

We had to reach the industrial port city of Gladstone by 30th December to catch the catamaran across eighty km of rough ocean swell to Heron Island, a coral key paradise at the southern end of the Great Barrier Reef. Most passengers were very seasick, but not us two hardy sailors and we were able to fully enjoy the free champagne as we cruised into the island's lagoon. A spot of true luxury living for the next five days with a cute little private cabin to ourselves tucked amongst the pisonia trees that cover the island. The trees are fully occupied by thousands of nesting Noddy Terns and the ground is perforated with thousands of burrows of muttonbirds (shearwaters) that come ashore at night to wail at each other like banshees. The island not only supports this posh all-inclusive resort but also a marine research station, and the entire island and its reefs are a Marine National Park.

A wonderful 60th birthday surprise the next morning was the return of sunshine accompanied by a beautiful basket of flowers, a chilled bottle of champagne and breakfast served on our patio by the Maitre d' himself. The resort had arranged lots of Hogmanay events that day starting with party hat and mask making, followed by a grand parade of costumed staff to lead us all down to the gazebo by the jetty to watch the sunset and indulge in complimentary champagne and canapés. Then a conga line danced us all off to the restaurant for a scrumptious seafood buffet, followed by a live band and dancing in the lounge till gone midnight. The resort had been extravagantly decorated and the usual net of balloons and streamers announced the arrival of the "real" millennium, seventeen hours ahead of our kids in Calgary and fifteen hours ahead of Ontario. It was an ideal night to wander along the beach at high tide at 1.00 a.m. and spot a huge green turtle laying her eggs, supervised by research station staff who patrol the beach each night. How lucky we were to spot the first one of the New Year.

Heron Island sits astride the Tropic of Capricorn. One of the Capricorn and Bunker Group of offshore islands, it has its own coral reef where you can snorkel or reef walk directly from the beach depending on the level of the tide. Many natural history walks through the woods, talks and activities were offered each day and a semi-submersible took you to the outer edge of the reef to let you view, not just the corals and highly coloured reef fish, but many turtles gorging on the jellyfish washed in by the previous day's wind. Rays were very common inside the lagoon and cruised happily amongst the snorkelers. We weren't so comfortable with the Red Lion's Mane jellyfish that also found their way into the lagoon on our final day and chased us out of the water. We left the island with a strong desire to return some day.

Returning south towards Brisbane, we booked a two day tour to the World Heritage Site of Fraser Island, 125 km by 14 km and the largest sand island in the world. It has many interesting features such as crystal-clear freshwater lakes and creeks, extensive rainforest, giant sand blows and a seventy-five mile stretch of eastern beach pounded by heavy surf. Unfortunately this is used as a main tourist highway with constant jeeps and trucks roaring past. Even small planes use it as a runway. Teenagers flock here for the all night beach party scene and even the less accessible areas of the National Park were disappointingly overused. We left with no strong desire ever to return.

Brisbane, the capital of Queensland, turned out to be a pleasant city and we enjoyed exploring it from the City Cat (catamaran) that plies the River Brisbane from Bretts Wharf all the way through the skyscrapers of downtown and out west to the University of Queensland. We were now flying on to Asia on this trip, but I will continue with previous and later memorable travels in Queensland starting with our visit to Cairns in 1993, which was the fourth destination on our "Four Cities by Air" deal.

QUEENSLAND THE TOP END

July 1993

Cairns is about as far north on the Queensland coast as the regular tourist ventures and it is a good stepping off point for the Great Barrier Reef. This we visited on one long July day with about forty other snorkelers and divers. Three hours and several seasick passengers later, we anchored off a small key on the reef and were ferried ashore to check our rental gear and practise our snorkelling techniques from the beach. However the sea was choppy and visibility poor on the reefs close to shore and so, as planned, our boat continued another few miles to the totally submerged outer reef.

Since then they have built a huge raft, with tourist facilities, where the boats can tie up and snorkelers can enter the water at leisure. In 1993, a boat was not allowed to anchor directly on the reef and there was nothing to see but the horizon and dark choppy ocean when the order came to just jump in and head for the reef "over there!" Several people were scuba diving and so the rest of us snorkelers had just one diving instructor in charge who shouted, over the wind, "If you follow me I'll show you around". There was a great thrashing of flippers which Peter and I tried to avoid by staying back, but by then we couldn't catch

Extraordinary Travels of an Ordinary Housewife

up. In those years we were still rookie snorkelers and were too nervous to venture far from the boat on our own, so we just puttered around the nearest reef, returning frequently to the boat for the occasional cough and splutter and a rest. We did enjoy what we saw and were impressed by the size of the fish and the enormous exotically coloured giant clams. The occasional harmless white-tipped reef shark would glide past far below. I gave the instructor a piece of my mind when he returned with the group and, as a result, was given a personal tour of the outer reef whilst I clung onto his hand. He would pass to me wonderful bright blue starfish, and black sea cucumbers to handle and then fed an enormous three-foot wrasse with some dead fish he was carrying. Actually he tempted the fish first of all and then, at the last moment, put the bait right in front of my mask and I thought I was going to be swallowed up too. Peter declined this personal tour as he was pretty waterlogged and, on the whole, we were disappointed with the Great Barrier Reef. Its claim to fame is that everything is bigger and more dramatic. True, including the waves and deep dark ocean.

Our guide in Kakadu recommended that, when we were in Cairns, we should book a trek in the outback called "Take a Walk on the Wild Side". I quote from the flimsy paper flyer he proffered. "The Cape York Peninsula is one of the remotest, wildest, least populated and unspoiled tropical wilderness areas of Australia. It is an area of unsurpassable beauty, an immense diversity of habitats, and flora and fauna of great biological significance........where the silvery sandy creek beds contrast with the yellow or red soils....... The country's life sources are its rivers. Our backpacking trek is designed to follow the Walsh River (a dry riverbed) walking between and camping at waterholes. The trekking at times is hard, and all participants must be fit. Each day we have plenty of time to rest and swim". (Might have been true if we hadn't spent so much time being lost!) "We have a rest day near hot springs to indulge and soothe our bodies" (The rest day was spent staggering up to a lookout point to see where we had gone wrong with our map reading, and the hot springs were barely ankle deep, unless you ventured to wriggle your bottom into the deeper pools of thick yellow slime.) It mentions an historical expedition. "Edmund Kennedy followed the Walsh River's tortuous course, its bed hundreds of metres wide and full of great boulders and fallen timber, its steep banks almost gorge-like. The weakened horses continually fell on the slippery boulders as they struggled along the riverbed" The brochure fails to mention the expedition ended when Kennedy was killed by the cannibalistic natives.

Unfortunately (or perhaps fortunately) our confirmation faxed copy of the trip details was foreshortened and omitted the bit about carrying all supplies and equipment on our backs. Unlike Kennedy, we would have no pack horses. Our guide only happened to mention this when we spoke on the phone to confirm we had arrived in Cairns and were expecting to be picked up at six the next morning. Continuing on the subject of packs on backs, I mumbled about creaking knees and greying hair and suggested that my pack (which was being supplied) might be filled with the group's ration of cornflakes and toilet paper. The guide must have panicked at the thought of his expedition being handicapped by these two Canadian wrinklies so, in the hours before departure, he persuaded a friend to come along for a free trip in return for his help with these two geriatric liabilities. This assistant guide was well qualified for all emergencies because, apart from currently being a diving instructor on the G.B.R., he had previously been a member of the London Police Tactical Squad and, before that, a Royal Marine Commando. In fact our total group for the trek turned out to be us, and one other couple in their thirties, two microbiologists from Cape Town. Avid birders like us, and carrying a heavy comprehensive bird book as well as more than their share of our supplies, they were a delightful couple with a great sense of humour. Just as well, as Mark (aged twenty-seven), our guide, was full of fun, and it was difficult to know if he was serious when he frequently said we were lost. We usually were, as he had only followed this cross country route once before. But Gavin, our quasi-assistant guide, was to be the biggest laugh of all. He had an irrepressible Cockney, slightly crude, always insulting or self-deprecating sense of humour, a never-ending supply of jokes and a razor-sharp wit. The fact that we were usually on our knees by the end of the day's hike was more due to incessant laughter than heavy packs and blistered feet.

The trip held true to its description - it just forgot to mention some of the bonuses: that we would be hiking mainly in the shade of the aromatic eucalyptus and melaleuca trees; the bird life would be as abundant as it was exotic and we would suddenly find ourselves wandering through clouds of butterflies. The yellow flowers of the kapok bushes, the orange blossoms of the bottle brush trees and the dried grasses ranging from bleached creams to rusty reds, gave vibrant colour to these dried arid lands. The fact that the bag of potatoes had gone missing from the start (honestly I did not leave them behind deliberately) meant that my backpack, at least, was of manageable weight, and the only downers of the journey, apart from the limited menu (more to follow), was the rubber vine which you would have to fight your way through whilst being careful not to get the irritating white latex, which would leak from its broken stems, onto your skin. Then there were the speargrass tips which would work their way through your gaiters and boots, then through your socks, till they pierced your skin like needles, and you had to stop, remove gaiters, boots and socks, and extricate the offending barbs.

Tents we had none, just lightweight nylon hammocks slung from the paperbark trees and a sleeping sheet. I can honestly say I had never slept in a hammock before, nor for the five nights of the trip.

Yes, about the food. Our menu was to have been potatoes and freshly caught fish. The fate of the potatoes remained a mystery and the fish did not quite come up to expectations. Our total catch in five days was three sardine sized black perch. We were, however, carrying a couple of folding net crayfish traps which we baited with precious salami and were rewarded with a few for breakfast each morning, but it was debatable if their food value was greater than the salami we had to sacrifice to catch them. Basically it was cereal for breakfast and copious cups of billy tea. Lunch required a two-hour stop in order to build a fire to provide ashes hot enough to bake our homemade bannock. We reluctantly took turns each day with bannock making as it was difficult to work up enthusiasm about a food that left one coated to the elbows in flour and water paste. At least it got the fingernails clean. This cardboard bannock would be livened up with sweaty cheese and crayfish bait. Dinner was pot-luck. That is, lucky if anything edible came out of the pot. We weren't too hopeful about gourmet suppers as we had only been supplied with a bowl, spoon and tin cup so we weren't too disappointed to have, what is called in the outback, Murray stew. The fact that we had it four nights running and that it never had the same ingredients at least kept us hopeful that it would taste better each time. But I can't say it did, perhaps because it was always made in the dark by pulling a variety of dried packets lucky-dip style from the food bag, and boiling on the fire with lots of water till it "looked" ready. We had no booze, too heavy to carry. Mind you, for a quick bush refreshment, you could always bite the green body from a tree ant for a refreshing splash of citric acid. You must be careful that the ant does not bite you on the lip first.

We were picked up by 4WD near Chillagoe, a tiny village which attracted a few tourists with its famous limestone caves, the relic of a coral reef from long ago when this area, in the centre of Cape York, was covered by an ancient sea. It was once a thriving gold rush town. Its central hotel was built in that era and style, and had not been renovated since. We are still not sure if the mail-ordered, non English speaking wife of the drunken owner thought that, as we had been sleeping side by side in hammocks for five nights, we would want to stay on these same intimate terms. She had obviously gone to some trouble to squeeze six tiny single beds, side by side, into one room. Not one other room in the inn was taken, so there was no obvious reason for this. It just meant that we had another sleepless night as Gavin had hit the bottle with great enthusiasm, presumably to celebrate the safe deliverance of his geriatric charges. He proved a very happy and entertaining drunk who kept us all in stitches with his carrying-ons till he eventually passed out quietly in his wee bed alongside us all. However our accommodation seemed deluxe since we all got a decent meal, a cold beer, a hot shower, and a seat on the can. With all these nasty creepy-crawlies about, you have to be careful where you drop your drawers in Australia!

North of Cairns is the famous crocodile infested Daintree River. These are the huge man eating "Salty" Estuarine Crocodiles and a tour boat on the Daintree is a tourist highlight. The freshwater crocodiles don't grow much more than eight feet and the ones we came across in Kakadu and Queensland were mainly in the creeks and billabongs, and humans are not normally on their menu. North of the Daintree River lies Cape Tribulation National Park where the virgin rainforest comes right down from the mountainous peaks of the Dividing Range to flank the beautiful deserted beaches where you may also find a Salty swimming along with you.

Our guide from the trek, Mark, also worked for Jungle Tours who are the main transporters of the backpackers who head up to the various hostels in Cape Trib and he had suggested it would be easier to hitch a ride with Jungle Tours rickety charabanc than catch the only commercial bus from Cairns. No hired vehicles are allowed beyond the Daintree River. However we didn't expect Mark to fix the company's manifest so that he could be the driver and guide of our bus on that Monday morning. He reserved us the best seats and gave a great detailed commentary all the way, adding the odd cheeky asides to the rest of the passengers (average age in their twenties) about these two oldies he had had to suffer on a trek the previous week. He had recommended, indeed insisted, that he book us into a famous hostel called Crocodylus. It is ranked #1 amongst Australia's hostels, and its tent style buildings are tucked unobtrusively amongst the dense rainforest. We couldn't resist its charm, despite its spartan dormitory living,

On arrival we were presented with bed linen and a blanket and a map through the woods to our airy dormitory cabin on stilts. We found the only two empty bunks out of twenty in the dorm, both on top and at opposite ends of the cabin. All the other bunks were covered in backpacks, or bodies sleeping off last night's party. There were lots of jungle trails to explore including the one to the washrooms! The central building had open sides and housed the large dining area and bar beside a small swimming pool for water babies who didn't want to catch the shuttle bus to the beach. Remember this was in July, Australia's winter, when you don't have to worry about Box Jellyfish in the ocean, only crocodiles! A communal kitchen served those doing their own cooking, with dire warnings about food being forbidden in the dorms. They also had good cheap wholesome meals for those, like us, who had not brought rations.

We took the opportunity of going on a guided night walk, seeing pademelons (little kangaroos), bandicoots, possums, forest dragons (lizards), fruit bats, enormous insects and pretty little melomys (hamster-like rats). These latter turned out to be the thieves of the dorm and I cursed the kids that had broken the rules and left food in their packs. I could hear their little teeth gnawing away all night and running around the room. Shame on me when, in the morning, I discovered my pack was the guilty one as I had forgotten about a little bag of bran in the front pocket which was now all over the floor.

Diane Jones

QUEENSLAND

Cairns to Sydney with Oz Experience

March-April 2003

We had flown across from Christchurch, New Zealand and, as expected, Cairns was very hot and very humid. We found an A/C cubbyhole on the Esplanade for two nights whilst we sorted ourselves out for our journey south with the Oz Experience Backpackers Bus.

Ten years ago we had gone north from Cairns to the Daintree and Cape Tribulation but we had not covered the 1,500 kms. from Cairns south to Gladstone. (We covered the coast as far north as Gladstone and Heron Island in 2000/01). We grabbed the front seat of the OZ Bus when we departed at 8.30 a.m. sharp. Our first stop, half an hour later, was at Kuranda, high on the escarpment behind Cairns. We ignored the tourist stalls and cafes of this "must do" small town and instead found a short walking track up Jum Jum Creek for a refresher taste of Queensland's rainforest. It was a long drive across the Atherton Tablelands with its rich red volcanic soil that is ideal for crops such as sugarcane, peanuts, vegetables and tropical fruits. These flat extensive plains, 900 m above sea level, give way to rolling pastures further south and the climate of the tablelands is mild, without the humidity of the coast, and therefore ideal for farming.

Mission Beach stretches along the coast for about fifteen kilometres. We stayed for three nights at the Wongaling Beach section, just south of the main centre. Gorgeous pristine beaches but not a soul in the water despite the heat. This is because, from October to May, it is Box Jellyfish season and we were smartly brought to attention when we heard that, on the afternoon we arrived from Cairns, a young boy was dead on the beach from cardiac arrest after being stung whilst paddling in the shallows. They are basically transparent and quite deadly if any of their trailing tentacles touch flesh. One or two areas of the beach had square netted enclosures called stinger nets, but the smaller jellyfish (only a centimetre or so) can get through. They are a favourite snack of turtles but, as we all know, the turtle populations have been dwindling. Therefore the populations of jellyfish, that breed in the shallow estuaries of Queensland and the Northern Territories, are increasing and serious injuries and death are not uncommon.

We were on the lookout for Cassowary birds in the Mission Beach area where they are regularly spotted except when you want to see one. We did spend one of our two days in the area hiking the Licuala Track through the Tam O'Shanter State Forest and Cassowary Reserve and were rewarded with a sighting of one solitary adolescent viewed through a tropical downpour and a cloud of vicious mosquitoes.

Much more enjoyable was our day spent hiking the forest trails on Dunk Island opposite Mission Beach. It is all National Park except for the fancy P & O Resort and airstrip at one end. A fabulous day climbing through cool rainforest to the top of Mt. Kootaloo Lookout at 271 m for views across to the other Family Islands, including Bedarra, another exclusive resort island well beyond our travel budget. All in all we hiked about twelve kms of trail, with a break on Coconut Beach for our picnic lunch. But no paddling! We did notice that all the beaches posted warnings, with bottles of vinegar on hand. Apparently vinegar is the first line of treatment for jellyfish stings of any kind.

We continued south on straight roads through endless plains of sugarcane. It was sunshine all the way, even when we passed through Tully, the wettest place in Australia at 450 cm per annum. This means triple cropping and very rich farmers. We hopped off the OZ Bus at Townsville and caught the afternoon ferry across to Magnetic Island, so named by Captain Cook because his compass went askew when he sailed past. Apparently the problem was the compass, not the island's magnetism. The island has several small towns connected by bus on the only ten kilometre stretch of road. Instead of catching the bus we hiked several trails through the dry tropical forest of the National Park and finally, very hot and dehydrated, arrived at Horseshoe Bay on the other side of the island from the ferry port at Picnic Bay. Our bird list was rewarded with a feeding frenzy of four big Black Red-tailed Cockatoos before we caught the bus back to our A/C Hideaway Backpackers and a soak in its shady pool. Next morning we were back on the ferry for the eight km crossing to Townsville to pick up the OZ Bus at lunchtime that would take us south to Airlie Beach.

I should mention that on our hikes on both Dunk and Magnetic Island we were met on the path by small thin snakes. Probably fallen out of their tree, where they would normally hang out, we were informed. Also we were being awakened each day at dawn by Australia's alarm clock, Blue Winged Kookaburras – laughing of course.

More sugarcane and flat plains eventually became more arboreal with fenced cattle pastures, whilst big articulated cattle trucks thundered past. By evening we were in Airlie Beach or Airlie No Beach, as it should really be called. However to compensate for their mud flats they have built a huge swimming pool lagoon with lovely shady landscaping, picnic shelters and boardwalks. Otherwise it is very much a young people's party town.

Diane Jones

Airlie Beach is the jumping off point for the Whitsunday Islands and we based ourselves here for five days so that we could catch one of the sailing trips. It has always been one of my dream places in the world and so I splurged on a three day, two night, sailing cruise that took off the next morning at nine. They had only one spot left on the eight-berth yacht, Mainstay, and offered it to me at a standby price that morning at 7.30 a.m. when I checked out the tours available. It suited us both, as Peter wanted to spend the time taking a four-day scuba diving course, and so we went our separate ways.

We continued to be so lucky with the weather, if not the wind, which meant that the sailing was gentle and suited me just fine. There were two young couples, and an older couple with their teenage daughter with whom I shared a cabin. The food was first class and appeared about five times a day. The company was bland but who cares. I was happy just enjoying the passing scenery, first of Hook Island and then the Pacific side of Whitsunday Island. At the southern end, where we anchored overnight, is the famous Whitehaven Beach, six kilometres of fine white silica sand with metre-long goannas hiding in the brush behind. At the northern end of Whitehaven is Hill Inlet with a huge spread of white sandbanks and turquoise sea. The view from the top of a steep trail above Hill Inlet is the postcard picture of everyone's image of the Whitsundays. Every day we stopped to snorkel where coral was colourful and varied and competed with the gaudy tropical fish, some ugly, some beautiful and all friendly. When the boat anchored, huge batfish and usually a giant wrasse who were all looking for kitchen scraps, immediately surrounded us. Because of the jellyfish problem we had to wear full-length stinger suits that covered all flesh except, of course, the face. You just prayed you would not meet up with one of these invisible terrors. My most memorable snorkel was at Manta Ray Bay at the north end of Hook, where I came across a green turtle and swam alongside with a lazy and languid stroke for at least a half hour. Also I thought it might gobble up any stingers that came our way.

On the last day of Peter's scuba course, I was able to join him on the dive boat, a racing catamaran. This was a fun day of sailing at about eleven knots and, although fast, it was very stable. Suited me just fine as I am a nervous-nelly yachtie. I was able to snorkel over the spot where Peter submerged for his final certification dive. He disappeared into the gloomy depths and resurfaced with a big smile, having passed. He was the oldest person that his divemaster had ever certified (seven weeks short of his 70th birthday) and they had a little ceremony on the Kat during our return to Abel Point Marina that afternoon.

I confessed to being a little disappointed with the Whitsundays. Of the seventy four islands, nine have resorts or private homes. Hamilton Island even has high rises! The other islands are National Park, all are forested and only a few have any inland walking trails. The beaches are mainly coarse coral, except the

Whitehaven and Hill Inlet Beaches. The snorkeling was over some good hard and soft corals but the water tended to be cloudy, either because of the tide or maybe just too many snorkelers and their attendant boats. We were ready to move on.

Next stop was a day's drive on a bright green OZ Experience Bus, painted with giant flowers, up and over the Dividing Range to the flat, dry, red plains of the outback. We'd reached Namoi Hills Cattle Station, near Dingo and southeast of Mackay. Here we had a Ute (utility truck) drive from one farm-steading to another where the family had created a Backpackers, and a nice source of income, with Oz Experience buses six nights a week for dinner, bed and breakfast. They can't have been too poor as they owned 43,000 acres and 3,500 Brahman beef cattle. We got the full ranch experience with whip cracking, boomerang and shotgun demos, followed by billy tea and damper (bannock) and a sunset drive across the station to visit cattle and watch the Eastern Grey Kangaroos amongst the dry grass and eucalypts.

We were on the Oz bus all the way through to Sydney for the next six days. From Dingo we headed back to the coast at Rockhampton and south to Bargara, the beach resort near Bundaberg. At Rockhampton we spent an hour in its terrific Botanic Gardens and small zoo where we finally had eye-to-eye contact with a big Cassowary with his red and blue neck wattles and heavy casque on his head. We had the odd tropical shower en route, but most of the time the skies were blue and the air hot and humid. Roos were visible by the roadside in the late afternoon.

Before reaching Brisbane we stopped off at the ubiquitous "Cuddle a Koala" Reserve and fed red and grey Eastern Kangaroos, Emus and Wombats. We could see the odd shaped volcanic plugs of the Glasshouse Mountains, the largest looking remarkably like King Kong. South of Brisbane Queensland's Gold Coast and Surfers Paradise may have vast stretches of good surf beaches but are just tacky, over-commercialized, high-rise crass resort cities with many theme parks and casinos.

We crossed at Tweed Heads into New South Wales and had an OZ bus compulsory overnight (guess where) at Granny's Backpackers in Nimbin, the druggie alternative lifestyle capital of Oz. We had passed through here briefly on our last visit to OZ. I insisted on the lock to our bedroom being repaired when I had a brief look at some of the residents walking as if on puffy clouds, rolling their tokes and sucking on their bongs in all the public areas. They may have chosen to drop out of society, but are very happy to pick-up their social security cheques. Drugs are on offer up and down the main street that boasts a cottage hospital, community health centre, doctors' offices, methadone clinic and even a police station. (No sign of any activity at the latter.) The town's psychedelic wall murals and human low-life in its sidewalk cafés were a complete turn-off for us. Fortunately spotting a duck billed platypus and a water dragon on my dawn walk gave the town a couple of good points to remember it by. I shall also remember it for the cigarette burn holes in our sheets!

Crossing the Dividing Range next morning brought us to Australia's most easterly point, Cape Byron, with its 1901 lighthouse whose beam can be seen forty kms away. Byron Bay is "Old Hippiesville" and surfing beaches its main attraction. Next day we retraced our footsteps of December 2000 by recrossing the Great Dividing Range via Waterfall Way and drove through, what are called, long yards of cattle. Stockmen can graze their cattle for free on the roadside vegetation and sometimes these long yards of wandering cows may stretch over half a mile or more, unperturbed at holding up the traffic. There is a stockman and his ute (pick-up truck) on watch at either end with his dogs ready to nip any stragglers.

Our OZ bus continued south across rolling red earth cattle and sheep pastures dotted with gum trees. This panorama could only be Australia. We were not looking forward to our last night at the Dag Inn at Nundle, southeast of Tamworth (the Nashville of Oz). Dag means the fecal dirt on the wool of a sheep's behind. This Dag Inn Backpackers was on a sheep station and designed to give every young Oz Experience kid a big piss-up party on either their first night out of Sydney going north or, in our case, last night before reaching Sydney. There were almost 100 people on both buses to be accommodated in five identical and very basic sheep-shearing shed dorms where rumours of bed bugs and/or fleas were visibly justified. There was a hurried introductory tour of "work on a sheep station" but basically it was to be one big roustabout. At least we got a good home-cooked soup, damper and roast lamb dinner and a few quiet hours in the twenty-bed dorm before the young 'uns had had their fill of booze and returned to flop one by one in the early hours. Our best laugh of the whole experience was when Peter admitted he had gone for a night pee, returned to the wrong dorm and climbed into bed with a surprised occupant.

Our last day on the OZ bus we rolled through the Hunter Valley with its horse breeders, coalfields and excellent vineyards. We followed the old convict road from Wollombi, with its preserved stone bridges and culverts built by penal colonists from 1826-1834. We rejoined the Pacific Highway at Hawkesbury River, through Ku-Ring-Gai Chase National Park to North Sydney and across the famous Sydney Harbour Bridge with the panorama of the bay anchored by the sails of the Sydney Opera House below.

Except when we were hunting for Cassowaries, we had never needed our brollies despite it being the rainy season in Queensland. The sun had blessed us all the way. What a country!

Diane Jones

House using bomb casings as stilts

Extraordinary Travels of an Ordinary Housewife

LAO

BACKPACKING
January 2001

The orchid corsage, presented by our Thai Airways hostess as we came in to land, seemed somewhat out of place on our well worn backpacker garb. Vientiane, the capital of Lao (you only call it Laos if you are French), sits on the eastern bank of the great Mekong River across from Thailand and north of Cambodia, and our plan was to spend a week exploring the country on our own. We were further spoiled by being unexpectedly met by a car from our hotel, The Asian Pavilion in the centre of town, where we were greeted like royalty. Was there some mistake?

However, we soon came down to earth and suffered immediate culture shock when we set off to find a bank and found that the sidewalks were riddled with bottomless potholes with open sewers of grey smelly water running alongside. To cross the street meant having to dodge heavy traffic, mainly mopeds, motorbikes and tuk tuks. Generally these created a great stour of dust to stick to your sweaty body, as the air was heavy and humid.

Fortunately the bank was air-conditioned so that we didn't get too flustered in trying to calculate exactly how many Lao Kip we had received for our US$200 traveller's cheque. They pushed a brick-sized wad of notes across the counter and assured us it was 1,628,000 Kip. They must supply wheelbarrows for customers with larger demands!

We tried the Lao buffet lunch at our hotel and found that, although all the dishes were cold, they set our palate on fire so much that even copious Lao beers could not help. Surprising, as we would consider ourselves fans of spicy-hot. From that meal on it was a challenge to find a meal that we could enjoy and tolerate. We ate many a mystery dish in the process. Vegetable spring rolls, fried vegetables and noodles and - forgive us - a plate of french fries became our staples for the week.

Diane Jones

We easily covered the sights of Vientiane in one full day of traipsing from one Wat (Buddhist temple) to another, nine of which had their own particular point of interest, but it wasn't too long before we couldn't see the point. One Buddha looks very much like the next. Then there was the Presidential Palace to squint at and a tuk tuk six km across the city to the World Precious Great Sacred Stupa – Pha That Luang - a must-see highlight of Vientiane. Apparently one of Buddha's breastbones was buried here in the third century. Frankly not worth the cost of the tuk tuk, but the orange-robed monks in all these Wats did lend some colourful human interest. Most of the monks are teenage boys serving only a few years to gain merit for their family and continue their education, particularly in languages, for their future benefit. They are often very happy to engage you in conversation, but they must not be nearer than one metre from a woman, nor touch anything a woman has just touched. This form of Theravada Buddhism is prevalent in Lao.

On day three we flew north with Lao Aviation to the old capital Luang Prabang. The plane was delayed for hydraulic reasons as explained to the few falangs (foreign tourists) like us looking anxiously at the old heap of a turbo prop sitting outside with its nose cone on the tarmac. However it eventually got us there safely, being only a forty-five minute flight and about 200 kms. The road infrastructure of Lao really doesn't make overland travel an option. A leaky ferryboat on the Mekong for several days did not appeal either, after we spoke to some young backpackers who had sampled river travel.

Luang Prabang is a World Heritage Site. It sits at the junction of the Mekong and Khan Rivers that create a small peninsula that contains most of the thirty-two remaining temples out of an original total of sixty-six. It is capped with a little hilltop stupa, Phu Si, from where you get wonderful sunset views over the old city when it is not covered in smog, as it often is. Most mornings and evenings, the air was what must be described as pea soupy.

It takes a couple of days of studious Wat watching to get round the most important temples and also there is the Royal Palace (now a museum) to visit. The last King and Queen were dispatched to a northern cave in 1975 where they expired in 1992. To get into the political history of Lao would take pages and pages; suffice to say that 1975 was the start of its first peaceful era in centuries and it is struggling to make up for many wasted years. Currently it is basically a nationalistic pro-communist pro-capitalist regime. Got that? Me neither!

We bargained for a day trip by private taxi-boat the twenty-five km upriver to the Pak Ou caves, set into a sheer cliff face on a bend of the Mekong. These were full of Buddha images of course, but much more interesting were the stop-offs at three of the river villages en route. The first was known for its distillation of rice wine, lao-lo or lao whisky. The second for its skilled weavers who were anxious that the falangs get their wallets out. However the third village was the best. It was the home village of our boatman and was in the process of preparing for a big festival feast later that day. Our boatman was warmly welcomed as were his two passengers and we watched with interest the entire involvement of the villagers, the women preparing food for the feast and the men decorating garish floats around the temple. One float was crowned with an open black business umbrella with banknotes hanging from the spokes all around. The village houses were raised above ground level and, though thatched with palm leaves, the walls were mainly planked wood. Only one bare room in each home, with all worldly goods stored around the walls. These are river people who are as comfortable in a simple shallow canoe on the fast flowing Mekong as we are on wheels. The trip up the Mekong River took two and a half hours, but only one hour to return to Luang Prabang.

By our third day we were running out of tourist attractions but did enjoy the big local Sunday market near our hotel, and noted packets of biscuits in the shape of life-size revolvers! It was also a pleasure to sit in an open-air café on the main street with a Lao beer and enjoy the unfolding scenes of locals going about their daily business. Tourists were browsing the many craft stalls and Buddhist monks walked purposefully past whilst protecting their shaved heads with black umbrellas. Sun protection whilst proselytizing must have reached Buddha.

Just a half-hour flight in an eighteen-seater, elastic-band-propelled plane found us deposited at a shack called the Phonsavan Airport terminal in Xiengkhouang Province. We had flown southeast through sharp-edged mountain peaks to a large central plain. Obvious from the air were the bomb craters that pock-marked the landscape, this being one of the most heavily bombed areas of the Vietnam War in an effort by the U.S. to destroy communist supply lines.

The capital of the province, Xiengkhouang, was completely destroyed and Phonsavan has become the main centre. However, one look at the town as we came in to land (a dusty rubble-strewn, sprawling place) was enough to have us change our tickets to the first flight out the next day. We had really only come here to visit the Plain of Jars, curious ancient urns, some six feet in height, carved from solid blocks of stone and strewn over several areas of the surrounding countryside. There are hundreds of them, and how and why such heavy pieces of solid rock, beautifully shaped and hollowed (some even with lids to fit the lipped rims) came to be placed over many square miles is still a mystery, as is their purpose. They are thought to be several thousand years old. Obviously they had been used as natural shelters during the war, as the various sites were splattered with bomb craters, and many of the jars had been shattered during these years. Walking amongst the rice paddies and grazing water buffalo to reach these sites was more interesting than the jars themselves. However there were many warnings about not straying off the path as the countryside is still littered with unexploded ordnance.

The farmers live simply and are perhaps amongst Lao's poorest. We visited a Hmong village nearby and were dismayed to see the squalid conditions and litter-strewn compounds with very rickety dwellings under which the black pigs and chickens scratched for a morsel. At least the Hmong had had initiative enough to use empty bomb casings as supports for their houses and a halved one made a fine pig's trough.

Our hotel proved to be of the minus five star category and we were glad to cover the dubious sheets with our own sleeping bags. The bathroom meant an involuntary paddle and cold water only. However it was close enough to walk to the centre of town to enjoy dinner at Phonsavan's best restaurant, a very shabby noodle shop. The town only had electricity from six till nine each evening. That is if there isn't one of the many blackouts. We found our plate plunged into darkness twice during the meal and were glad that we remembered our flashlight to help us stumble down the uneven dirt road back to our hotel. It was with a sigh of relief that our plane actually arrived to fly us back to Vientiane without mishap the next morning.

The general view of our visit was of a struggling, impoverished, war-ravaged country desperately trying to catch up with its Asian neighbours. However, the people were charming and helpful and anxious to welcome tourists whom they have been educated to understand will help their economy. You did not feel hassled, nor ripped off, except by that Vientiane Bank that had peeled 10,000 Kip off that brick of banknotes! That's all of US$1.25 - the price of two plates of french fries!

Extraordinary Travels of an Ordinary Housewife

Ngo Dong River near the Tam Coc caves

Coracle transport near Nha Trang

Extraordinary Travels of an Ordinary Housewife

VIETNAM

BACKPACKING - HIRED CAR & GUIDE
January-February 2001

What a treat for two weary backpackers to slump into the soft backseat of their own air-conditioned limo. Everyone in Hanoi, Vietnam's capital, must have a motorbike or pedal-bike, for the streets were a nightmare of traffic going in all directions. Smog masks were de rigueur and very necessary because of the heavy vehicle pollution that blankets the city. Even trying to walk along the sidewalks was impossible, as they were cluttered with parked bikes and impromptu noodle vendors, and our first afternoon spent trying to cross the road to reach the bank was enough to persuade us to go first class.

Recommended by our Lonely Planet guidebook, we dropped into Ann Tours who were very happy to put together a twenty-eight-day all-inclusive tour in our own chauffeur driven car, plus our own personal guide to ease the way and fill us in on everything one could possibly want to know about Vietnam. It turned out to be a bargain at $50 each per day including flights. We had landed in Vietnam just before the Chinese New Year (Tet) which meant the closing down of just about everything for at least a week. Better to make that into Ann Tours' problem to figure out how to find us lodging, food and entertainment over this period.

Our driver was an expert at squeezing between all those bikes, most now carrying on their pillion a potted peach blossom tree or one loaded with tiny oranges, the Tet equivalent of a Christmas tree. One day pretty well covered the highlights and museums of Hanoi starting with the required visit to pay respects to the embalmed body of a very dead Ho Chi Minh (d.1969). He is considered the saviour of Vietnam and much revered. The more I learned about him the more I liked him. A very worldly-wise old geyser not unlike India's Mahatma Gandhi. Uncle Ho, they still affectionately call him. He never married and had no children.

We took several day trips out of Hanoi, first to Hoa Lu, the old capital up till the 12th century. Its nondescript ruins are only worth the visit because they

Diane Jones

are near to the Ngo Dong River where a woman, rowing a bamboo skiff, took the pair of us through a magical world of limestone beehive domes towering above the river which meandered between flooded rice paddies. The women, in their ubiquitous coolie hats, were up to their armpits planting rice seedlings. The river's course we followed actually flowed through some of these limestone outcrops, creating the three Tam Coc Caves, one 300 ft in length from daylight to daylight.

Two days were required to visit Halong Bay in the Gulf of Tonkin, east of Hanoi. The roads were dreadful, full of traffic and travel was slow. However the endless rice paddies and villages that stretched themselves out along the roadside were a constant visual delight and one had to marvel at how a motorbike could carry such unwieldy loads. For instance, on different occasions, we spied four pillion passengers, three big pigs in elongated baskets, a coffin, a dressing table with mirror, pannier baskets of live ducks and chickens, and heavy loads of market produce. Strapped to one pillion were tables, stools, charcoal brazier and pots of food, all that was required to set up an instant roadside cafe. Helmets, of any kind, were few and far between.

UNESCO has declared Halong Bay to be a World Heritage Site. It's a place I've often dreamed of visiting. A limestone mountain chain tumbles into the sea and creates over 3,000 steep-sided peaked islands covering 1,500 sq km of ocean. Our own private tour boat took us to visit several stunning caves and our camera shutter worked overtime as the boat slipped in and out amongst these dramatic out-crops. It's a truly special place and one I have enjoyed returning to on cruise ships in later years.

A visit to the famous Perfume Pagoda, south of Hanoi, might have been a tour worth reconsidering. To view the piece de resistance, a pagoda within a cave at the top of a mountain, we first had to take a rowboat along a lazy river, again lined with rice planters up to the thighs in mud. From a landing stage it was a stagger two and a half kilometres up a steep cobbled holy path to reach the temple and, apparently, "Nirvana". It was hot, humid and no sign of Nirvana. It was time to head for the hills!

Four hundred kilometres and a ten-hour drive took us to Sapa, a hilltop town near the northern Chinese border crossing of Lao Cai. Sapa sits in the shadow of Fransipan (3,143 m), Vietnam's highest mountain. Usually the town is enveloped in cloud but, when we arrived, a gale was blowing (most of it through our hotel bedroom) and the weather was surprisingly sunny and warm for our two-day visit. With the wind at our back we walked through terraced valleys to visit local ethnic tribes. We covered fifteen km on foot the first day, out-striding our guide who had to thumb a lift on a motorbike back to Sapa. Celebrations for Tet were in full force, which meant everyone was dressed in their ethnic best and was in a hospitable mood. We were invited to share in green tea and rice wine hooch with the Flower Hmong, who wear brightly coloured pleated skirts and shirts, and we were honoured with the presentation of a large slab of sticky rice, bean curd and minced pork. To organize some gift wrapping, an elderly lady whipped her checkered wool headscarf from her matted locks. What a thoughtful gesture! The Black Hmong at another village were, not surprisingly, dressed all in black with the women sporting snazzy pillbox hats. Subtle and intricate embroidery ameliorated the gothic look. If they didn't have black teeth from betel nut use, they displayed glamorous gold capped teeth. Again, after being served tea in little cups, which had probably never seen a washing-up bowl, we were honoured with a stack of pork fat patties, this time gift-wrapped in an embroidered drawstring bag. Of course, for these gifts we felt obliged to leave an unobtrusive "donation" towards their houskeeping budget. We kept these gourmet gifts in the back of the car until we could dump them far away from Sapa, but I still have the pretty drawstring shoe bag The houses of these villages were mostly of woven bamboo slat walls, thatched roofs and mud-packed floors. No chimneys for the indoor cooking fires, so interior decor was considerably smoke distressed. Partitions gave some privacy to family members, but there was next to no furniture save some small low tables and six-inch high stools to squat upon. Raw pork hung over the fire to be slowly smoked, perhaps beef also as they seemed to manage herds of very healthy cattle in addition to pigs, chickens and ducks.

We also paid a visit to the Red Dao (Zao) fifteen km from Sapa. I suspect that our arrival in a posh car brought out the materialistic yearnings of the villagers and they were not impressed with our gift of a big box of Tet Green Bean Candies. We managed to snap a few pictures of their red turbans and embroidered dresses before fleeing back to the car and heading for another ethnic village of the Cay (Zai). Here the women wore black bell-bottoms and jewel coloured cheongsam blouses. One of the ubiquitous tartan checkered headscarfs, worn like a flattened turban, topped it all off. The men were in simple dark Chinese style tunics. We hit the jackpot by being invited into the hut of a well educated, recently married young man and noticed how clean and well organized it all was. His new wife was obviously still playing house. His old father joined us for tea and beer and finally shots of throat searing rice wine but nothing to eat as it was explained that the dubious looking snacks arranged on the kitchen table were gifts for the ancestors. That was a relief!

The hotel staff very kindly insisted we join them to celebrate the arrival of the "Year Of the Snake" at midnight on the 24th of January, as we were the only hotel guests. They phoned our room at 11.45 to wake us up in time for the television countdown. An earthenware pot of hooch was put on a central table and rattan curved straws issued to the ten of us with instructions to get sucking. The Karaoke machine was brought out and we managed to give our best to the party till two in the morning, just before the local police arrived for their "protection" drinks. At breakfast time we were honoured guests at the Tet first meal of the New Year. A solid square of rice, pork and beancurd cake, spicy noodle soup, bony boiled chicken, and other very unappetizing dishes. Mind you, for two nights the alternative hotel meal had been boiled rice and cabbage. We had endured some very disappointing meals in Hanoi (always careful to check dog was not on the menu) and were now beginning to wonder where we could find some enjoyable Vietnamese fare.

Certainly not on the plane that took us from Hanoi to Hue, halfway down Vietnam's 1,700 km length. Air "fare" was a stale bun, filled with a slab of grey pate, garnished with what looked like a piece of frayed string. Pork products, we believe!

The Citadel in Hue, another UNESCO World Heritage Site, with its moat and three separate encircling walls, was the centre of the Nguyen (Huwen) Dynasty from 1804-1945. The Emperor, his wife, mother and harem of concubines isolated themselves within the central core, called The Forbidden Purple City. It was from here that Bao Dai, the 13th Emperor, abdicated to Ho Chi Minh in 1945 and skedaddled off to France for a cushy life till he died in 1991. The Citadel has been much restored after being heavily bombed by the U.S., and walking around the two and a half kilometres of its six metre walls was quite a workout.

We now followed the coast road south, over the Hai Van Pass to Danang, an ugly port city but host to the Cham Museum where we were introduced to this Hindu influenced culture of the south. Later we visited Myson, the ancient holy city dating from the 2nd-13th centuries. (Another UNESCO World Heritage Site). Its Cham Towers of religious temples are Vietnam's answer to Cambodia's Angkor Wat but, once again, U.S. bombs have reduced several towers to rubble. What is left of the red brick structures, with intricately carved pink roofs and statuary, give insight into this important culture of ancient Vietnam.

U.S. bomb damage was also very evident at the Marble Mountains (five rocky, cave riddled outcrops) where hilltop caves are now flooded with natural light from the bomb holes in the roof. They were a Viet Cong hideout and strategic spot. Nearby, famous China Beach, the Americans' R & R base, reminds you again of their presence from 1965 to 1973. It is now a tawdry littered beach, but you can imagine the old loudspeakers on the changing room walls booming "Good Morning Vietnam" across the sand.

We based ourselves for two days at Hoi An, our fourth and final UNESCO World Heritage Site. The old town has narrow streets lined with tiny terraced houses influenced by French, Chinese and Japanese settlements over the past two centuries. As the old town is flooded each rainy season, there was some charm in the houses' green tide-marked walls and tiled roofs overgrown with damp moss. It has a bustling fish market, as it sits on an island-strewn delta five km from the ocean and is also the centre of Vietnam's silk industry. A charming place to wander around for a couple of days, with excellent restaurants where we were able to enjoy some local dishes, whatever they were! We declined a drink from a large glass jar full of dead snakes. I suppose it was Vietnam's version of "Kiss the Cod."

Highway #1, as we headed south along the coast, was a potholed slow ride but not without charm. If you do not have a vista to the horizon of rice paddies, dotted with conical straw hats and water buffalo ploughs, then you find the highway lined with simple dwellings. The homes open onto the road, which serves as their front yard, and they use the hard shoulder to dry their rice, shrimp, cassava slices, coffee beans etc. There must be a few tire marks across their harvest by the time the sun goes down. Our guide would frequently order the car to stop so that we could jump out for an impromptu visit to one of the cottage industries, be it rice paper making (for spring rolls etc), fish sauce fermentation, joss stick production, tea, coffee and sugar processing or maybe rattan furniture and basket weaving.

We stopped at the Mai Lai Massacre Memorial Peace Park for a gruesome reminder of the barbaric behaviour of a few U.S. soldiers. It was Americans of conscience who have chosen to build the Memorial and fund a local hospital to try to heal the psychological wounds of war and not allow such atrocities to be forgotten.

Qui Nhon boasts of being a beautiful beach resort, but our hotel room balcony looked down on a narrow brown sand beach crossed by excavated ditches in which they were laying large sewage pipes. No doubt this is all in anticipation of resort venture capital scrambling to invest in this rather dismal town, whose image is not enhanced by the large leper village at its southern end.

At least Dai Lanh and Doc Let, a little further south, had white sand beaches where we were encouraged to take a swim. Surely they were joking. This part of the coastline, north of Nha Trang, is Vietnam's pride and joy and they must be surprised that Club Med has not yet moved in. However, no doubt Club Med, like us, has been turned off by the amount of garbage, not just on the beaches, but continually washing up with the surf. Swimming through jellyfish is one thing but plastic bags and kitchen waste is another.

We kept our swimming for the Mun Islands off Nha Trang. Our private charter boat took us first to a new aquarium built of cement in the form of a huge sailing ship. This introduced us to the many tropical fish we were about to see when we snorkeled on the coral reefs that surround Ebony Island, an uninhabited and delightful spot to anchor off for most of a day. Unfortunately the water was a little chilly and climbing a rickety ladder back onto the boat, wearing flippers, was a complicated procedure. However, I spent as much time in the water as my goose bumps would allow, as the coral and size of the fish were remarkably good for a spot that is popular with daily tour boats.

At the end of our eight-hour cruise we stopped at a little old-fashioned fishing village on Mie Island just off Nha Trang harbour. It is so old-fashioned that you are ferried ashore in a coracle, a circular woven and tarred bamboo basket with a paddle. The very same were used in Britain in the dark ages! Your balance has already been tested by the time you have to disembark onto floating walkways that encircle submerged net tanks of live cuttle fish and other marine life. This way the villagers can store their catch live until the market price is right. Cuttle fish the size of rugby balls with highly patterned backs were a sight not often seen.

Compulsory stops at 13th century Po Nagar (Nha Trang) and Po Klong Garai, both Cham Towers further south, reminded us that we may well suffer cranial overload if we have to absorb much more of Vietnam's religious and cultural heritage. However these towers were in good condition, having been spared military action, and as the Cham culture worshiped the Linga and Uni (male and female stylized genitalia) you could at least find some interest in comparative altar studies.

After Po Klong Garai we left the coast just north of Phan Rang and headed for the hills. The Ngoan Mue Pass takes you over the first 980 m and you continue to climb to 1,400 m before you reach the French hill station of Dalat on a high plateau. Coffee and tea plantations and cut-flower market gardens support the communities. Dalat itself nestles in a valley and still exudes much continental charm in both its French style mansions as well as its good restaurants, for which we were truly grateful. We spent a recovery day wandering round the botanical flower gardens and incredible orchid house before touring the Emperor's Art Deco Summer Palace built in 1933. The palace is in sharp contrast to The Crazy House which is a fantasy themed guesthouse, designed by a well known architect who should perhaps have been, or seen, a psychiatrist. It is like a giant strangler fig tree full of narrow stairs that twist and wind to exotic little bedrooms. The mirrors above the beds were interesting but the cement furniture and damp smell very unappealing. To match Crazy House there is also a Pagoda with a Crazy Monk who lives alone and paints pictures at the rate of about one every five minutes. If he likes the bulge of your wallet when he peeps through his gate, he will let you in and then hold court from a reclining chair whilst encouraging you to buy one of his awful scribbles. We gave in for the sake of our guide's commission prospects and were lucky to get out with some scribbled Chinese characters with, apparently, some hidden meaning! He certainly adds colour to Dalat which, we found, was a vibrant and well heeled resort town, known as "The City of Eternal Spring".

It was downhill all the way to Saigon where we spent a day north of the city exploring the famous Cu Chi tunnels, the 250 km of underground routes of the Viet Cong. Started during the war with the French in the 1950s, they were extended throughout the U.S. war and even ran underneath some U.S. bases. They proved a dreadful nightmare for the G.Is. The booby traps, hidden trap doors, underwater entrances to bunkers, field kitchens and dormitories were ingenious, all manufactured with what the VC could steal from the U.S. bases and what they could find in the local villages and fields. In fact, from early in the war, Viet Cong bases surrounded Saigon. Even the head cadres had an underground secret base at Xeo Quit, which we visited during our trip to the Mekong Delta. Here they actually grew, in five years, a 100 acre patch of melaleuca forest in a swamp to disguise their permanent camp, most of it in waterproofed underground bunkers. Called the Rung Tram Forest, it was the only bit of wild woodland we got to visit and we were just as fascinated by the birds, butterflies and flower-covered swamp vegetation as we were by the clever fortifications. One has to remember, many of the forests in Vietnam were destroyed in the war with the dreadful herbicide, Agent Orange.

The canals of the Mekong River Delta are lined with houses, most on high stilts, and there was much human activity to observe. These people are amongst Vietnam's poorest and life is a continuous uphill struggle. Fish is a daily staple and lots of simple shallow boats and ingenious fishing methods allow them to use the canals as an extension of their homes. In fact, boat trips in several areas of the Mekong over four days were the most interesting part of our visit. We spent a night at a beautiful restored hotel on the river at Chau Doc on the Cambodian Border. French windows, opening onto our balcony, offered an ever changing vista of river life. It was a hotchpotch of boats, barges, overcrowded ferries and islands of floating vegetation, all travelling on the fast current of the mighty Mekong. Cantho, further to the south, had a wonderful floating wholesale market where all the tiny shallow boats of the local farmers, top heavy with fresh produce, met with the bigger merchant boats. These would in turn sell to land markets or even ship to cities like Saigon. Little noodle shop boats hustled in between and, as we were in our own small private tour boat, we too could bustle in amongst them all. Afterwards we cruised through palm fringed narrow canals amongst orchard farms full of tropical fruits.

Diane Jones

Near Chau Doc we rose at dawn and climbed sacred Sam Mountain. A party of wealthy Vietnamese from Saigon were going through many religious and expensive gestures at the little shrine on the summit. After much joss stick waving and offerings of barbecued sucking pigs, beer and US dollar bills (fake?) they lit a big bonfire. On this they burned ceremonial paper clothing plus their wish lists written by an old female "scribe" who pocketed large bills for her calligraphy. A cage full of birds were released one by one and finally rice and paper flowers were thrown all over the place. More litter! As usual there were several tombs, pagodas and temples to visit on Sam Mountain. All were full of superstitious Vietnamese making bigger and better offerings than their frugal lifestyle could afford. However, all goes towards merit points in the next life and, if we had to live the way they do in the Mekong Delta, we too would surely hope for promotion next time round.

Quite a number of Catholics are to be found in the south, a hangover of the French influence. However there is another modern religion found in this area. Ngo Minh (Van) Chieu founded Caodaism in 1926. It now has as many as 30,000 followers and its headquarters, The Caodai Holy See, is in Tay Ninh Province, north of Saigon and near the Cambodian border. We were lucky to attend their huge cathedral on a special festival day. It resembled a colourful Klu Klux Klan meeting. We were able to observe, from a high balcony, the priests in yellow, blue or red gowns with very imaginative hats, nuns in long white habits with muslin draped helmets, and white-robed male and female worshippers. Caodism is an attempt to create the perfect religion using both secular and religious philosophies and incorporates a mix of Buddhist, Catholic, Tao, Confucianism, Spiritualism and Islam. Sun Yat-Sen and Victor Hugo as well as the Vietnamese poet Nguyen Binh Kheim apparently gave their suggestions from the afterlife. I don't know who the divine architect was, but he pulled out all the stops in birthday cake colours, dragon wrapped columns, a ceiling full of astrological meaning and topped the fancy altar off with a big eye looking out from a great orb. Plenty of highly-coloured statues representative of all the above religions (Jesus looking a bit embarrassed at being amongst the more garish) adorned the proscenium. The cathedral had twin towers at the front of the building for Catholics, a dome in the centre for Islam and a pagoda roof and tower at the back for the Orient. All quite fascinating but you had to wonder if this is Oriental Evangelism at work on simple minds. Certainly much money has had to go into the pot to produce all this pomp.

Our final two days in Vietnam were spent touring the important pagodas, museums and markets of Saigon, now known officially as Ho Chi Minh City or HCMC for short. The War Remnants Museum, with its grisly photos of the French and U. S. war atrocities, was surprisingly the most popular with tourists. Also interesting was a tour of the Revolutionary Palace, built in 1966 as the Palace of Independence until 30 April 1975 when a North Vietnamese tank rolled through the front gates. On that date Vietnam became one unified country, with its capital in Hanoi. Touring the markets with our guide was always fun, as he was able to identify in English all the mysterious fruits, vegetables and dry goods offered for sale. We found a market for secondhand military clothing, medals etc, but most fascinating of all was Binh Tay Market in Chinatown with its Chinese medicine shops. Dried worms, horse penises, feathered coucals soaked in jars and, of course, that popular snake wine with sometimes several different snakes in one bottle. We also sat down at some local restaurants for lunch and let our guide select something for us. Not always a great idea but at least he confirmed if it was safe for foreigners' consumption. The funny thing is that the tables and chairs in these restaurants were nursery size, possibly allowing the proprietor to pack more into his noodle shop and even more onto his patio, which meant the dirty public sidewalk. However it was not an elegant squat, and guaranteed laundry problems when presented with no alternative cutlery but chopsticks.

My impressions? I think that if Buddhist demerit points were handed out for littering, Vietnam's natural beauty would soon be rid of this eyesore. Apart from discomforting pestering by opportunistic souvenir sellers at the tourist sites, we really appreciated the warmth and gentleness of the Vietnamese people who, despite having lived through tumultuous times, were hauling themselves up by their bootstraps to make their mark on the 21st century. They have continued to be one of the world's biggest exporters of rice. and I shall always think of Vietnam as one vast shimmering rice paddy dotted with industrious conical hats.

Mekong River Travel

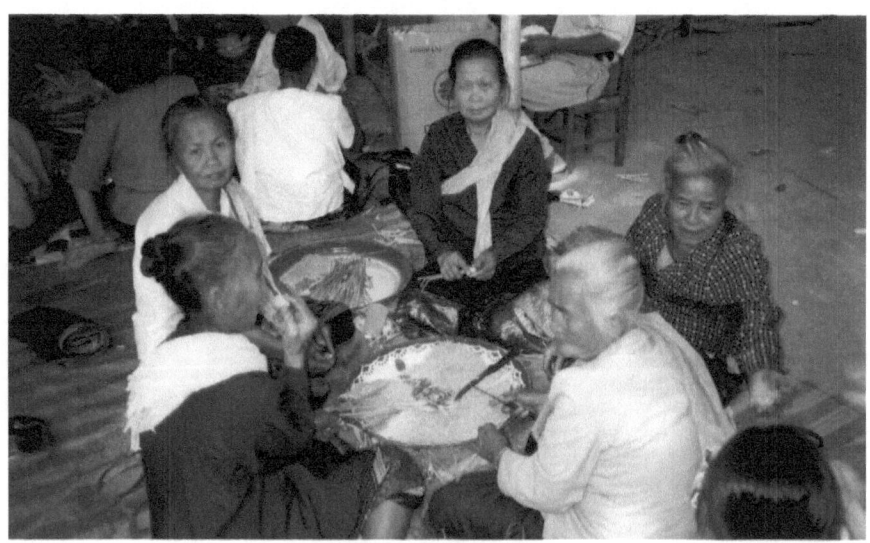

Luncheon companions

Extraordinary Travels of an Ordinary Housewife

CAMBODIA (KAMPUCHEA)

BACKPACKING - HIRED CAR & GUIDE
February 2001

On arrival in Phnom Penh we immediately noticed battle-scarred buildings and potholed roads. Between 1975 and 1979 Pol Pot's Khmer Rouge were responsible for the disappearance of three million of the country's seven million population at that time. We had been told that we would find very few middle-aged people in Cambodia and most of those we met were indeed young.

It was a city full of contrasts. Some of the buildings from French Indochina times had been beautifully restored and painted and the Royal Palace, once again inhabited by King Norodom Sihanouk, was a delightful compound of Thai influenced buildings set in manicured gardens and surrounded by high walls. Similar to the Grand Palace in Bangkok, and likewise home to an Emerald Buddha (in this case jade), its highlight is the Silver Pagoda so called for the 5,329 solid silver tiles that cover the floor. The Royal Residence is behind closed gates, but the public can visit the Throne Room, Banqueting Hall, Treasury, Elephant stables and Napoleon III Pavilion (a gift from the same).

However, poor roads, crumbling public buildings, and impoverished dwellings were more the norm in the capital, but the people seemed to have sunny dispositions towards the tourist and were very anxious to please. Beggars were ever present and there were many amputees amongst them, the result of the minefields that riddled the countryside.

Straight from the beauty of the Royal Palace we went to visit the Killing Fields of Choeung, fifteen km south of the city. Here the Khmer Rouge exterminated at least 17,000 Cambodians and buried them in mass graves. 9,000 have been exhumed from 86 of the 129 graves and their skulls (men, women, children and babies) displayed in a tall glass tower memorial. Many of them came here from Tuol Sleng S21 Prison in Phnom Penh, now called the Genocide Museum. This gives detailed graphic accounts of the incarceration and torture of the

Diane Jones

country's intelligentsia, religious right and anyone whom Pol Pot felt was a threat to his regime. It was Cambodia's holocaust and most every Khmer living today was touched by these horrors in some way or another. We found, not surprisingly, that those Khmers we spoke with avoided a discussion on the painful subject of Pol Pot's genocide.

We hired a car and driver/guide as it proved a cool and inexpensive way to travel around the capital and enjoyed the same for our visit to Angkor Wat. This meant it only required a day and a half to cover most of the items of tourist interest, and we enjoyed a little bit of the old colonial lifestyle still to be found on the upper verandah of the Foreign Correspondents' Club. This overlooks the confluence of the Mekong and Tonle Sap Rivers and we were happy to slump into big leather armchairs in the airy restaurant bar with European food, good coffee and most of the other tourists in town.

On our third day we caught the express boat for the five-hour trip up the Tonle Sap River and across the great Tonle Sap Lake to Siem Reap. This was a floating coffin if ever I've seen one. One hundred filled seats in a narrow enclosed speedboat with only one exit at the very front and made top-heavy with the luggage piled high on the roof. The alternative was a regular ferry that takes twenty-four hours, so we chose the five-hour coffin and took our chances. We were right at the back with twenty-four rows of seats between us and the only exit. The boat was absolutely loaded to the max. Some other tourists were so white-knuckled that they chose to scorch themselves by joining the luggage on the roof under a blistering sun. However we made it, and the most dangerous moment was trying to disembark, from the prow of the boat, down a forty-five-degree narrow wooden plank clutching our luggage. One fellow did take the plunge when he missed his footing, but managed to keep his suitcase above water.

Siem Reap is the northern city that supports the huge tourist trade that comes to Cambodia to see Angkor Wat or, to be exact, the ancient 10-13th century Khmer capital city of Angkor. Angkor Wat is the main temple and the most impressive of the 100 or more religious buildings that have been discovered in the jungles north of Tonle Sap Lake. A vast Khmer Empire existed at this time and stretched from South Vietnam to Yunnan in China and from West Vietnam to the Bay of Bengal. It was influenced by Hinduism and the Gods Shiva and Vishnu. However Buddhism took over at the end of the 13th century.

Thousands lived within the walls of these great cities of Angkor. Angkor Thom covers ten sq km and each side of its square wall is three km long. All dwellings and structures, apart from religious ones, were built of wood and have long since rotted away and returned to the jungle. Jayavarman VII, who ruled from 1181-1201, was responsible for many of the temples, especially the fifty-four towers of the Bayon Temple in the very centre of Angkor Thom. The towers represented the fifty-four provinces of the Khmer Empire at that time and, to leave his mark on the place, he had his divine face carved on the four sides of many of them. He even had his face look down from the five city entry gates on everyone who passed within. The temples are guarded by nagas and dragons and the walls covered with detailed bas reliefs of Hindu Legends and beautiful individually detailed dancing girls, Apsaras, are carved into the walls everywhere. The ceremonial reviewing platform, the Terrace of Elephants, has its façade covered with a parade of marching elephants.

Thirty-eight km along a dusty rural road is Angkor's gem, Banteay Srei or The Citadel of Women. Built of pink sandstone by a high ranking Brahman in the 10th century, it is full of intricate three-dimensional floral carvings and finely sculpted Apsaras and Vishnu characters. Monkeys and Garudas guard the doors.

However, by far the most popular temple is Angkor Wat which is encircled by a 200 m wide moat stretching 5.5 km around. Approached by a causeway across the moat to the central gate of the Western wall, you then pass through to walk a further 350 m towards the five-towered temple along a raised and balustraded promenade. On either side are lawns, libraries, and ponds. The first walled level of the temple has fine bas reliefs along its four 800 m cloisters. The most famous is known as The Churning of the Ocean's Milk, interpreted as a Tug of War between gods and devils. The second and third levels enclose a square with interlinked galleries and the central tower rises fifty-five m above ground. A very steep climb up some leg stretching narrow steps leads you to the holy of holies, now a Buddhist shrine but originally a funeral pyre dedicated to Vishnu. To get back down you hang onto a cable and try not to step on the head of a nervous nelly tourist on their way up.

We visited almost twenty temples and important sites and have to say that two and a half days spent at Angkor's World Heritage Site were almost too much. We certainly suffered temple overload and by the afternoon the temperatures were in the mid 30s. We were wise to hire a car and driver and would take off at 7.30 in the morning when temperatures were cooler, visit some temples, and return to our hotel in Siem Reap for a couple of hours at lunchtime. The temples stand in "tamed" jungle" and driving around the temple circuit in an air-conditioned car was a great pleasure, even spotting monkeys and parrots, in what has technically become a well managed parkland.

It is the vast area of the site, hidden in the jungle, that makes Angkor impressive. It is the largest religious complex in the world but the original stonework seemed to be in poorer condition than other famous structures from the same period. Probably the occupation of several of the sites during the

Khmer Rouge guerrilla campaign has also taken a toll. We climbed the Phnom Bakheng hill to watch the sun set on Angkor Wat. It is the only temple with towers high enough to rise above the trees that makes it rather special and it was a memorable view for our last evening in Cambodia.

The archaeologists will continue to rescue the temples from the giant banyan and fig trees that have woven themselves into the ruins over the centuries and hopefully the rising tide of tourism will bring much needed help to the country's economy and cultural heritage. However, a recent visit on a cruise ship to the port of Sinanhoukville showed heavy financial investment by China which, unfortunately, may not be in the best interests of these gentle people.

Everest Sherpas

In the distance, Everest (8,848 m) and Lhotse (8,516 m)
On their right, two peaks of Ama Dablam (6,856 m)

NEPAL

PEREGRINE TRAVEL
November 2003

Nepal is not a particularly large country, being only 800 km east to west and between 90 and 230 km north to south. On its northern boundary with Tibet it soars to almost nine kilometres above sea level and is home to many of the world's highest peaks. The most famous of these Himalayan mountains is the world's highest at 8,848 metres, Mount Everest, also known in Nepalese as Sagarmatha and by the local ethnic group, the Sherpas, as Chomolungma. Our secret ambition was to be able to climb high enough into the Himalayas that we would be close enough to actually see Everest itself. This is no mean feat, as it requires mountain goat tactics to hike over rough dusty trails and up steep gorges for at least three days before you can catch a first glimpse, provided it is not covered in cloud. To this should be added the discomforts of freezing cold nights, no running water and the threat of altitude sickness. The closest starting point is to fly (no road transport) into Lukla, 240 km northeast of Kathmandu. On reflection this was one tough trip. By comparison our first week in the Annapurna region of Nepal, 250 km west of Kathmandu, was a cakewalk.

About half a million of Nepal's population of twenty-two million live in the sprawling capital, Kathmandu. It sits in a broad central valley at 1,360 m and is one of those impoverished, polluted, construction-challenged cities. No high-rises, just dusty pot-holed streets lined with houses either half-built or half-demolished. Difficult to know which. Being both a Hindu and Buddhist country, cows and monkeys are allowed to wander at will without fear of harm. In fact, I had to laugh as we watched a cow and its calf wander down a narrow city lane, reach up and snatch a corn broom from a hardware shop's display. They only managed a few mouthfuls before the owner persuaded them to return his merchandise. Big bright-bottomed monkeys are happy to hold up the choking traffic whilst they check the street litter for food scraps. Nobody chases them away. Cows sleeping in the traffic lanes of a busy highway are just another reason why vehicle travel is frustratingly slow. All that, plus many police and military checkpoints, made a 200 km journey to Pokhara, Nepal's second city, a nine-hour waste of a day. However, we had to travel there and beyond by chartered bus to trek into the Annapurnas after we had explored the capital.

Nepal in 2003 was still a Constitutional Monarchy (or rather a Monarchical Dictatorship) which meant that palaces were pretty important. Kathmandu is really made up of three old kingdoms, Kathmandu, Patan, and Bhaktapur, and there are three Durbar (Old Palace) Squares that must be visited. Durbar Square, in Old Kathmandu, has amongst its many temples and palaces the Kumari Ghar which is the home of The Living Goddess. Any female five-year-old can apply for the position provided she can prove to be the reincarnation of the Goddess Taleju and provided the position has become vacant due to the previous Kumari having spilled a drop of blood. She can sometimes be spotted at an upstairs window mouthing, "Let me outta here, I want to play with the other kids!" Also in the square is the shrine of Kaal Bhairav, a big black scary representation of the Hindu God, Shiva, in his destructive mode, and the Monkey God, Hanuman, covered in red drool, guards the Golden Door to the Hanuman Dhoka Palace. You had better remember your binoculars as close scrutiny of the roof struts of the temples, Maju Dega, Jagannath and Basantapur Tower will reveal some very revealing erotic sculptures. The idea was that these would so embarrass the modest Goddess of Lightning that she would avoid such temples.

The kingdom of Patan is the oldest of the three, dating back to 650 AD. It is now just an upper-class suburb of modern Kathmandu and its old streets are full of colourful saris and well-to-do merchant classes. Again it has its own Durbar Palace Square with intricately carved stone and wood adornments on many of its temples. The Charnarayan Temple's roof struts are said to depict eighty-four positions of the Kama Sutra, but I got a strained neck and forgot to count. Peter's camera was shaking too much to focus his shots. There is a comfortable relationship and many similarities between Hinduism and Buddhism, such as karma and reincarnation, and so it's not surprising to find an important Buddhist shrine, the Golden Temple, adjacent to the Durbar Square. In fact the most important Buddhist temple, the Bodhnath Stupa or Temple of Enlightenment, is an impressive place to visit in Kathmandu. It is encircled by a storied enclave inhabited by Tibetan Buddhist refugees and this circular terrace also incorporates a small monastery devoted to the Dalai Lama. Approached through a narrow laneway, the huge central dome of the Stupa represents water, its square base the earth, the piercing eyes atop the dome represent fire, the stepped steeple above is the air, and the umbrella style pinnacle the very ether itself! Being a Stupa, (a type of memorial), it has no interior. The third kingdom, Bhaktapur, about eight kms from the centre of the city, is geared a little more towards the tourist. Much of it was destroyed in an earthquake in 1934 but it still remains impressive with very ornate 17th century wood and metal carvings by skilled artisans of the Newars, a very cultured Tibet-o-Burman people who ruled the valley. The Teleju Chowk, accessed through the Golden Gate, has the most intricate and finest of the temple carvings. Here 108 buffalo are still sacrificed at an annual festival. The Nyatapola, with five pagoda style platforms, is Nepal's highest temple whereas the Dattatreya Temple is both Hindu and Buddhist. Being on the outskirts of the city, the inhabitants are still mainly farm workers and the women wear red saris with a wide black border. There was an interesting paper factory, making their paper from the bark of the Daphne shrub, which we saw amongst the forests of Annapurna. Also Bhaktapur is famous for its potters, and Pottery Square is covered with basic clay pots drying in the sun.

The final attraction of Kathmandu one must not miss is the Shaivite Temple of Pashupatinath on the Bagmati River, a tributary of the Ganges. I use the term attraction loosely as we were taken there first thing in the morning, specifically to watch cremations in progress. Yes, there was a very dead yellow-clad body, lying on a wood pyre being chanted over and sprinkled with marigolds before the addition of a layer of straw and final ignition. Another white-wrapped body lay nearby, perhaps hoping to share any remaining embers, as wood is very expensive and not everyone can afford a full burn. Fortunately, we were looking down on all this from the opposite bank, but not so far as to be unable to read the notice on a shed behind the ghats which said "Cornea Excision Centre". Just down the road was the Eye Hospital. Well, that's pretty practical, isn't it? Further along from the cremation pyres, and high above the sacred river, was the temple proper with steep steps leading down to the water's edge. A mass of colourful women and white dhoti-clad men (well sometimes not clad as they performed their ritual bathing in the murky river) continually moved up and down these steps caressing and blessing lingams (see below) and sending little floral boats adrift on the river. There were many Brahmin (priests) squatting on both sides of the steeply stepped banks offering blessings. Many skinny dirty sadhus were wandering about hoping to find themselves in the centre of your camera lens so that they could demand some rupees.

Here is some basic info about Hinduism - for adults only! The Hindu God Shiva is considered to be both the destroyer and the regenerator of the Hindu world. The central altar of his temples will be a stone lingam, a phallic symbol that represents both male and female genitalia in the sexual act of consummation. His wife is Parvati (alias Durga, or Kali) and their son Ganesh has an elephant's head. Shiva's devotees, called Shaivites, paint horizontal bands across their foreheads. The other two main gods of the Hindu Trinity are Brahma, the Creative Principle and Vishnu the Preserver. Vishnu sometimes appears as Rama whose helpmate is Hanuman the Monkey God or in his other reincarnation, Krishna the mischievous God of Love. Vaishnavites paint three vertical lines on their foreheads. To complete your forehead makeup for the day, any of the priests hanging around your temple of choice will give you absolution and add a bright red thumbprint to the middle of your forehead. If you like, you could strip to the buff, cover yourself with ashes, and become a Sadhu, dependent on the charity of others for the rest of your life. These holy beggars are a bit scary to meet in the street with their attempts to extort money, either by posing for a snapshot, or by sticking a red tikal mark between your eyes.

Of course, in the very centre of Kathmandu is the current Royal Palace, hidden from the public by a high wall and guarded by soldiers, many of them traditional Gurkhas. Our Hotel Shankar was close by and pretty luxurious by our budget standards with satellite TV, good inexpensive food, big baths and tons of hot water. Here we assembled for our six-day circular trek with Peregrine Travel up into the foothills of the Annapurna Range.

We had an exhausting 250 km nine-hour trip by private bus held up by all the police and military checks, landslides and traffic jams. When we finally set out on foot from the road end at Naya Phul it was now too late to reach our planned overnight stop in daylight and so we spent our first night in a teahouse at Birethanti (approx.1,600 m), all of a half-hour hike from the bus. This was our first taste of the cell-like accommodation that was to be the norm. Two wooden bed bases with a variable thickness of foam mat, covered with a flimsy sheet and a hard pillow with dubious provenance. No hooks, no shelves, just a padlock for your door. Toilet facilities usually meant negotiating some kind of rickety stairway to a cupboard with a china squat toilet sluiced down with a bowl of water. If there was electricity in a village, then you might be lucky enough to have your room "lit" by a twenty-watt bulb. Enough to deal with the padlock, but never enough to read by or write a journal.

Each day we were awakened by our three Sherpas bringing mugs of hot tea at 6.30 a.m. followed shortly after by a small bowl with an inch of warm water for our daily bathe. To allow our three porters to get a head start on the day, we would have until 7.30 to pack our Peregrine special issue duffel bags, which meant a daily struggle to stuff the big down jackets, sleeping bags and sheet liners they supplied. Breakfast consisted of porridge and two eggs, various styles, and by 8.30 we would be ready to hit the trail. There were only nine of us in the group, and as Peregrine is an Australian Tour Company, the majority were young Aussies. Good fun. We had a Sherpa guide, Nima who, having been brought up in Darjeeling, spoke excellent English. Our three Sherpas walked with us, organized and served our meals and made sure we all had our hands rinsed with potassium permanganate solution before every meal. Peregrine were very strong on hygiene, thank goodness. I was really appalled to find that most of the teahouses we stayed in did not have a washbasin and not even a water tap where you could wash your hands with good old soap and water. Our small bottle of bacterial hand-wash was a blessing. Meanwhile the three porters sped off each morning, loaded with our gear, and were never seen until that evening when you had to pry them from the prized spots around the teahouse's wood stove. If you weren't within about two feet of the stove, then you had better have on your down jacket, long underwear, and everything else for that matter. When the sun dropped behind the hills, and the clouds came over the higher villages, I declared I have never been so cold in all my life. We had to wear hats, socks and long-johns in our sleeping bag, and cuddle our water bottles that were refilled each night with boiling water. This would be our drinking water for the following day.

Our delayed start meant we had to cover a two day hike up to Ghandruk on our first full day. Not really a problem as the weather was fine and, almost immediately, we could see snow-capped Machhapuchhre (The Fishtail) standing guard over the Annapurna Sanctuary. It was fairly easy following the sub tropical valley of the Modi Khola on a well defined stone flagged path that contoured through terraced rice paddies and stands of bamboo, with yellow primula peeping from the grassy verge. We were finally tested by a steady ascent up a stone staircase and a welcome break for lunch. We were forever passing donkey trains as well as groups of other trekkers. There is only one central vehicle road in Nepal and so, to get anywhere, you have to travel over these mountain paths on foot. If you can't afford a donkey to carry your supplies then you put them in a big conical basket supported by a tumpline on the forehead. If granny or granddad can't walk anymore then you put them in a basket on your back too. These are small people, but wiry and fit. It's no wonder as everyone farms and the hillsides are covered with steep terraced fields growing rice, millet, corn and winter wheat. Water buffalo pull ploughs and supply milk. They were harvesting millet as we passed, making huge straw stacks, threshing with sticks and winnowing with flat baskets. The turbulent mountain streams turn water wheels for milling and villages had at least one communal standpipe.

We were a little taken aback at our lunch stop when it was announced that one of the Sherpas would be going ahead to negotiate with the Maoists and pay them the necessary bribe for our safe passage! No one had mentioned we were going into Maoist held territory. We had heard that there were problems in Western Nepal with terrorists, but didn't realize that they had a hold on the Annapurna Region. We were firmly told that, when we reached their check point, we should say nothing and just quietly listen to what they had to say. Well, this very erudite Maoist leader, with an Oxbridge English accent, told us that we had nothing to fear as they are not terrorists but a political party attempting to change the present monarchical control of the government. We would have safe passage throughout our trek. He had me convinced and I was happy that Peregrine was stumping up 1,000 rupees per head for their cause. I'd say it was CAN$20 well spent.

We now had a long steady climb, high above the river valley, with Annapurna South and Hiunchule coming into view as we reached the overnight village of Ghandruk, (1,950 m). A sign said "No Admission without Maoist Permission"! Many of its Gurung villagers served in the British Ghurka regiments and there is an interesting little museum and monastery in this village perched high on a ridge. To visit them meant climbing up and down the village's almost vertical lanes, grumbling all the while about our aching muscles. But we had wonderful views to reward our efforts, until the afternoon clouds rolled in. However, our teahouse, perched on a misty cliff edge, spoiled us with a hot shower, which was sadly to be our last on this trek.

Leaving behind the terraced hillsides and the neat gardens of the whitewashed stone houses of Ghandruk, we found ourselves in pretty rhododendron woods with birdsong and tumbling waterfalls. Spanish moss hung from the trees and it was like a goblin forest. Cloud cover was low, so no distant views of the mountains and, when we reached Tadapani (2,700 m) by late afternoon, we were very glad of the charcoal braziers that they had under the big dining table of the teahouse and as much hot tea as we could drink.

Neither sunset or sunrise of the eastern Annapurna Range were as promised in the brochure. The little village was still in thick cloud when we left the next morning. We had a series of ascents and descents through rhododendron forest and across several mountain streams before we reached Deurali (2,987 m), the highest village of our trek, by early afternoon. We were beginning to notice the effect of altitude on our lung power and the last steep muddy section was a hard slog. The teahouse was cold, despite a big oil drum wood stove that was always being stoked. There was even a TV but only a local station. The others would bring out the cards when the lighting became too poor to read by, to fill in time whilst keeping warm. Peter and I climbed the steep hill to the lookout platform above the village. However, the clouds refused to clear and offer the grand panorama, another supposed highlight of our itinerary. Fortunately, next morning at 5.30, we were told that it was clear and we all stumbled up the hill by flashlight to be at the lookout tower as the sun came over the distant horizon. We were rewarded with the grand panorama of Annapurna I (8,091 m) in the east, Annapurna South (7,219 m) before us, and Machhapuchhre (6,993 m) with Annapurna III (7,855 m) and Annapurna II (7,937 m) behind it, one to the west and one to the east of its fishtail ridge. The sun was here to stay.

From Deurali we followed a narrow-wooded ridge to an open alpine meadow high above the blue roofed village of Ghorepani. Here was a great viewpoint up the valley to Jomsom with the towering peaks of Dhaulagiri I (8,167 m) and

Nilgiri (6,940 m) behind. We were so high that the flight paths of the small planes heading for Jomsom were well below us. From here on it was very much downhill. Steep downhill! Ghorepani (2,780 m) is an important stopover on the old trading route to Tibet. Indeed, we saw several flocks of sheep and goats being herded down the valley by Tibetans hoping to sell them in Pokhara. In fact, this was a very, very busy route, with many locals, donkeys and trekkers headed for the Dhaulagiri area. We stopped for the night in Ulleri (2,070 m), perched high on the hillside overlooking the Bhurungdi Khola valley. Next morning we had an immediate drop of 500 metres on a stone staircase down to the river. It was agony on the knees and calf muscles. You had to concentrate on every single step as we had been warned that, one immobilizing accident and they would need to call for helicopter evacuation, at a cost to your personal credit card of US$2,500. Alas, instead of the anticipated gentler path that was to follow on the other side of the river, we found it had been obliterated in a landslide and we were forced to walk down the stony riverbed, criss-crossing the river every now and again on some pretty shifty stepping stones. We were quite exhausted when we finally reached Birethanti for a very late but much deserved lunch. This was the village where we had spent our first night, so all we had to do was stagger uphill to Naya Phul where our bus was waiting to deliver us to our deluxe hotel in Pokhara, fifty km east, for a couple of nights R&R.

Amazing how you can go from the ridiculous to the sublime. From a shabby cell to a deluxe ensuite with CNN and British soccer on the TV. Our teahouse fantasy of soaking in a hot bath along with our week's laundry came true. Pokhara is Nepal's second largest city, an unattractive sprawl and home to a large Tibetan refugee community. Fortunately it has a decent lakeside suburb with a main street of tourist shops and a café that serves real coffee. I spent much time there. Opposite, on a hilltop above Phewa Lake, was the World Peace Pagoda. Peter had developed a cold so he was happy to hole up in the room and watch soccer. I found a curbside shoe-shine boy who did a fine job of gluing and sewing-up my hiking boot, which had taken a bit of a beating. I also shopped for a famous Pashmina shawl that every unfashionable matron like me must include in her world wardrobe.

We had to suffer the same slow, hot and sticky ride back to Kathmandu. It is a very scenic mountain drive but unnerving when you creep round huge roadway landslides and watch yesterday's unlucky vehicles being hauled up from seemingly bottomless gorges. It was interesting to see the many stages of river rock processing, from collecting at the riverbeds to crushing the rocks into gravel using very primitive machinery. Obviously it's an important industry and much of it is still manual and backbreaking. Driving through the central valley west of Kathmandu, most of the people were Hindu Chattri Brahmin, (the highest of the caste system). The women always wear red, and the men white tight cotton pants and tunic (Dhaura Sural), often with a western jacket or vest and an embroidered "glengarry style" soft fez. How they look so clean and fresh with all the dust defeats me. This road joins in with the main route south to India. After umpteen traffic and cow snarl-ups plus road tax, police and military check-points (we didn't mention we had met the Maoists), we only had the evening left to be reassigned new duffel bags, down jackets, warmer down sleeping bags and cotton liners. We said goodbye to our guide and most of our group. Next morning at 6.00 a.m. we were to leave by plane for Lukla, the start of our Everest trek. First we enjoyed another soak in the tub at the Shanker Hotel. We didn't know it then, but this would be our last scrub down for nine days!

The half-hour charter flight, about 200 km east northeast by Twin Otter along the southern edge of the Himalayas, is spectacular. In fact it's quite hair-raising when you skim across a high ridge, do a quick left turn and come into land on a very short, very steep uphill runway. Brakes on full, tires screeching you pull up just in time in front of a vertical cliff-face. Yeti Airlines barely pulled off onto the arrival apron before all thirteen of us leapt out, duffel bags were exchanged and a group returning to Kathmandu jumped aboard. Within minutes the plane shoots down the runway and hopefully is airborne before it runs out of tarmac. No second chances, no aborted take-offs or landings at Lukla. As it takes five days on foot to reach Lukla from the nearest vehicle road, flying is the only way to go. The weather must be clear both in Kathmandu and Lukla simultaneously, so frequently these flights can become very backed-up because of cloud cover, sometimes for days! However we were fortunate to be delayed by only one hour on the way there, and three hours on the morning we returned from Lukla. Both delays due to fog (smog) in Kathmandu!

Three of our Annapurna group continued with us and eight new Aussies and Brits joined us for a total of thirteen plus our new Sherpa guide, Lakpa. Sadly, Lakpa spoke at high speed so that we would not notice his English mispronunciation. We were in for nine days of confusing instructions. Fortunately our four new Sherpa helpers knew the score and our bags just miraculously appeared each evening in our assigned cell.

We had the morning to stroll the main streets of Lukla. This is only a narrow dirt lane, between houses and the occasional shop, crowded with yaks and overloaded porters. These local Sherpa porters can carry as much as eighty-five kilo, at ten rupees per kilo, for the two whole days it takes them to climb up to the market town of Namche Bazaar, the last shop stop before Everest. They are tiny people, with brown leather faces and Mongolian features. Often they have nothing on their feet but rubber thongs and they carry a homemade T-shaped stick that they prop under their load when they want to remove the tumpline and take a breather. Apart from the obvious cartons of food supplies, they had crates of beer, pieces of furniture, cages of live chickens and the obvious trekkers' duffel bags, tents etc. No wonder their average lifespan is only fifty-seven years.

We had now entered the Khumbu, home of the Sherpas. They originally migrated about 400 years ago from Eastern Tibet, (Sher = East and Pa = people), and brought with them the traditions of Tibetan Buddhism and built many important monasteries. Namche Bazaar was always a trade centre with Tibet and in fact, in the warmer months, it still has an influx of Tibetans who cross the border at the 19,000 ft high pass of Nangpa La. They load their yaks with cheap Chinese household goods to sell to the local people, and live in a squalid flimsy tented temporary camp in the centre of the town. However, since the Tibetan border was closed in 1950, Sherpas have wisely turned their attention from trade to trekking. Many Sherpa families migrated to anglicized Darjeeling and their progeny have such excellent English that they become well-paid trekking guides. Unfortunately Lakpa had never been to Darjeeling. He had learned his English in Germany!

Sherpa houses have a solid timber frame and dry stone whitewashed walls with mud caulking. Roofs are either corrugated tin or planked boards weighted with stones. Roofs and window frames are often painted royal blue. The ground floor is used for livestock and storage and an internal stair leads up to living quarters with an open hearth, bed benches and low tables. Poorer homes are single storied planked boards and the smoke just leaches through the wood shingled roof. Most Sherpa villages face south for maximum sunshine and, as with the ones we visited, are usually perched, like Phortse, in a hanging terrace or, like Khumjung and Kunde, in a glacial trough or, like Namche Bazaar, in a bowl or cwm. The villages range between 7,000 and 15,000 ft in altitude and the climate is too cold to have more than one harvest a year. Their staple crops, grown on terraced hillsides, are barley, buckwheat and potatoes. Their longhaired Yaks and female Naks need cold weather and so for journeys to lower altitudes they interbreed them with cattle and produce less hairy Dzopchioks (m) and Dzooms (f). Both are sterile but they make excellent docile pack animals, as sure footed as the Annapurna donkeys, and they are happy to help with the ploughing of the tiny drywalled fields.

In the afternoon we began our trek towards Everest by descending down to the Dudh Kosi River and joining the main trail to Namche Bazaar. It was an easy start and we stopped overnight at Phakding (2,652 m), 200 metres lower than Lukla. Our well-appointed teahouse with "western toilets" gave us false hope that those ahead would be similar. Next day we crossed the wide glacial river on a long high swing bridge, the first of many, and followed the trail through blue pine and rhododendron forest before recrossing the river on a new swing bridge, with the old bridge broken and hanging helplessly below. As you must share these single lane bridges with porters and yaks, you sometimes have to delay and choose your moment to cross. We reached our overnight teahouse in Monjo (2,835 m) by lunchtime. This gave us the afternoon to stretch our legs even further and visit the local school, abandoned monastery and prowl around an expensive new German hotel. Also, high on the sheer mountain slopes on the opposite side of the valley, we could discern the wreckage of a plane that had crashed in 1999. Before the cloud descended in the late afternoon, we climbed to a lookout point from where we could just see the village of Namche Bazaar high up the valley. That was to be our destination tomorrow. However this evening, after our vegetarian meal, (meat and booze are discouraged when climbing at altitude,) we huddled around the stove which was being stoked frequently with yak dung patties, and tried to ignore the sleet outside. Difficult to ignore during the night when you had to visit the outhouse some distance from the building. Coping with a big down jacket, long johns, a flashlight and a slippery hole in the floor is not easy. Was I detecting a tickle in my throat?

The trail had so far been relatively easy, though dusty when the yaks passed or there was a sudden rush of wind on the more exposed slopes. A scarf to pull across your face was a good idea. Along the way were huge boulders called Mani Stones, covered in Buddhist writings painstakingly carved in relief - by long suffering monks? Also there were many poles decorated with flags, called chhotar. These and the Mani Stones had always to be passed on the left. Often there would be prayer wheels inside a village gateway or decorating a stupa, all of which had to be spun for good karma. Just after the village of Monjo we entered Sagarmatha National Park, Sagarmatha being the Nepalese for Everest. The National Park has been developed to promote environmental aspects, manage a reforestation programme and deal with the garbage that trekkers once left behind.

Bridges became higher and we had a serious uphill climb to the village of Namche Bazaar at 3,446 m. The altitude was reducing our hiking to a snail's pace and our hiking boots seemed to be encased in concrete blocks. We needed frequent stops to catch our breath, which gave an opportunity to examine the flora of the region. Forests of silver birch, silver fir, blue pine and whitebeam gave way to more open hillsides of juniper, cotoneaster, rhododendron, berberis and potentilla. Gentians of various hues were tucked into sheltered banks and cushion and mat plants covered the upper alpine meadows. There was one lookout point on this steep ascent where we had our first view of Everest. It was just a pimple rising behind the Nuptse Ridge, but it was cloud free. Its near neighbour Lhotse was more impressive, but most striking of all was the spiky peak of Ama Dablam (6,856 m) just to the east and a real mountaineering challenge. This one became my favourite and was most often in view. My nose was beginning to run. Peter's Pokhara cold?

The blue roofed whitewashed houses of Namche Bazaar looked as if they had been hooked onto the steep hillsides in uniform rows around three sides of a natural bowl. The fourth side falls away to dear knows where. Our teahouse was perched on one of the higher terraces. Although it had magnificent views of the village all the way down to the Tibetan market at the bottom of the bowl, the thought of climbing down the hundreds of steps to the market and back up again was just too daunting after such a hard day. Instead Peter persuaded me, with my weak legs and runny nose, to climb up to the Visitors' Centre on a high point behind the village, and there we had a great view of Everest (8,848 m) and Lhotse (8,501 m) in the late afternoon sun. The place was deserted apart from a few bored soldiers who man the adjacent military station and we enjoyed the very interesting interpretive display about the Khumbu Region. Our teahouse accommodation was pretty miserable and very chilly. The toilets out back were long drops, (they looked bottomless in fact) with a wood floor, too narrow a slot for those without perfect aim, and a pile of leaf litter. Stoutly padlocked, so as not to be used by passers by, getting in and out at all hours was challenging.

Altitude seems to put pressure on the bladder combined with the effects of having to continually make sure you stay hydrated. There was no running water to wash hands and I was beginning to become very disenchanted with our living conditions. However it was better than being in a tent, as I watched the shiverings of a camping group on a narrow terrace adjacent to our teahouse. Our vegetarian food was excellent and plentiful and despite pigging out on our three meals a day I managed to lose weight. Lots of carbohydrate loading with potatoes, rice and pasta, often all three on the same plate! There were always cups of tea, instant coffee or hot chocolate after meals and mid-morning and afternoon.

We spent two nights at Namche to help us acclimatise. On our "day off'" I had planned to rest up and maybe check out the Tibetan Market below. However we were awoken at 5.00 a.m. to stagger up the hill once again to the Visitors' Centre to watch the sunrise on Everest. It was wonderful and worth the effort to see the snowy ridges edged in gold. We estimated we were about fifteen miles as the crow flies from Everest but, of course, to get up close and personal requires about another four or five days' trek by a circuitous route to even reach the base camp on the Khumbu glacier. Peregrine did offer treks to Base Camp, which we were led to understand has become a one thousand tent slum with no permanent structures, but it would have been beyond us and also for many that tried. Of eleven trekkers on Peregrine's concurrent Base Camp trip, six were brought back to our teahouse in Namche with altitude mountain sickness. Headaches, nausea, coughing and insomnia are the preliminary symptoms but it can quickly become a serious and deadly condition. A figure of four deaths from AMS the previous week was casually mentioned. Some just go to bed and don't wake up. Despite Peter and I being by far the oldest in our group, we were every bit as able as the younger ones and fortunately we had no altitude symptoms apart from heavy boots and all round lassitude. No energy left to write up the day's log, or even read a book. Those 20-watt bulbs were partly to blame. You just wanted dinner to be over so that you could get inside your sleeping bag, cuddle your hot Sigg water bottle and get warm. Oh yes, and wonder how many times you will have to go outside to that awful loo before dawn.

After returning for breakfast, we were persuaded to go on an "easy" day-hike up to Khumjung and Kunde villages that sit in a glacial trough behind Namche Bazaar. Well, it was basically a vertical climb up a goat path of loose stones, and me with my runny nose. We were rewarded at the top with a cup of coffee at the posh Everest View Hotel, catering to the rich and lazy who arrive by helicopter. Its views under blue skies and wispy clouds were worth the climb. We continued over the hill and strolled down through rhododendron woods to Khumjung Village, the Beverly Hills of the Sherpa community, where the most successful in the mountaineering and tourist business have built their retreats. Khumjung is famous for its monastery where they are the proud possessors of a genuine red-haired scalp of a yeti! If you make a monetary donation they will unpadlock the cupboard and let you have a dim view of it in a glass case. It looked as if it might be half of a coconut shell. The village is also proud of its large school built by the Sir Edmund Hillary Foundation. A new statue of him had been erected the previous May to celebrate the first ascent of Everest fifty years ago: the 29th May 1953. He has contributed enormously to the Sherpa peoples and he is revered like a God. In the adjacent village of Kunde is a small hospital run by The Sir Edmund Hillary Trust. Another of his schools in Lukla encourages and funds the education of less privileged children.

It was getting cold, as the sun had set by the time we scrambled back down to Namche, but despite being quite exhausted, we forced ourselves to go down into the Tibetan market at the bottom of the village. It would be our last chance as apparently the next day they had to pack up their tents, load up their yaks and return to Tibet before the high pass would be closed by winter snows. They were wild looking people, tall with long faces and sharp features. Both men and women had long unkempt hair (not combed in years) which was braided with red cloth and wound around their head. Both sexes wore earrings, mainly turquoise stones and amulets around their necks which they kept offering to sell to us, but we were never hustled. There was no language communication. I gather they barely speak Nepalese. Cheap Chinese-made goods to sell to the locals (not the tourists) were spread on the dirt in front of their tents. These were of striped woven plastic sacking, very basic and with an open cooking fire "inside". Their yaks, in an adjacent dirt compound, looked strong and healthy and better groomed than their owners. I found the Tibetans sinister, especially as it was dusk and I didn't know how I would find the strength to climb the million steep steps back up to my teahouse cell. I certainly didn't want anyone with wild wooly hair chasing me.

Next day was our final climb from Namche Bazaar to Thyangboche Monastery at 3,875 m, a strenuous day and with a streaming cold to boot. However it was the most scenic and dramatic path of our entire trip and I really enjoyed it, especially when Shree, a serious and devoted Sherpa, was assigned to carry my daypack. I must have been looking fragile. Apparently we had been nicknamed Grandma and Grandpa in Sherpa language. They were not used to having such old dodderers to look after but I am sure they were impressed by our stamina. I certainly was! Peter, of course, was fitter than any of our party and always up front. I chose to hang back and stop frequently to pretend to enjoy the view whilst I searched my blood for oxygen.

The first half of the day we followed an almost level contoured trail along the steep mountainside, high above the milky turbulent waters of the Dudh Kosi. We spotted wild Thar (like large brown shaggy goats) on the grassy mountainside above and kept our eyes open for Danphe pheasant, almost identical to Indian peacocks. This is the National Bird of Nepal. We were lucky enough to spot several on our return the next day. A large Griffon vulture cruised overhead, probably waiting for a trekker to miss their footing and fall over the edge. I should have known that, to reach Thyangboche, you had first to cross the river which meant a steep descent, stop for a carbohydrate loading lunch, negotiate a very high swing bridge blessed with hundreds of prayer flags and struggle up the final long and very tough climb wearing "concrete" boots.

It was late afternoon when we staggered into the hilltop village located in a beautiful meadow surrounded by towering peaks, a truly peaceful and tranquil setting. The most notable peaks to be seen from here are the black sacred mountain of Kumbila just to the west of the village and north of Namche. Its black rock peak is too sheer for snow to stick. We had skirted its lower flanks en route. To our east Kantian and Ama Dablam towered over us and, due north, framed beautifully by our bedroom window was the Nuptse ridge with the peaks of Everest and Lhotse behind. However, we only had time for a quick cup of tea before we were rushed off to the Monastery's Interpretative Centre, followed by the opportunity to slink into the holy of holies, making ourselves as unobtrusive as possible, to observe evening prayers. Thyangboche is an important Buddhist centre having been founded in the 17th century by a Lama from the Tibetan Monastery at Rongbuk. It was destroyed by an earthquake in 1933, rebuilt and again badly damaged by fire in 1989. It was reconstructed in

Diane Jones

1992. Two rows of monks, heavily clad in maroon cloaks, sat cross-legged on platform benches facing two rows of monks on the opposite side of the central aisle. They were wearing those wonderful yellow gladiator style hats, with the big cockscomb running fore and aft on the helmet. There was continual chanting accompanied by intermittent gongs, bells, horns and drums. All very spooky. There were a couple of dozen monks at any one time, but there seemed to be a bit of coming and going, and steaming kettles carried by minion monks would deliver hot cuppas. No wonder, as it was freezing cold especially as we had had to remove our shoes. The Abbot of the Gompa, the Reincarnate Lama Remproche, sat closest to the altar area and directed proceedings. The only procedure we understood was when a monk walked past the spectators with a sign that read "Please leave now before the end". The monastery hosts the Mani Rimdu Festival in the late autumn each year. Apparently it's a great gathering with much pomp and ceremony, processions and dancing. Sadly we had missed it by only a few weeks.

It was a freezing cold night, especially as my "headboard" was a flimsy piece of linoleum which I discovered was to cover up the gaps in the wood planked wall. The stove in the dining area was frequently stoked with yak dung patties but, despite the place being packed with trekkers, we needed to wear our big hooded down jackets. A young Glaswegian doctor arrived who was doing research on precursors to altitude sickness. She was glad to test a couple of older guinea pigs, as she said this would raise her average sample age. No surprise that Peter came out with the best results and lowest heart rate of everyone, and I came a close second despite my cold. Both of us were circulating sufficient oxygen in our bloodstream and were suffering no ill effects, unlike some other poor souls who had severe headaches, coughs and upset tummies. We were truly tested the next morning when we climbed high above the monastery on a ridge, past Stupas and stumpy pine trees festooned with prayer flags like lines of washing. The yellow flags represented earth, the red ones, fire, green for wood, blue for sky and water, and white for iron. They not only adorned trees and Stupas but roofs, bridges, paths and passes. We climbed to exactly 4,000 metres (13,000 ft). However we were a bit, well a big bit, whacked and we both admitted that if a helicopter arrived and said it had two free seats back to Canada we would have both jumped at the chance.

It was downhill, both physically and mentally, from here on. We returned to Lukla in three days by the same route that had taken us five days to ascend. Descending steep paths of loose rock with windy squalls stirring up the dust, made it into a bit of a slog. We needed that hot bath. We were ready to go home. A highlight apart from the scenery? The happy Sherpa children with dumpling cheeks, rouged by sun and wind.

Extraordinary Travels of an Ordinary Housewife

Pashupatinath Temple, Kathmandu

Whale bones on the beach, Arctowski Base, Antarctica

Our beach fale, Savaii, Samoa

A – Z

of

MY MOST MEMORABLE MOMENTS

A   **ANTARCTICA** *December/January 2003, 2014, 2017, 2020 Cruiseships*

For me this is the most dynamic scenery in the world. The landscape's dramatic monotones of black and white seen in the sheer cliff faces, the snowfields, the rocky shoreline and even the ocean, are often enhanced by the shadows caused by a brilliant sun in a blue, blue sky. The fissures in the glaciers and icebergs surprise you with glimpses of brilliant purple and azure hues, and where the snow appears pink you know there is penguin activity. In 2003 I was fortunate to sail on the "Nordnorge", a Norwegian ship that had zodiacs to take us ashore to visit research stations and penguin nesting colonies. Four of these were on the mainland peninsula and four in the South Shetland Islands of Antarctica. We even had the good fortune to take the zodiac very close to the tiny beach on Elephant Island where some of Shackleton's crew spent four months sheltered under two lifeboats before being rescued. I shall never tire of Antarctica and its ocean wildlife. Every visit has been different and magical.

MMMM (My Most Memorable Moment) The ship had to squeeze through Neptune's Bellows into the active volcanic caldera of Deception Island where I was proud to win the Ice-Dipping Award. Very few ventured to wade out from Whalers' Beach and submerge, up to the neck, in the frigid water before the ship's doc warmed us up with a brandy and a hot bath. This was a hole, dug in the sand at the tidal edge of the volcanic beach, which promptly filled with extremely hot water.

Diane Jones

ARCTIC (THE POLAR ICE CAP) August 2016 HAL's "Prinsendam"

After cruising the fjords of Spitsbergen in the Svalbard Archipelago, where we had spotted polar bears and their cubs on land, our ship sailed north to within sight of the Polar Ice Cap.

MMMM Suddenly we came across dozens of playful walruses on an icy haulout and in the sea. They were tussling with one another and showing off their long, slightly curved tusks which are, in fact, their canine teeth. Both male and females have tusks which continue to grow throughout their lives.

B BURMA (MYANMAR) January 2005 Peregrine Tour

As a young child I was intrigued by WWII stories of Burma and the wartime song "The Road to Mandalay..." When it gained independence in 1948 from Britain, it returned to its pre colonial name of Myanmar and its main city, Rangoon, became Yangon. It took an entire day to visit the many temples and shrines of the Golden Shwedagon Pagoda which dominates Yangon, before flying north to Mandalay and its hill resort of Maymyo. A ferry took us down the Ayeyarwady River to Bagan where thousands of decaying pagodas rise majestically from the plains. We drove east to the tall volcanic plug of Mount Popa and climbed to the top to visit its shrine, dedicated to animist spirits known as Nats. Further east, at Inle Lake, life is lived on the water with floating farms and villages built on stilts. There the famous leg-rowing Intha fishermen row their skiffs standing on one leg, with the other leg wound around the paddle.

MMMM In a village near to Inle lake I met a group of Padaung women from the Shan region, further to the east near the Thai Border. From as young as five they have had their necks extended to twice their normal length with brass rings. These are really brass coils which can be removed and new longer ones added. This results in the shoulders being gradually pushed downwards with the pressure from added rings and it does not affect their spinal cord. Legend has it that it was to protect from tiger attacks, but more likely to make them less attractive to other men. In many societies they are considered beauty accessories and the long necked women I met were happy to pose for my brass-necked photographic request.

C CHINA July 1983 & March 2013

On my first three-week visit to China with Globus Gateway Tours, the country was just emerging from the Cultural Revolution of Mao Tse Tung who had died in 1976, and there were very few tourists. The people seemed shy and submissive towards us and were still wearing the ubiquitous khaki caps with the red star. When I returned thirty years later to visit the old cities of Yunnan Province, I was surprised to find myself being elbowed aside by wealthy Chinese tourists, loud mouthed and ill mannered. In July 1983 our tour started with the Forbidden City and Temples of Beijing; we walked on the Great Wall; saw all 600 terracotta warriors so far restored near Xian; flew to Nanking on the Yangtze River; and took the train to Wuxi where we caught an ornate barge down the Grand Canal to Suzhou, a miniature Venice of canals and little bridges. In Shanghai we walked down The Bund alongside the Huang Po River; flew by military plane to Guilin to lose ourselves in the maze of limestone pinnacles rising from the rice paddy plains; watched the tethered fishing cormorants, with rings around their necks, during our cruise down the scenic Li River; flew to westernized Guangzhou (Canton) and visited the Giant Pandas at the zoo. Our tour finished with three days in Hong Kong. I hired a car and guide for my 2013 week-long visit to Kunming and the Stone Forest, picturesque Dali, the old capital of Lijiang, Jade Dragon Snow Mountain, Tiger Leaping Gorge on the Yangtze River and Shangri La (Zhongdian) where I hiked in Potatso National Park on the Tibetan Plateau.

MMMMs In 1983 I watched snakes being skinned alive, coiled up and tied with a carrying string in Nanking market; moxibustion (cupping) being performed on a volunteer's bare back in Guangzhou market and tapeworm cures displayed beside a large jar containing a specimen!

D *DUBAI, U.A.E. January 2015 HAL's "Rotterdam" Grand Cruise*

How can one not be stunned by the incredible architecture of this city? The Dubai Mall, one of the largest in the world, is at the base of the largest tower in the world, the Burj Khalifa. In the mall you can walk through a glass tunnel inside the huge aquarium zoo and, in the Emirates Mall, you can top this experience by taking a slalom run down the piste of their indoor ski resort! Our "Hop on Hop off" bus first visited the 18th century port with its traditional dhows and drove on through the old town before whisking us into the 21st century to view the 7 star Burj Al Arab. This hotel is shaped like a ship in full sail, with its prow just touching the shoreline. Beyond, formed by land reclamation, is a residential island shaped like a palm tree, The Palm Jumeirah. Four kilometres offshore and similarly created are The World Islands which, when viewed from the air, are shaped like a map of the world.

MMMM Sailing down the Red Sea, through the Gulf of Aden and into the Arabian Sea, our small cruise ship had been told to take action against possible pirate activity. So it was with some surprise when, suddenly, our cruise ship went into total blackout at night. Fire hoses were hooked up and laid out along the decks ready to repel boarders, floodlights were at the ready and CCTV cameras monitored the sides of the vessel. Suddenly I realized that this might be serious when bullet proof vests and helmets appeared at various points along the decks. Fortunately the pirates failed to show and we arrived at Dubai without being held to ransom.

E   *ETHIOPIA March 2006 Explore Tour*

After acknowledging Lucy, who is three and a half million years old and lives at the National Museum in Addis Ababa, our Explore Tour bus took us from the capital to overnight at Lake Tana and visit the source of the Blue Nile. Further north we investigated 17th century Emperor Fasilides' castle and his lion cages at Gondor before hiking for two days in the 4,000 m Simien Mountains with the Gelada baboons. We drove on to the sacred city of Axum in the Tigray region, famous for its many granite stelae obelisks. This was the centre of the Aksumite Empire from the 1st to the 10th centuries and Axum declared itself the birthplace of Christianity in the 4th century. Claimed to be the final resting place of the Ark of the Covenant, its guardian monks bring it out for a quick peek once a year from St. Mary of Zion Cathedral. Further south, Lalibela is famous for its rock hewn churches built at the end of the 12th century. These are all free-standing churches, with sculpted exteriors and hewn-out interiors, which sit entirely within a deep excavated square in the solid rock terrain and below ground level. It is a living site with priests and monks holding active services that have not changed in 800 years, and Ethiopia's Orthodox Christians consider it a second Holy Land. They were a wonder to see and on UNESCO's World Heritage list. Lalibela was in marked contrast to Harar, an old walled Moslem city to the east of Addis and the fourth most holy place in Islam after Mecca, Medina and Jerusalem. With few tourists these Adare Moslems were curious and friendly, the latter perhaps being due to the amount of the stimulant Qat (or Chat) leaves that groups of men meet to chew at the end of each day. Could this be where the term Chat Room comes from?

MMMM I discovered why some Jamaicans call themselves Rastafarians. The last Emperor of Ethiopia, Haile Selassie, was born Ras Taferi Makonnen in 1892 in Harar and was a cousin and the successor to Emperor Menelik. On a visit to Jamaica he made such an impression that he became the key figure of a cult called Rastafari formed after he became Emperor in 1930.

EGYPT December 1987 Transglobal for the Imaginative Traveller

We did all the must see tourist sites of Egypt. These included the pyramids at Giza and Saqqara, train to Aswan, bus to Abu Simbel, and we slept on the deck of a small boat from Aswan to Luxor with stops at Kom Ombo and Edfu en route. By bus we visited Tutankhaman in the Valley of the Kings and the many other sites on the West Bank except that we saved the Tombs of the Nobles for a very hot, bum numbing, all-day donkey ride. The tour ended with a few days at the resort town of Hurghada on the Red Sea, snorkeling off the sandy islands, before returning to crowded Cairo where its dreadful traffic promises a one in three chance of an accident.

MMMMs Two memories but only the first was painful: Our obligatory camel ride at Saqqara; our taxi's minor accident on the way to the airport.

F   *THE FALKLANDS Winter 2014, 2018, 2020 Holland America's "Zaandam" & "Volendam"*

The capital, Stanley, reminded me of a smart seaside town in the UK. Freshly painted houses, picket-fenced front gardens with English shrubs and perennials, and a red telephone box and mailbox to complete the picture. We joined a nature hike out to the windy headland, where the ship's tender had had to negotiate the narrow entrance into the bay, and found flightless Steamer Ducks and fearless Magellanic Penguins sitting outside their burrows. Between stops, to observe the native moorland plants, our guide filled us in on the war in 1982, when Argentina had failed to win back what they considered their Malvina Islands. A special highlight of our day was meeting up with a solitary King Penguin that had lost its way. We stopped the bus to ask if he needed a ride to the beach but he just wanted his photo taken.

MMMM In 2018 we set off to look for two King Penguins in moult who were stranded at the west end of the bay. The heavens opened as we passed the supply vessel wharf on the coastal path and were invited to shelter in the Seamen's Mission. There we were declared bona fide seamen as we had come from a ship, and were welcomed with coffee and biscuits. After continuing for several miles in the ensuing drizzle to find these two AWOL King Penguins, we were happy to return to the Mission, by now deserted, to dry our clothes, enjoy a hot drink, and peruse their free bookshelf. I did, but I am afraid I forgot to return the book on my next visit in 2020.

G   *GREECE September 1966 Horizon Holidays*

In England, in the mid sixties, Greece was considered the new and upcoming honeymoon destination from London. Our all-inclusive tour offered a fortnight in Athens, Crete and Rhodes plus a day-trip from Piraeus port to the islands of Aegina, Hydra and Poros. Included were trips to Delphi from Athens, the Lindos acropolis in Rhodes and the Palace of Knossos near Heraklion in Crete. I have embarked on a cruise from Athens many times which has been an opportunity to spend time with my Canadian girlfriend, now living in a small village near Sparta. Ports of call have been the Greek islands of Corfu, Lefkas, Kos and, my most favourite of all, Santorini with its white villages perched

Diane Jones

high on the cliffs of an old crater. Of course, I must include the Greek half of Cyprus, with ports of call at Limassol and Paphos.

MMMM Tourism had not overwhelmed Athens in 1966 as it has today, and the public were at liberty to wander at leisure all over the Acropolis and visit the Parthenon and the many other treasured ruins of this ancient city.

H   *HUNGARY & EASTERN EUROPE October 2004 Craig Tours*

My visit to Budapest was the first stop on an all-Canadian bus tour, which continued through Slovakia's High Tatra Mountains to Krakow, Warsaw and Poznan in Poland, before crossing the River Oder in East Germany to visit Berlin, Potsdam and Dresden. All these cities have been beautifully restored since WWII. Next was Prague in The Czech Republic, before finishing with a few days in Vienna, Austria. I have visited all the countries bordering the Baltic Sea except Latvia and Lithuania but since the break up of Yugoslavia I have never quite made it to the Balkan states except Croatia, Monte Negro and, of course, Greece.

MMMM Having visited the ghettos of Warsaw and Krakow, my visit to Auschwitz, one of the Nazi Death Camps, was an optional tour which I chose to take. It was a very moving experience to see the gas chamber and the human furnaces next door. It was a period in our history that the world must never forget.

I   *INDIA February 1997 & January 2004 Explore Tours*

Our first of these tours with Explore, out of the capital New Delhi, covered the Golden Triangle. This area included Jaipur, The Amber Fort, Fatehpur Sikri, Agra with its famous Taj Mahal, plus three game parks: Sariska Wildlife Sanctuary, Ranthambhore Tiger Reserve and Keoladeo Bird Sanctuary. Heading southeast we stopped at the Gwailor Fort and the Orchha Palaces and spent two days gawking, with open mouths, at the 11th century Hindu and Jain temples in Khajuraho, famed for their erotic carved friezes. We had two days to spot a spectacular array of wildlife, including tigers, in Bandhavgarh National Park where we enjoyed the view perched atop an elephant. We returned to Delhi on the overnight train from Varanasi after visiting the sacred Buddhist shrine at Sarnath. In 2004 our Explore Tour visited the southern state of Kerala where we took a houseboat on the famous lagoons, drove up to Periyar National Park in the Western Ghats, and down to hot and humid Cochin, just in time for a parade of elephants in jewelled carapaces at a Temple Festival.

Extraordinary Travels of an Ordinary Housewife

MMMM At dawn in Varanasi, the spiritual capital of India, we took a small boat on the misty Ganges River past the steep steps of the Ghats with their funeral pyres and pilgrims. India's devout Hindus believe that they will be purified by submersing their naked bodies in the sacred Ganges. This looked questionable judging by the state of the river!

J   JORDAN & ISRAEL *February 2000 Explore Tour*

A circular tour from Amman in Jordan took us to the Roman city of Jerash; Mount Nebo where we had a view of the Promised Land; the Sea of Galilee where we found our salty swim suits, when dried, were stiff as a board; the Crusader castle of Karnak; a camel ride and sleepover in a Bedouin Tent in Wadi Rum; two days scrambling all over the 2000 year old city of Petra before relaxing with a swim in the Gulf of Aqaba in the Red Sea. We entered Israel at Eilat and drove through the Negev Desert in 4WD vehicles and stayed overnight at two Kibbutz. The ancient besieged fortress of Masada was our next stop and Qumran where the Dead Sea scrolls were found. We had several days in Jerusalem to wander at leisure along the Via Dolorosa; visit the Church of the Holy Sepulchre; the Wailing Wall; Al Aqsa Mosque and the Dome of the Rock, which protects the hoof print where Mohammed dreamt he ascended to heaven on his horse. Visiting The Church of the Nativity in Bethlehem was a simple journey as there were almost no security check-points in Jerusalem to pass through twenty years ago. We drove across the Judean Desert to Jericho and on to Nazareth and the Sea of Galilee where we climbed up to the Church of the Beatitudes. From Capernaum, we took the "Jesus Boat" across the Sea of Galilee to Tiberius, and spent our last night at a resort on the Eastern shore under the Golan Heights.

MMMM Walking out of the dark shadows of the two kilometre narrow slot canyon (the Siq), the only entrance to Petra. Here we were dazzled by the stunning sunlit facade of The Treasury, carved into the pink rock face opposite, as picture perfect as every Petra brochure.

K   KOMODO ISLAND, INDONESIA *January 2019 HAL's "Maasdam"*

Apart from Irian Jaya and Kalimantan, both in Indonesia, I have had several visits to Bali with its gentle Bali Hindu culture. On cruises I have also visited several ports in Java including the overcrowded capital, Jakarta. From Semarang we took a tour bus to 9th century Borobudur, the world's largest Buddhist Temple. In Udang Prabang (Makassar), capital of Sulawesi, I had a visit to old Fort Rotterdam and the new Floating Mosque built on pillars over the sea. Dili, in Timor Leste, was another port of call but it became independent from Indonesia in 2002.

MMMM The Komodo Dragons, of course! Our small group, with a local guide carrying his dragon deterrent stick, came across a nine foot specimen on the open hillside. It looked us up and down for a while, before it gave us a flick of its white forked tongue and ambled off to find some better company. We saw several others, zonked out, having a siesta at the waterhole.

L   LUXEMBOURG & WESTERN EUROPE 1968......

I don't remember much of my car trip through the mountains of Luxembourg in the sixties on what was called a Benelux Tour (Belgium, Netherlands, Luxembourg) but I have chosen it as representative of all the countries of Western Europe I have enjoyed before and after emigrating to Canada. Some of these were visits to family or friends, some were vacations and some were by car, by bus, by train, by plane and in recent years by cruise ship. I include the islands of The Azores, Madeira, The Canaries, Gibraltar, The Balearics, Sardinia, Sicily, Malta and Cyprus as European. Mustn't forget the little principality of Monaco.

MMMM Part of my childhood ukulele repertoire was a song about the Zuiderzee. (Zing, Zing, Zing...it went). When I visited a cousin in Holland in the mid-fifties I resolved to visit the Zuiderzee and took a day trip by ferry from Volendam to the Island of Marken. I was totally charmed by this pretty fishing village where the people were still wearing traditional dress with starched caps and wooden clogs. Eager to visit again on our Benelux tour in 1968, I was disappointed to find that a road now stretched all the way to the island, across the reclaimed polders, and Marken had reinvented itself as a tourist attraction.

M   THE MALDIVES *February 2004 Explore Tour*

Twenty-six atolls and over a thousand islands stretch 750 kms north to south in the Indian Ocean. I spent a week on a Dhoni (converted fishing boat), with six guests in three small double bunk cubicles, plus a captain and a cook. We sailed south to three of the atolls during that week and, twice each day, I had the best ever snorkeling experiences in each of the lagoons, plus visits on shore to some of the small villages. I returned with Holland America's "Maasdam" in 2019 to atolls further north.

MMMM Spotting a Whale Shark from our Dhoni as we sailed the deep channel between two of the atolls.

Extraordinary Travels of an Ordinary Housewife

***MALAYSIA** January 2005 Imaginative Traveller & Explore tours*

Kuala Lumpur, with its famous Petronas Towers landmark, is the capital but Georgetown, on the Island of Penang, was a strategic base for The British East India Co in the 18th century. After touring these cities, the Taman Negara National Park, the cooler Cameron Highlands and Langkawi Island, we flew to Malaysia's two states in N.E. Borneo. In Sarawak we explored the caves in Niah National Park where bat guano for fertilizer, and Swiftlet's nests for Chinese bird nest soup, are harvested. We lived with Kayan tribes in Home Stays and Longhouses, and in Mulu National Park's tropical jungle we took the three km boardwalk at dusk to see the three million bats stream, in tight formation, from Deer Cave. Kota Kinabalu (4,095 m), Asia's highest mountain, anchors the state of Sabah, and Peter bravely joined the two-day climb to the summit. We visited the Orangutan Sanctuary in Sepilok and fought off the leeches on a Kinabatangan River canoe trip to see the Proboscis monkeys that hang about there. A bonus was to come across the world's largest flower, the Rafflesia, in bloom at Poring Hot Springs.

MMMM Idyllic Pulau Tiga, off the coast of Sabah, was the first Survivor Island of the TV series in 2000. We stayed for two days at the small resort built for the film crew, and enjoyed exploring the trails and mud pools of this tiny tropical island. For those who dared, there was the opportunity to go over to Snake Island where a show's participant had had to spend a lonely night. The rocky shoreline was writhing with poisonous sea snakes. Our boatman showed how to safely pick up these venomous sea kraits, stating that they were very docile and "prefer" not to bite. I preferred to just observe!

N   *NORWAY 1974......till 2011*

I had a Norwegian best friend, my next-door neighbour in London in the late sixties. She moved back to Oslo and I to Canada in the mid seventies but we met many times either in London or Oslo or Canada or at her cabin in the mountains outside Oslo. In April 2007 we took the Hurtigruten Coastal Ferry from Bergen to Kirkenes next to the Russian border and back. The ferry stops to service all the ports en route over the eleven days, allowing us to go ashore for a few hours to explore, including a bus tour across the Lofoten Islands.

MMMM Trying to avoid stepping on the zillions of fearless lemmings whilst walking in the mountains during one of their periodic population explosions.

O   *OMAN January 2015 Holland America's "Rotterdam" Grand Cruise*

Muscat, the capital of The Sultanate of Oman, is an absolute monarchy, and one of the safest Islamic countries in the Middle East. It is backed by arid jagged mountains and surrounded by desert. We enjoyed its early morning fish market and the Mutrah Souq. In the cooler hours before sunset, we walked the beautiful corniche to the government buildings in the Old City and looked through the gates of the Al Alam Palace where the Sultan resides. Two ruined 16th century forts guard the harbour on the rocky point that separates Sultan Qaboos Port from the Old City.

MMMM Many years ago we had a very long transfer wait at Muscat Airport. It was a relief to find we could rent an ensuite bedroom within the transit lounge, although it was a very short night as our connecting flight back to Canada left in the early hours. Next morning we had to check out of our room to be allowed to leave the premises. The check-in desk for our flight was only a few yards across the transit lounge where we were horrified to find there was a three hour delay. I couldn't believe we were refused re-entry to our warm bed in the room we had left five minutes before. In an absolute monarchy, unfortunately for us, the Sultan's rules are rules.

P *PANAMA December 2002 Backpacking*

We backpacked for two weeks, spending a few days in Panama City where our hotel wisely insisted on us using their "safe taxi" man. He turned out to be an excellent tour guide but, more importantly, our personal bodyguard. He never left our side as we sussed out the canal locks at Miraflores and Fort Amador on the canal's breakwater, the Bridge of the Americas that crosses the canal, and Casco Viejo with colonial buildings and the Presidential Palace. This became the main city after 1671 when Panama Viejo was sacked by pirates. We left the city and took local buses to Boquete to hike trails in Volcan Baru National Park before heading for the archipelago of Bocas del Toro on the Caribbean coast, considered to be the poor man's Costa Rica. Both places were not what they were cracked up to be in our Lonely Planet guidebook. However, El Valle de Anton, sitting in an extinct crater, was the weekend retreat of the wealthy with grand homes and luscious gardens full of exotic birds. We found a biologist who was happy to take us on hikes with his students along the crater rim each day. Fortunately this was Panama's one redeeming feature as we never felt truly safe. Since 2002 I have passed through the Panama Canal several times on cruise ships and tendered to the San Blas Islands off the north coast of Panama. These flat islands, with streets of hard sand lined with basic thatched dwellings, are home to the friendly Guna people. Molas are their traditional textile, created by layering several coloured materials into very unique applique designs. I treasure my little mola purses which have been much admired and have since travelled the world with me..

MMMM Security guards, with big guns, outside every bank and hotel in Panama city. Our hotel's hitman was usually to be found with his feet up in the lobby, with coffee and a cigarette, and his loaded weapon slung casually across the table.

Q QUEBEC, CANADA *(Emigrated 2nd April 1976 from the UK)*

All provinces have been thoroughly explored on car trips except Nunavut and the NorthWest Territories. I had the chance to join an Arctic canoe trip out of Pond Inlet on Baffin Island but declined when I heard a high calibre rifle must be taken to guard against polar bear attacks.

MMMM In 1984 an eye injury, whilst on a whitewater canoe trip down the Coulonge River with professional guides, meant I had to be evacuated solo to hospital. With a blindfold tightly covering both eyes, I was canoed down a long and isolated lake. Our guide, using a small mirror, attracted two fishermen in a distant boat. They sped me to a fishing camp with the hope I could catch their plane, but it had just left. This meant spending several hours in a trailer at the camp where they were very kind, but there was little communication as they only spoke Joual, the (to me) incomprehensible local french dialect. Finally a 4WD truck and driver were commandeered for the three-hour bumpy sightless drive down remote logging roads to the nearest rural police station. Again language still proved an issue and, unfortunately, the truck had driven off forgetting that my garbage bag of belongings, including all my ID, was still in the back. The police seemed slightly surly and inconvenienced at having to drive me to Shawville hospital but, after my eye was anaesthetized and I could see again, I realized what an unkempt sight I was. My face and clothes were disgusting after twenty-four hours of eating with filthy campfire-blackened greasy fingers. No wonder the Surete du Quebec had been somewhat abrupt with me as I looked like a filthy bag lady who had been living rough in a tent in the woods. How right they were!

R RUSSIA *December 1985 British Airways Tours*

British Airways celebrated their new air route to Russia with an all-inclusive land tour. In Moscow I toured the Kremlin and Red Square, with St. Basil's Church and Lenin's tomb, and checked out the half empty shelves of GUM, the department store. There were other visits to the Monastery of St. Andronikus, the Novodevichy Nunnery and the Kuskovo Palace of the Shermetov family, considered Moscow's Versailles. We were entertained with an opera at the Bolshoi, the Russian State Circus, and the Red Army Choir at the Palace of Congress inside the Kremlin. In Leningrad we had a private tour of the Hermitage and walked down Nevsky Prospect and on to the Admiralty with the statue of Peter the Great. There was a visit to Pavlovsk Palace outside Leningrad and an evening at the Kirov Ballet. British Airways had certainly pulled out all the stops to promote this all-inclusive grand tour which had begun in Toronto and included a stopover in London with hotel and two free theatre nights. What a great start to my plans to see the world.

MMMM I had to share a four person compartment with three strangers on a very old overnight train from Moscow to Leningrad. It was December and so cold that I slept in my fur coat and had the guard fill my hot water bottle from his samovar in the corridor. The window did not close properly and in the morning I had a neat little pyramid of snow on top of my thin blanket.

S SOUTH PACIFIC ISLANDS *Winter months 1997, 2006, 2009, 2013, 2016, 2018*

I have often thought I may be the reincarnation of a dusky maiden from the South Seas. I have a great affinity for the South Pacific and have visited many of the islands by backpacking in 1997 and later on cruises, always with my snorkeling gear at the ready. The Cook Islands (Rarotonga and Aitutaki); Fiji (Taveuni, Viti Levu, Savusavu, Dravuni); Kiribiti (Fanning Island); The Marquesas (Nuku Hiva); New Caledonia (Lifou, Ile de Pins); Philippines (Manila, Puerto Princesa); Robinson Crusoe Island (Chile); American Samoa (Pago Pago); Western Samoa (Upolu and Savaii); The Society Islands (Tahiti, Moorea, Raiatea, Bora Bora); Tonga (Nuku'Alofa, Vava'u); Tuamotos (Rangiroa, Rotoava); Vanuatu (Port Vila, Aneighowhat).

MMMM Five days relaxing in a fale at a small family resort on Savaii Island, Western Samoa. There were only six of these open-sided thatched huts on stilts with double mattress, mosquito net and reed blinds that could be lowered for privacy. They were spaced apart on a white sand beach by a perfect lagoon, sheltered within a bountiful reef. Idyllic, and I wouldn't mind returning there by outrigger canoe in my next life.

SRI LANKA *February 2004 Explore Tour*

In the north of the island are to be found the vast ancient Buddhist cities of Anuradhapura and Polonnaruawa. At Mihintale the Ambastalee Dagoba requires a climb of 1,840 steps (I counted them) plus a final stout metal rail and a rope to reach the top of Meditation Rock for a view of the northern plains. The Caves of Dambulla are another sacred site for Theravada Buddhism. After all this religious overload we were glad of the 200 metre climb up the perpendicular volcanic plug of Sigiriya with the 5th century Sky Fortress on its flat top. We had a breather halfway to enjoy the naughty Sigiriya Damsel Frescos on an overhang. Nestled in the central mountains is The Sinhalese Kingdom of Kandy where Buddha's incisor tooth, which was snatched from his funeral pyre, is secreted under seven golden stupa caskets inside the Temple of the Tooth. It is paraded each summer on the back of a magnificently carapaced elephant. We visited one of the many Plantations where the crew-cut tea bushes cover the hillsides before our descent to the south coast, past the famous stilt fishermen hugging both their pole and fishing pole. After two days at Unawatuna Beach Resort and a visit to the old port of Galle, we returned to Colombo. Here the bombed buildings were a reminder of the ongoing civil war.

MMMM In February 2019 HAL Maasdam docked at Hambantota in southeast Sri Lanka and spent a day at the Bundala Bird Sanctuary. After thirty years of hopeful searching I spotted my first Bird of Paradise, an Asian Paradise Flycatcher with its long ribbon tails floating in the breeze..

T   *THAILAND December 1992 Passages Trek*

After exploring The Grand Palace with its Emerald Buddha and Bangkok's many Temples (Wats) we took the night train to the old capital, Chaing Mai. We visited its many Wats by bicycle and took a tuk tuk to the Royal family retreat at Doi Suthep. Avoiding the commercial trekking areas north of Chiang Mai we headed south east where we trekked for nine days between the Black Lahu, Lisu and Karen hilltribes observing and participating in their everyday lives. We slept in their huts or, if in the jungle, under bamboo and banana leaf shelters. (No tents). One day we were transported on elephants and another day travelled downriver on bamboo rafts. Our trek ended at Mae Sot on the Burmese Border where we were kept awake that night by the noise of gunfire on the far side of the river due to the war between Burma and their Karen tribespeople. We continued to the ancient city of Sukhothai before an overnight on a riverboat on the River Kwai at Kanchanaburi, notorious for the WWII Japanese prisoner of war camp. It was significant that someone was playing the British POW's marching song, Colonel Bogey, on a tin whistle as we crossed the bridge.

MMMM On the Thai Island of Phuket in 2019, I discovered that my booked pedicure had been relocated. Horrified but game, I had to hop on the back of a motor-bike and be transported, a couple of miles at great speed, to the reassigned beauty salon whilst wearing no helmet, just windswept hair. There was also a massage parlour at the rear of the salon and there were some sheepish smiles from male crew of my cruise ship as they passed me on their way out. The madam of the salon kindly returned me to the ship in her chauffeured car which was, surprisingly, ushered straight through security and right up to the gangway. I was almost eighty and am still terrified of motorbikes.

Diane Jones

U   UNITED STATES OF AMERICA 1976......

From Alaska to New Orleans, San Francisco to Cape Cod, I have visited forty three of America's fifty States and many of its famous National Parks, mostly on road trips from Ontario. Our first in 1979 was a fly/drive around Florida with our two sons. We drove the Big Sur from San Francisco to Los Angeles in 1983 and in 1986 flew into the Grand Canyon on a day trip from Las Vegas. We drove to the Four Corners in 1995 and visited many of the National Parks (Zion, Bryce, Bandolier etc.) and in 2018 a cross country car trip included Yellowstone, Grand Teton, Rocky Mountain and many other National Parks in between, such as Sleeping Bear, Mt. Rushmore, Black Hills of Dakota, Badlands etc. The Hawaiian Islands have been visited on several cruises and it was exciting, one evening after dark, to sail close to the coast of the Big Island. Here we could see the rivers of red hot lava from the Kilauea Volcano toppling into the ocean, creating great clouds of steam.

MMMM In July 1980 we sent the children off to camp and, as two totally novice sailors, joined business friends (a crazy Quebec couple) in Connecticut on their unsinkable C&C yacht. Day one, we took the wrong way around a buoy, hit the keel on a rock and lost the winch plus our chart overboard. Only our intrepid captain dared to leave Rhode Island's safe harbour in the next day's high winds. As he began to raise the sails, the hatch cover blew away and our host, without life jacket or lifeline, was knocked overboard by the boom. I threw him the life belt, whilst his wife had hysterics, and Peter released the dinghy line to help get him back on board. Unfortunately our novice sailor's dinghy knot failed and it was some time before we fortunately noticed our dinghy cresting a wave some distance away. Day three, leaving Cuttyhunk Island, we ran aground on a sandbank and had to wait for the tide to release us and, as we were now navigating with a our car's CAA road map, we continued to Martha's Vineyard by the treacherous southern route of endless skerries. Next day's thick fog meant we had to navigate with the sound of buoys to eventually reach Nantucket. This is where I mutinied, left the boat, took the commercial ferry back to Cape Cod and have refused all further yachting invitations.

V   VIRGIN GORDA The Caribbean 2007, 2013 Winter cruises.

I could make-up a calypso alphabet about all the Caribbean Islands I have visited, something like...... Aruba, Bahamas, Cuba, Dominica,.......Barbados, Curacao, Jamaica, The Caymans.....St. Lucia, St. Maarten, St.Thomas, Tortola.... etc, etc. All have been visited on cruises except Cuba in 2002 where we joined an excellent two week Explore Tour in Havana and travelled the length of the country.

MMMM Exploring hidden coves and swimming in crystal waters amongst the huge boulders of "The Baths" on Virgin Gorda in the British Virgin Islands.

W   *WESTERN PACIFIC ISLANDS March 2008 HAL "Statendam" Cruise*

This was a Memorial Cruise to the islands involved in World War II: New Caledonia; Guadalcanal in the Solomons; Rabaul in the New Britain Islands; Yap in the Caroline Islands; Guam and Saipan in the North Marianas; sail past of the Island of Iwo Jima, Japan; ports of call in Okinawa and Nagasaki (Site of the 2nd Atomic bomb in 1945); disembarked in Osaka, Japan

MMMM Whilst we were ashore in Rabaul, the Turvurvur volcano, that sits at the narrow entrance to the bay, erupted. The choking black ash rained down over the small town and we had an emergency call to return to the ship for immediate departure. We all returned with black faces and white eyes behind our sunglasses and the outer decks were closed off for some days until several inches of black ash had been cleared.

X   *XUNANTUNICH Central America December 2001 Explore tours*

Pronounced "Tunasandwich ", these Mayan Ruins are on the border of Belize with Guatemala and not far from the famous Mayan ruins of Tikal. It was simple to cross to Guatemala for two nights to allow us to climb to the top of one of Tikal's pyramids at sunrise. Howler monkeys enjoyed scaring the daylights out of all early risers. Belize has several other Mayan cities dating back to 200 BC and worth visiting, such as Caracol, Altun Ha and Lamanai where a thirty mile boat trip up river through thick jungle was the only access. I was fascinated to learn that a basketball type of game was played by the Mayans using only shoulders and hips to propel a ball through a hoop. Every fifty-two years (being the Katun cycle of 18,980 days) they held a special game where the winner was duly sacrificed. I can't imagine how the runner-up was rewarded! Not far away is Chichen Itza in the Yucatan Peninsula, Mexico. We flew there for a day in 1987 when we were vacationing in Cozumel. Belize has a 200 mile long coral reef close to shore with excellent snorkeling off its many cayes and we spent several days on Caye Caulker.

MMMM In Tortuguero National Park in Costa Rica, a fist sized black Tarantula had dared to take over the shower stall in a young couple's stilted rain forest cabin. None of the males in our group seemed to want to volunteer to solve the matter for the hysterical female. All that needed to be done was throw a towel over the hairy spider, scoop it up, and toss it into the jungle. I guess it was still angry with me when I found it hiding under my duvet at bedtime. No wonder it scurried quickly out the door.

Diane Jones

Y YAP ISLAND *Caroline Islands of Micronesia March 2008 Cruise*

The state capital, Colonia, still retains its traditional culture as there are few foreign visitors to this tropical island of rolling green hills and lush mangroves. It gained independence in 1986 from post war administration by the U.S.A. In Yap the trading currency used to be Stone Money, which are very large stone discs much too heavy to lift, sometimes measuring feet across and with a hole in the middle. These are still displayed, standing on their edges, outside village houses. The Yapese continue to wear traditional dress. Women do not include a blouse or top with their grass skirts and the men only a Thu'us, a type of loincloth. Through dance, legends are passed down and, from an early age, dance is considered an important part of their culture.

MMMM I won't forget the look on the faces of many of the less worldly passengers when the Yapese, in traditional minimal garb, arrived en masse at the gangway. They lined up, one by one, to come on board that evening to enthusiastically perform, on stage. some of their colourful and raucous dances. I can confirm that much was revealed!

Z ZINGAPORE *2015, 2019 Holland America "Rotterdam" & "Maasdam"*

Poetic license I know, but Singapore is my favourite city in the world and it seemed appropriate to book-end it with my favourite continent in the world, Antarctica. The obvious alphabetical countries would be Zambia and Zimbabwe but they have already been thoroughly examined in this book. Singapore is both a city-state and an island with Chinese, Malay, and Indian cultures all living in harmony. Although the country's national language is Malay everything is also transcribed or spoken in English which, with an excellent transport system, makes getting around very simple. It's very clean, very safe and everyone is respectful of each other and the law. It has beautiful colonial buildings juxtaposed to some very imaginative architecture encircling the bay.

MMMM Gardens of the Bay are part of the city's core and we spent an entire day wandering the multitude of gardens representing horticulture in different regions around the world. The entire area of the park could all be viewed from the high walkway connecting the structures of the SuperTree Grove. We climbed the path through the rainforest vegetation and exotic butterflies to the top of the Cloud Forest Biosphere Dome and continued on to the dry heat of the Flower Dome. In the cool of the evening we joined the crowds at the Super Tree Grove to enjoy the classical music of the Garden Rhapsody Lite Show. It was, quite simply. magical and one of many memories of my favourite city.

REFERENCE

WORLD TRAVELS SUMMARY

(New country, state, province in **bold**)

1956 August	**WEST GERMANY** Village near Mannheim (High School Exchange)
1966 September	**GREECE** Athens, Aegina, Hydra, Crete & Rhodes
1967 Spring	**AUSTRIA** Brand via Zurich **SWITZERLAND** 1967 and Solden 1968
1968 August	**BELGIUM, NETHERLANDS, LUXEMBURG** trip by car
1970 May	**CHANNEL ISLANDS** Jersey
1971 June	**PORTUGAL** The Algarve
1973 July	**THE BALEARICS** Menorca
1973 October	**FRANCE** Paris w/e
1974 September	**NORWAY** Oslo visit to friends
1975 December	**ITALY** Rome, Sorrento, Capri - Tour from UK
1976 July	U.S.A. **New York State**, Finger Lakes car trip
1979 January	U.S.A. **Florida,** Orlando, Ocala, Cape Canaveral, Florida Keys, Everglades, Gulf Keys
1980 July	U.S.A. **Vermont, New Hampshire, Connecticut** (New Haven), **Rhode Island,** (Newport, Cuttyhunk Island), **Massachusetts** (Martha's Vineyard, Nantucket, Cape Cod), Car camping trip and New England sailing trip

Diane Jones

1983 July	**JAPAN** (Tokyo, Mt. Fuji) **CHINA** (Beijing, Xian, Nanking, Wuxi, Suzho, Shanghai, Guilin, Canton), **HONG KONG** Globus Gateway Tour. **California** Big Sur by car
1985 Nov/Dec.	**RUSSIA** Moscow & Leningrad – British Airways Tour
1986 January	U.S.A. Las Vegas, **Nevada** & Grand Canyon, **Arizona**
1986 July	U.S.A. **Pennsylvania, Maryland, Virginia, Washington DC** Car tour from Ontario
1986 November	**KENYA** Camping Safari out of London **U.K.** On my own
1987 January	**MEXICO,** Cozumel. All-inclusive resort and day trip to Chichen Itza, Yucatan.
1987 December	**EGYPT** Cairo, Luxor, Aswan
1988 July	California, San Francisco to Crater Lake, **Oregon** return via Cascades. Car & camping
1989 October	**IRIAN JAYA, INDONESIA** Baliem Valley to the Asmat (Expedition)
1989 December	**DOMINICAN REPUBLIC** All-inclusive resort
1990 December	**COSTA RICA** Eco Lodge, Monteverde Cloud Forest
1991/92 January	**THAILAND** Tour Bangkok, Chiang Mai, trek & camp with Hill Tribes, Sukhothai, River Kwai
1993 June/July	**AUSTRALIA** Sydney, Melbourne, Darwin, Cairns by air
1994 August	**KALIMANTAN** (overland trek Dayak Tribes & Orangutans) & **BALI** (Ubud)
1995/96 Dec/Jan	U.S.A. **Ohio, Indiana, Illinois, Kansas, Missouri, Colorado, Utah, Arizona, New Mexico, Oklahoma** (Monument Valley, Moab, Bryce, Zion, Bandelier N.Ps, Taos) Roadtrip
1996 February	**MOROCCO** Casablanca, Rabat, Fez, Marrakesh & Explore trek across Jebel Sahro

1996 Nov/Dec	**SPAIN** Andalusia (Rhonda, Grenada, Seville, Cordoba, Malaga, Nerja) **GIBRALTAR** from Marbella. Backpacking with local buses
1997 February	**INDIA** New Delhi, Jaipur, Agra, Khajuraho, Varanasi, 4 Tiger Safari Parks (Explore)
1997 Nov/Dec	**COOK ISLANDS** (Rarotonga & Aitutaki) **FIJI** (Taveuni, Nadi) **NEW ZEALAND** (by Kiwi Experience Bus)
1998 Jan/Mar	**WESTERN SAMOA** (Apia and Savai'i). Backpacking
1998/99 Nov/Feb	**ECUADOR, PERU, BOLIVIA, CHILE, ARGENTINA, PARAGUAY, BRAZIL** by Tucan overland truck **URUGUAY** 2004 by ferry from Buenos Aires.
1999 Aug/Sep	CANADA Ontario, Manitoba, Saskatchewan, Alberta, British Columbia, Yukon, Alaska, Montana, Nth Dakota, Minnesota, Wisconsin, Michigan camping by van.
1999 Oct/Dec.	KENYA, **TANZANIA**, Zanzibar, **MALAWI, ZAMBIA, ZIMBABWE, BOTSWANA, NAMIBIA, SOUTH AFRICA** by Exodus overland truck
2000 Feb/Mar	**JORDAN, ISRAEL, TURKEY** Explore tours
2000 Oct/Jan	AUSTRALIA, Perth to Darwin tour, Alice Springs, **Tasmania**, Heron Island, Brisbane
2001 Jan/Feb	**LAO** Vientiane, **VIETNAM** North & South, **CAMBODIA** Phnom Phen, Angkor Wat
2001 Mar/Apr	ITALY and **SICILY** Messina, Etna, Palermo, Tuscany, Venice (British Tour Bus)
2001/02 Dec/Jan	**BELIZE**, COSTA RICA, **CUBA** Explore Land Tours
2002 Mar/April	**CANARIES**, (Tenerife, Hierro, Gomera - Explore) **EIRE** and **N. IRELAND** by car
2002 Nov/Dec	**VENEZUELA** Dragoman Truck, **GALÁPAGOS by** Yacht, **PANAMÁ**, Backpacking

Diane Jones

2003 Feb/Mar	NEW ZEALAND by car, AUSTRALIA Oz Experience bus. Backpacking Cairns to Sydney
2003 November	**NEPAL** Annapurna and Everest trekking with Peregrine Tour from Kathmandu
2003 Dec/Jan	**ANTARCTICA** Santiago to Buenos Aires on "MS Nordnorge" 9 Landings. Antarctic Peninsula, Deception & South Shetland Islands, Elephant Island
2004 Jan/Feb	INDIA, **Kerala** (Cochin & Lagoons) **SRI LANKA**, (Anuradhapura, Sigiriya, Kandy, Colombo) **MALDIVES** by Dhoni boat (Sth Male, Felidhe, Mulaku, Meemu Atolls)
2004 October	HUNGARY, SLOVAKIA, POLAND, EAST GERMANY, CZECH REPUBLIC, AUSTRIA
2005 Jan/Feb	**MYANMAR** (Mandalay, Bagan, Inle Lake, Yangon) Peregrine & Imaginative Travel, **MALAYSIA** (Kuala Lumpur, Cameron Highlands, Penang, Langkawi); **SARAWAK**, (Kuching, Mulu N.P, Miri); **SABAH** (Kota Kinabalu, Sepilok, Sukau, Pulau Tiga)
2005 April	New York to U.K. Queen Mary II (visit family and friends)
2005 Fall	U.K. FRANCE, ITALY, NORWAY (visit family and friends)
2006 January	**HAWAII, SOCIETY ISLANDS, MARQUESES** HAL "Amsterdam" South Pacific
2006 March	**ETHIOPIA** (Addis Ababa, Bahar Dal (Blue Nile), Gondar, Axum, Lalibela, Harar)
2006 Aug/Sept	Newfoundland & Labrador via Quebec, New Brunswick, Nova Scotia. Road Trip
2006 November	BALEARICS, Majorca (visit to cousin) & U.K. Family Visit
2007 January	**GRAND CAYMAN, COLOMBIA, SAN BLAS ISLANDS, NICARAGUA, GUATEMALA,** Mexico & Baja Peninsula HAL"Ryndam'" Tampa to San Diego

2007 Feb/Mar	BAHAMAS, ST. MAARTEN, ST. LUCIA, BARBADOS, MARTINIQUE, U.S.VIRGIN ISLANDS (St.Thomas) BRITISH VIRGIN ISLANDS (Tortola), DOMINICA, CURACAO & ARUBA, HAL"Maasdam" Ft.Lauderdale return.
2007 April	NORWAY, MS Polarlys "Hurtigruten" Bergen to Kirkenes (Russian Border) return
2007 November	ITALY, **MONACO,** SPAIN, GIBRALTAR, **MELILLA**, MOROCCO, CANARY ISLANDS, (Lanzarote & Tenerife) **MADEIRA** HAL"Prinsendam" to U.S.
2008 Feb/Mar	AUSTRALIA, NEW ZEALAND, **NEW CALEDONIA, SOLOMON ISLANDS** (Guadalcanal), **NEW BRITAIN ISLANDS,** (Rabaul), **YAP ISLANDS, GUAM, SAIPAN** Nth Mariana Islands, JAPAN (Iwo Jima, Okinawa, Nagasaki, Osaka) HAL"Statendam" to Osaka.
2008 Nov/Dec	**TURKS & CAICOS**, COLUMBIA (St. Andras), Panama Canal, ECUADOR, PERU, COSTA RICA (P. Limon) HAL "Statendam" Inca Discovery Cruise Ft.Laud. return
2009 Jan/Feb	HAWAII Big Island, Maui, Oahu, Kauai, SOCIETY ISLANDS (Raiatea, Bora Bora, Tahiti, Moorea), MARQUESAS (Nuku Hiva). HAL"Ryndam" Sth Pacific, San Diego
2009 April	UK. & Whiting Bay, Isle of Arran Family Reunion
2010 January	CANADA, fly to B.C. family visit and tour Vancouver Island by rental car.
2010 Mar/Apr	**AZORES** and MADEIRA Long Term Stay
2010 August	U.K. Family visit
2010 October	Italy (Venice) **CROATIA** (Dubrovnik) **MONTENEGRO** (Kotor), GREECE (Corfu), **MALTA** (Valletta), SICILY (Trapani), ITALY HAL "Westerdam" Athens to Rome:
2011 April	U.K. London, FRANCE, ITALY, NORWAY (Oslo), Scotland
2011 Oct.	GREECE (Santorini, Rhodes) TURKEY (Ephesus, Kos, Antalya), ISRAEL (Ashdod, Haifa), **CYPRUS** (Paphos) Cruise Azamara "Quest"Athens rtn

Diane Jones

2012 April	U.K. Scotland. Family visit
2012 Nov.	U.K. Queen Mary II New York to London rtn by air
2013 February	BRAZIL (Salvador, Recife, Belem) **FRENCH GUIANA** (Devil's Island), BARBADOS, B.V.I. (Virgin Gorda) Cruise Azamara "Quest" Rio to Miami
2013 March	CHINA Private Tour 1 week (Kunming, Dali, Lijiang, Zongdian (Shangri-La)
2013 April	JAPAN, CHINA, **S. KOREA**, Alaska Cruise HAL "Volendam" Osaka to Vancouver
2013 June	GREECE, ITALY, FRANCE. U.K. by car
2013 November	NEW CALEDONIA, FIJI, **VANUATU** Snorkel Cruise HAL"Oosterdam" Sydney rtn
2014 January	CHILE, ANTARCTICA, **FALKLAND ISLANDS,** ARGENTINA, HAL"Zaandam"
2014 Feb/Mar	MADEIRA, (The Lido Funchal), Long term stay
2014 May	U.S. Ohio, **Kentucky, Tennessee, Alabama, Mississippi, Louisiana** Ottawa Valley Bus Tour to New Orleans
2014 July	NEWFOUNDLAND, (St. John's B&B) by air
2014 Jul/Aug	Alaska, (Anchorage, Denali, Fairbanks, Ketchikan) Yukon, (Dawson City, Whitehorse, Skagway) Glacier Bay, Vancouver HAL Land & Cruise "Zuiderdam"
2014 November	ITALY Florence, cruise to Monte Carlo, Barcelona, Corfu, Kotor, Dubrovnik, Venice, CUNARD "Queen Elizabeth II" Rome to Venice
2015 Jan/Feb	Cruise from Southampton U.K. to Lisbon, Tangiers, Malaga, Athens, Suez Canal, **OMAN** (Muscat), **U.A.E**, (Dubai), **GOA**, India (Cochin), **ANDAMAN and NICOBAR** (Port Blair), MYANMAR (Yangon), THAILAND (Phuket), **SINGAPORE** HAL GRAND CRUISE "Rotterdam"

Extraordinary Travels of an Ordinary Housewife

2015 Jul/Aug	Across Canada car trip Ottawa to B.C interior and Sunshine Coast. (6 weeks)
2015 November	Family visits to Arran, Glasgow and rental car Otley, (H&R) Droitwich, Southport, Lake District, Dumfries, Bute (R & M), Oban, Ballachulish, Glasgow to Toronto
2016 January	COSTA RICA; PANAMA Canal; MARQUESAS; **TUAMOTUS** (Rangiroa); FRENCH POLYNESIA (Tahiti, Moorea); COOK ISLANDS (Rarotonga); NEW ZEALAND (Pahia, Auckland, Picton); AUSTRALIA (Melbourne, Sydney, Townsville, Cairns, Darwin); BALI, INDONESIA, Java (Semerang, Jakarta); HONG KONG. HAL WORLD CRUISE "Amsterdam" Fort Lauderdale
2016 Jul/Aug	**DENMARK** (Aarhus, Copenhagen); **ESTONIA** (Tallinn); RUSSIA (St. Petersburg); **FINLAND** (Helsinki); GERMANY (Warnemunde, Kiel Canal); NORWAY (Oslo, Hardanger Fjord, Eidfjord, Bergen, Alesund); **SVALBARD** Archipelago (Longyearbyen, Ny Alesund); **POLAR ICE CAP; ICELAND** (Akureyri, Isafjordur, Reykjavik); SCOTLAND (Edinburgh) HAL "Prinsendam" Amsterdam return.
2016 Oct/Nov	HAWAII (Honolulu, Maui, Nawiliwili, Hilo, Kona); **KIRIBATI** (Fanning Island); **U.S. SAMOA** (Pago Pago), WESTERN SAMOA (Apia), FIJI (Savusavu, Suva, Latauka, Dravuni Island), **TONGA** (Nuku'Alofa, Vava'u), **NIUE**, COOK ISLANDS (Rarotonga), SOCIETY ISLANDS (Bora Bora, Raiatea, Tahiti, Moorea) TUAMOTUS, (Rangiroa, Rotoava), MARQUESAS (Nuku Hiva) HAL "Amsterdam" San Diego rtn.
2016 Dec/Jan	NEW YORK at New Year. Ottawa Valley Bus Tour
2017 April	MADEIRA, SPAIN, FRANCE, ITALY, **SARDINIA**, (Cagliari); PORTUGAL (Lisbon, Vigo); FRANCE (Le Havre); U.K. (Portland Bill); NETHERLANDS Rotterdam train to Amsterdam. HAL "Rotterdam" Ft.Lauderdale-Rotterdam
2017 Aug/Sep	U.S.A. Chicago - Ottawa Valley Bus Tour Michigan, **Indiana, illinois**
2017 October	UK Otley, Yorkshire; Edinburgh, Rabbie's Tour Skye & Orkneys; Arran; Bute; Glasgow

Diane Jones

2017/18 Dec/Jan	ANTARCTICA & FALKLANDS. HAL "Zaandam" Chile to Buenos Aires
2018 Feb/Mar	NEW ZEALAND (Auckland, Napier, Dunedin, Fiordland); AUSTRALIA Tasmania (Hobart, Sydney, Kangaroo Island, Adelaide, Albany, Fremantle); BALI; **PHILIPPINES** (Puerto Princesa, Manila) H.K. HAL"Amsterdam" WORLD CRUISE
2018 May/June	U.S Road trip to Michigan (Sleeping Bear N.P.) Wisconsin; Minnesota; **Sth. Dakota** (Badlands N.P., Black Hills, Mount Rushmore N.P.**)**; **Wyoming** (Yellowstone & Grand Teton Nat. Pks); Colorado (Rocky Mtn. NP); **Nebraska; Iowa;** Illinois; Indiana
2018 October	Cruise Quebec (Montreal, Quebec City); Nova Scotia (Sydney & Halifax); **Maine**; (Bar Harbour); Massachusetts (Boston); New York; **South Carolina,** (Charleston); Florida, (Key West, Tampa). HAL "Rotterdam"
2019 Jan/Mar	Western AUSTRALIA (Geraldton, Exmouth, Broome, Kuri Bay, Darwin); **TIMOR LESTE** (Dili**); KOMODO ISLAND; SULAWESI** (Ujang Padang); BALI (Celukan Bawang); JAVA (Probolinggo, Surabaya, Semarang); SINGAPORE; MALAYSIA (Malacca, Penang, Langkawi, Port Klang for Kuala Lumpur); SINGAPORE; MALAYSIA (Malacca, Penang, Langkawi); THAILAND (Phuket, Leam Chabang for Bangkok); SRI LANKA (Trincomalee, Hambantota, Colombo); MALDIVES (Male, Himmafushi, Male Atoll, Utheemu in North Thiladhunmathi Atoll); CAMBODIA (Sihanoukville); VIETNAM (Nah Trang, Da Nang, Hoi An, Halong Bay, Ho Chi Min City (Saigon); HONG KONG. HAL "Maasdam" Fremantle to Singapore
2019 May	Quebec; Maine; New Brunswick (Saint John); ferry to Nova Scotia (Yarmouth to Cape Breton); **Prince Edward Island**; Gaspe Peninsula. Maritimes Road Trip.
2019 Oct/Nov	GREECE (Katakolon, Athens, Rhodes, Crete); ISRAEL (Ashdod, Haifa, Acre); CYPRUS (Limassol); ITALY (Messina, Naples, Civitavecchia); SPAIN (Barcelona, Malaga, Cadiz); MOROCCO (Casablanca, Rabat); TENERIFE; MADEIRA. HAL "Rotterdam" Rome to Ft. Lauderdale.

2019 December	Half Moon Key; **JAMAICA** (Falmouth); GRAND CAYMAN (Georgetown); MEXICO (Cozumel). HAL "Eurodam" Family Seven Day Xmas Cruise. Fort Lauderdale return.
2020 Jan/Mar	GRAND CAYMAN; PANAMA Canal; ECUADOR (Manta); PERU (Trujillo, Callao, Lima, Pisco); CHILE (Coquimbo, La Serena, San Antonio for Santiago); **ROBINSON CRUSOE ISLAND**; CHILE (Puerto Montt, Castro, Puerto Chacabuco, Punta Arenas, Ushuaia); Cape Horn, ANTARCTICA; SOUTH SHETLANDS; THE FALKLANDS (Stanley); URUGUAY (Punta del Este, Montevideo); ARGENTINA (Puerto Madryn, Buenos Aires); BRAZIL (Santos for Sao Paulo, Ilhabela on São Sebastião Island, Armacao dos Buzios, Rio de Janeiro, Ilhéus, Salvador de Bahia, Recife & Olinda), AMAZON RIVER (Belém, Santarem, Boca de Valeria, Manaus, Parintins, Alter do Cho); BARBADOS. HAL "Volendam" GRAND VOYAGE. Fort Lauderdale return: 75 days
2022 Oct/Dec	**NEW COUNTRIES I PLAN TO VISIT** TUNISIA; SEYCHELLES; MADAGASCAR; COMOROS ISLANDS; MOZAMBIQUE; ANGOLA; GHANA; IVORY COAST; GAMBIA; SENEGAL; CAPE VERDE; PUERTO RICO.

www.ingramcontent.com/pod-product-compliance
Lightning Source LLC
Chambersburg PA
CBHW030255100526
44590CB00012B/403